THE AMERICAN ESTABLISHMENTS SERIES
EDWIN M. SCHUR, *general editor*

Each book in the AMERICAN ESTABLISHMENTS series examines a single, broadly defined "vested interest" in our society. The volumes focus on power and resistance to change in these American institutions, providing a radical reassessment of their future influence.

Gaye Tuchman, editor of this volume, is Assistant Professor of Sociology at Queens College, City University of New York. She has published several articles on news and is presently researching aspects of social memory.

THE TV ESTABLISHMENT

PROGRAMMING FOR POWER AND PROFIT

edited and with an introduction by GAYE TUCHMAN

Babson College
Library

A SPECTRUM BOOK

PRENTICE-HALL, INC., *Englewood Cliffs, New Jersey*

Library of Congress Cataloging in Publication Data

TUCHMAN, GAYE, comp.
  The TV establishment.

  (A Spectrum Book) (The american establishments series)
  Includes bibliographical references.
  CONTENTS: Epstein, E. J. News from nowhere.—
Molotch, H. and Lester, M. Accidents, scandals, and
routines: resources for insurgent methodology.—Nix, M.
The Meet the press game. [etc.]
    1. Television broadcasting—Addresses, essays,
lectures. I. Title.
PNI992.5.T8   384.55'44   74–3206
ISBN 0–13–902403–4
ISBN 0–13–902395–X (pbk.)

© 1974 by PRENTICE-HALL, INC.
Englewood Cliffs, New Jersey

A SPECTRUM BOOK

10 9 8 7 6 5 4 3 2 1

Printed in the United States of America

PRENTICE-HALL INTERNATIONAL, INC. (*London*)
PRENTICE-HALL OF AUSTRALIA PTY., LTD. (*Sydney*)
PRENTICE-HALL OF CANADA, LTD. (*Toronto*)
PRENTICE-HALL OF INDIA PRIVATE LIMITED (*New Delhi*)
PRENTICE-HALL OF JAPAN, INC. (*Tokyo*)

Contents

Introduction*

GAYE TUCHMAN

The notion that television reflects society is called "the reflection hypothesis." At its simplest, it states that a medium's content reflects its society's values, goals, ideals, aspirations, and shortcomings. The definition of society used will vary. Society is sometimes understood as just a specific class; or at other times as either its socio-economic or political structures, or as both. Whatever definition is used, the reflection hypothesis applies to television, just as much as to magazines, movies, art, music, poetry, and novels. Viewing society socio-economically, this book uses the reflection hypothesis to explore the ways in which American commercial television legitimates the status quo and truncates the range of ideas admissable to the legendary free marketplace of ideas.

Guided by the reflection hypothesis, the book asks four basic questions.

Who owns and who regulates the television industry?

How do ownership and regulation, coupled with organizational factors, influence news and public affairs programming?

How do they influence entertainment programming?

What is the long-range effect of television?

To introduce the argument, let me briefly review some aspects of the reflection hypothesis.

As Lowenthal demonstrated, the reflection hypothesis insists that a medium's *content reflects economic relationships in its society*.[1] Examining biographies in popular magazines, Lowenthal noted that

---

* Carolyn Etheridge and Harvey Molotch criticized an early draft of this introduction. The accessibility of the library of the Television Information Office, the public relations wing of the National Association of Broadcasters, facilitated the research.

[1] Leo Lowenthal, "Biographies in Popular Magazines," in Paul Lazarsfeld and Frank Stanton, eds., *Radio Research 1942–43* (New York: Duell, Sloan and Pearce, 1944).

at the turn of the century, they concerned "Heroes of Production," such as Andrew Carnegie. By World War II, they dealt with "Heroes of Consumption," such as Howard Johnson and golfer Bobby Jones. This change, to Lowenthal, reflected the shift in emphasis of the American economy: consumerism had become more important than production.

But the reflection hypothesis goes beyond content. *The structure of a medium also reflects the structure of its society.* Ian Watt showed that both the rise of the novel and its form reflected the growing importance of the middle class in English life.[2] Not only was the new middle class the audience for novels, but also, the bookseller replaced the patron as the author's source of income. Writing very explicitly, as Richardson and Defoe did, enabled less educated readers to understand novels. Writing quickly and copiously brought more funds to the author.[3]

Unfortunately, it is difficult to show conclusively that the industrial structure of a medium reflects the society, just as the form of the medium and its content does. At the very least, one has problems locating data on the common enterprises and operations of the noncentralized media. More generally, problems arise in establishing operational definitions of the phenomena being examined. It is also difficult to demonstrate what interrelation exists between these factors and whether their impact reinforces existing social structures. At best, and then even rarely, mass communications theorists try to outline the media as systems encompassing both forces of production and of audience consumption.[4]

THE TV ESTABLISHMENT

In using the reflection hypothesis, I will first look at the largest possible units, the economic and political structures, asking how these affect the ownership-patterns and the regulation of television by the Federal Communications Commission and by the White House Office of Telecommunications. The American media are privately owned.

2 Ian Watt, *The Rise of the Novel: Studies in Defoe, Richardson, and Fielding.* (Berkeley: University of California Press, 1957).

3 *Ibid.*, p. 56.

4 One attempt at outlining the mass media as a coherent system in Melvin DeFleur, *Theories of Mass Communication* (New York: David McKay and Co., 1966). A less successful effort is John W. Riley, Jr. and Matilda White Riley, "Mass Communication and the Social System," in R. Merton, L. Broom and L. Cottrell, eds., *Sociology Today* (New York: Basic Books, 1959). These and other attempts are reviewed by J. D. Halloran, "The Communicator in Mass Communications Research," *The Sociological Review: Monograph No. 13* (1969), pp. 5–21.

When compared to countries in which the media are state monopolies, they are frequently lauded as "free" and "uncensored." Although broadcasting is subject to some regulation, these "restraints and pressures . . . only qualify the notion of independence of the communications media from state direction and control; they do not nullify it." [5]

The predominance of private ownership in the broadcast industry does not mean that radio and television are either socially or politically independent of the corporate capitalism that dominates the American economy.[6] Using the reflection hypothesis, one expects to find patterns of ownership within broadcasting that are similar to patterns in other industries. In fact, as in other industries, the ownership-pattern of television stations is one of local monopolies, regional concentrations, multiple ownerships, multi-media ownerships, and conglomerates. Similarly, one might further expect to find shared social and political values. (This does not mean that all stations are either Republican or Democratic. Rather, they share elements of corporate philosophies, particularly the drive toward profit.) Theorists of all viewpoints have argued that the mass media are central agencies in the legitimation of existing socio-economic and political patterns.[7] This generalization applies both to American television and to media that are run as state monopolies in other countries.

But, stating that television acts as a conservative force raises more issues than it settles. How do ownership patterns influence the types and content of programs that are broadcast? Do the actions of network-owned stations differ from those owned by other corporations? Does a station that is one of several owned by a corporate group (termed a "group station") differ from one that is not part of a group? Does a network-affiliated station air different types of programs than an unaffiliated station? If, as will be argued, the search for profit influences all types of stations and all networks, does federal regulation

5 Ralph Miliband, *The State in Capitalist Society: An Analysis of the Western System of Power* (New York: Basic Books, 1969), p. 219.

6 For a general discussion of this dominance, see Pam Tate Eversole, "Concentration of Ownership in the Communications Industry," *Journalism Quarterly* 48 (1971), pp. 251–260, 268; Miliband, *The State in Capitalist Society*; *cf.* Paul A. Baran and Paul M. Sweezy, *Monopoly Capital* (New York: Monthly Review Press, 1966); Gabriel Kolko, *Wealth and Power in America: An Analysis of Social Class and Income Distribution* (New York: Praeger, Inc., 1962), *cf.* Leo Bogart. "How the Mass Media Work in America," *Violence and the Media: Volume 9* (Washington, D.C.: U.S. Government Printing Office, 1969), pp. 165–216.

7 For instance, Paul Lazarsfeld and Robert Merton, "Mass Communication, Popular Taste and Social Action," originally published in 1948 and reprinted in Bernard Rosenberg and David Manning White, eds., *Mass Culture: The Popular Arts in America* (New York: The Free Press of Glencoe, 1964), and Herbert Marcuse, *One-Dimensional Man* (Boston: Beacon Press, 1965).

decrease the industry's ability to use the public airwaves for private profit?

It is naive to claim simply that private and even conglomerate ownership of the public airwaves explains television programming. As business enterprises, the media are organizations dedicated to the constant task of getting the daily work done. Though their profit margins might justify the description, the mass media are not just money-making machines.[8] They are, also, organizations in which people work, and are thus subject to organizational pressures common to all work. Take, for instance, the matter of professional networks, the inter-connections shared by professionals who know one another and can personally contact, and be pressured by, the friend of a friend of a friend. Elliott, explaining that both the staff and those interviewed on a series of BBC documentaries were contacted through professional and personal networks,[9] argues that this "contact chain" in part determined the character of the broadcasts. Clearly, the BBC is not privately owned. How, then, does the task of getting work done influence television programming? Like economic concerns, do organizational and professional factors act as a conservative force to maintain the existing "social and economic status quo?"

Finally, one must ask about the television audience. Can it influence programs? Is its influence as direct as that exerted by the owners? by the regulatory agencies? by the staff members of television programs? All available research indicates that the influence of the audience is, at most, indirect.[10] Highly organized owners confront a disorganized audience, whom they sell to advertisers at varying rates of x dollars per thousand viewers. Also, in spite of their frequent arguments that programming is what it is because the audience wants it so, producers of programs have little knowledge of the audience for whom they are designing shows.[11] Using ratings, they supposedly know the size and demographic composition of the audience, but even this information

[8] For instance, from 1960 to 1969, net industry income rose from $244 millions to $553.6 millions. Profits fell in 1970 and 1971, totalling only $389.2 millions in the latter year. In 1960, broadcast revenues were $1,268.6 millions; in 1971, $2,750.3 millions. Sources for this information are Federal Communications Commission, "Television Broadcast Financial Data—1970," publication no. 71434 (September 7, 1971) and "Television Broadcast Financial Data—1971," publication no. 87384 (August 15, 1972). According to trade reports, net income was rising in 1972.

[9] See Chapter 4.

[10] See DeFleur, *Theories of Mass Communication,* pp. 165–66; cf. Herbert Gans, "Broadcaster and Audience Values in the Mass Media: The Image of Man in American TV News." (Paper presented at 6th World Congress of Sociology, Evian France, 1966).

[11] Denis McQuail, "Uncertainty about the Audience and the Organization of Mass Communications," *The Sociological Review: Monograph No. 13* (1969), pp. 75–84.

is inexact. The adequacy of the ratings have been seriously challenged by experts on sampling and other facets of statistical measurement.[12]

Since both audiences and federal agencies have little impact upon television programming, power to determine what American television is rests by default with its owners and the staff members of individual programs. Enmeshed in corporate concerns, these persons are hardly likely to challenge the legitimacy of existing institutions. Rather, shackled to the corporate structure, television does more than legitimate and conserve the status quo. It also encourages *hegemony,* "an order in which a certain way of life and thought is dominant, in which one concept of reality is diffused throughout society in all its institutional and private manifestations, informing with its spirit . . . all social relations, particularly in their intellectual and moral connotations." [13]

My purpose here, then, is to study the ways in which television maintains hegemony and legitimates the status quo. I will argue that the programming activities of all networks and stations are dominated by the search for corporate profits realized by selling audiences to advertisers. This is as true of the proportion of programs devoted to news, public affairs, and entertainment (those proportions being regulated by the FCC) as it is of the content of individual programs. Furthermore, though federal regulation is at best symbolic, even the FCC's symbolic efforts are being challenged by the White House Office of Telecommunications Policy, presently allied with the broadcasting industry.

The introduction will suggest that the press for profit leads to programming designed to appeal to the lowest common national denominator, a phenomenon that violates the notion of local broadcasting that supposedly ruled when federal regulation was introduced. In the face of the profit motive, individual programmers are shackled and prevented from introducing new forms and new ideas. However, they are not directly controlled by station owners and network officials. Rather, they perpetuate the status quo in the process of doing their work in the most expeditious manner. Further, as upper middle class and upper class Americans, they too subscribe to the status quo. The net result of all of this, I will argue, is the perpetuation of

[12] Senate Committee on Interstate and Foreign Commerce, *Evaluation of Statistical Methods Used in Obtaining Broadcast.* (Washington, D.C.: U.S. Government Printing Office, 1961.) A major difficulty reported is the high rate at which more educated families refuse to participate in the studies. This problem has yet to be solved.

[13] G. A. Williams, "Gramsci's Concept of Egemonia," *Journal of the History of Ideas 21* (1960), p. 587, quoted in Miliband, *The State in Capitalist Society,* p. 180.

hegemony, television programming that reflects and reinforces the
economic and socio-political structures of the United States.

OWNERSHIP AND REGULATION
OF TELEVISION

To understand the patterns of ownership and regulation of today's
television industry, one must understand the patterns established in
the early days of radio.[14] In the United States, as in most other countries, the system devised for radio was extended to the newer medium.
From the beginning, the profit motive ruled the American industry,
squeezing out competition from those who claimed radio could be
used for educational purposes. From the beginning, federal regulations were designed to aid the industry as opposed to the individual
citizen.

RADIO, THE PRECEDENT FOR MONOPOLY

Two factors are particularly germane in the history of American broadcasting. First, *programming was a secondary concern of the early radio
industry.* Second, *governmental regulation began during a period of
chaos on the airwaves, and it was requested by the radio industry.*

Like the telegraph, radio was originally thought to be a medium
by which businessmen could communicate with one another. Although some educators hoped to use it to elevate the masses, the
nature of radio programming was of minor importance in the early
days of the industry. As they were subsequently to do with television,
Americans bought crystal sets to hear scratchy sounds, not to hear
specific programs. And, for the early broadcast industry, profit was *not*
made in supplying radio programs, but in the manufacture and sale
of radio sets. The major manufacturers began broadcasting radio
signals so that their customers would have signals to listen to, so that
more people would buy radios, so that profits would be increased by
those sales.

To be sure, in the teens of this century, non-manufacturers also
established radio stations. Businesses used radio as a means of corporate communication. Educators used radio to teach whoever would
listen. Some small businesses, such as hardware stores and car dealers,

---

14 Information in this section is drawn from Erik Barnouw, *Mass Communica-
tion* (New York: Holt, Rinehart and Winston, 1956); Barnouw, *A Tower in Babel:
A History of Broadcasting in the United States, Volume I* (New York: Oxford
University Press, 1966); DeFleur, *Theories of Mass Communication*; Erwin G.
Krasnow and Lawrence D. Longley, *The Politics of Broadcasting Regulation* (New
York St Martin's Press, 1973). Generally, these sources argue more for an ad-
versary relationship between the FCC and the industry than I do. But none of the
sources argues that the FCC enforces its own reguations.

set up stations to play music to glean the "good will" of potential customers. Then, in 1922, the American Society of Authors, Composers, and Publishers (ASCAP) insisted that royalties be paid to its members for the use of their work on radio. Radio stations no longer had a viable economic base. And so, the future economic base and character of radio became an important public issue.

Like all such issues, it was debated endlessly by concerned parties. An assortment of plans—alternatives to corporate capitalism—were propounded. Some resembled plans now governing television in Europe—subscription, support by foundations, state monopolies. Some groups recommended that manufacturers continue to supply programs. In the midst of the debate, a station in New York introduced an idea that had accounted for most of newspaper profits since the mid-nineteenth century. As Barnouw put it, "It was no accident" [15] that in the year ASCAP insisted upon royalties, WEAF, owned and operated by American Telephone and Telegraph, broadcast a ten-minute advertisement to sell real estate on Long Island. Cutting through the diffuse notion that through starting a radio station a business could profit from "customer good will," WEAF had produced a more direct way of gleaning profit—selling commercials that deliver an audience to advertisers.

With the introduction of advertising, broadcasting's fate was sealed. New ways of turning a profit had been discovered: (1) Manufacturers, such as RCA, could consolidate their stations into networks, now profiting from the sale of advertising as well as sets. Indeed, RCA started two networks. One became NBC; the other, ABC, after the Justice Department insisted upon divestment under the anti-trust act. Some independent stations banded together to start another network,* subsequently sold to CBS. (2) Individual stations could sell commercial time to advertisers, affiliates reserving the right to use certain portions of each hour for local ads. (3) It became profitable for an individual station to be affiliated with a network. An unaffiliated station had to produce its own programs; if a station affiliated, it was paid by the network to air preproduced programs designed for a mass market. It could still reserve time for the sale of local ads. In sum, when advertising was introduced, *programming became a tool with which to sell the audience to advertisers*. Earning a profit was seen to be more important than the equally ill-defined notions of the public welfare and the welfare of the individual citizen.

---

* A network is a corporation that seeks stations as affiliates. It leases airtime from its affiliated stations and sells portions of that leased time to commercial advertisers. Networks also own and operate stations. For intance, ABC, NBC, and CBS each own and operate five affiliated television stations, the maximum permitted under FCC regulations.

15 Barnouw, *Mass Communications*, p. 32.

The introduction of government regulation is also intimately related to the growth of radio In the early 1920's. Now, any group or
individual who wanted to could set up a radio station. Equipment,
an engineer, and the money to pay ASCAP, were all that was needed.
To get a sense of what this involved, suppose that Company A started
a radio station at 100 Main Street, and Company B, located at 200
Main Street, established a radio station on the identical frequency.
The result—two overlapping stations—would be perfectly legal, and
perfectly cacophonous. Both stations would find it difficult to sell advertisements profitably. After an abortive attempt at regulation by
the Secretary of Commerce, bedlam on the airwaves and the inability
of station owners to agree about broadcast frequencies prompted the
radio industry to request government regulation. Owners asked the
government to assign frequencies and to limit the number of stations
in any given community.

Although, at the turn of the century, the meat industry had requested government regulation in order to compete internationally, it
is unusual for an American industry to ask for government regulation,
and at the time, President Hoover mistakenly reported that this was
the first such request ever. As a rule,[16] groups claiming to represent
the public interest apply so much political pressure that a regulatory
agency is established over the strong protests and lobbying efforts of
the concerned industry. Generally, the industry can apply enough
pressure to take the "bite" out of the watchdog agency by convincing
Congress to limit the agency's powers. Then, after a period in which
the agency remains fairly vigilant to its limited mission, its vigilance
wanes, and the agency becomes in effect the handmaiden of the industries it supposedly regulates. It engages in "symbolic politics,"
or "symbolic regulation," that is, "tangible resources and benefits are
frequently not distributed to unorganized political group interests as
promised in regulatory statutes and the propaganda attending their
enactment." [17] Instead, the agencies make highly publicized statements
about reallocating the distribution of resources in the society, sometimes accompanied by actions that *seem* to reallocate resources, while
their non-public actions (their non-symbolic actions) insistently uphold
the existing and highly organized industries whom they purport to
regulate.[18]

That the broadcasting industry requested government regulation
certainly suggests that the initial relationship between the industry
and the regulatory agency was not exactly an adversary one, but more
like a "sweetheart" contract between a business and its house-union.

[16] For a general discussion of regulatory agencies, see Murray Edelman, *The
Symbolic Uses of Politics* (Urbana: University of Illinois Press, 1964).

[17] Edelman, *The Symbolic Uses of Politics*, p. 23.

[18] *Ibid.*, p. 24 ff.

For significantly, although both the 1927 Federal Radio Commission and the Federal Communications Commission, to which it expanded in 1934, were instructed to "frame responsible public policy regarding broadcasting," [19] *they were neither to monitor nor to regulate programs.* To be sure, forbidding this type of regulation meets the requirements of the First Amendment, long established for the press and reaffirmed at the turn of the century, when the "yellow press" [20]—faced with government intervention—improved itself. Forbidding the examination of specific content also enables ruling groups to insist that the American broadcast industry is "free" and "uncensored" in contrast to the state monopolies found elsewhere. It is important that *the so-called "broad-based powers" of the FCC have historically been the power to grant and to renew licenses according to fairly limited criteria, and that these activities were initially requested by the industry which exerted an influence upon the enactment legislation.* (These criteria will be discussed later in this section.)

Five characteristics of either the FCC or its commissioners emphasize the extent to which the FCC resembles a "sweetheart union" and engages in "symbolic politics." (1) *The issues with which the FCC have been concerned at any particular point in time have always been questions with which the industry itself is concerned.* For instance, when ultra-high frequency channels (UHF) were developed, a discovery that would have permitted more stations to broadcast in any community, the FCC froze the licensing of more stations and launched an extensive study of the problem. Meanwhile, the existing very-high frequency stations (VHF) already granted licenses maintained their hold on the market, and manufacturers continued to make television sets without a UHF capability. By the time the FCC "unfroze" its licensing, the VHF stations—many affiliated with networks—had established economic predominance, *as had been desired by the broadcast industry.*[21]

At the present time, competing segments of the telecommunications industry are claiming the right to own cable television companies. The FCC has ruled that owners must carry at least one "public access" channel. (A "public access" channel is a frequency for use by individuals and groups who may produce and broadcast their own programs. For instance, in New York, public access has been used to

[19] Krasnow and Longley discuss the amorphous meaning of this directive (*The Politics of Broadcast Regulation*), pp. 16, 17 *passim.*

[20] Named for the "Yellow Kid," a comic strip printed in color, this term refers to the American press at the turn of the twentieth century. Furor for regulation arose because of the newspapers' sensationalism. For a brief general review of this history, see DeFleur, *Theories of Communication.*

[21] Krasnow and Longley, *The Politics of Broadcast Regulation,* pp. 19, 20. A more radical view is found in The Network Project, *Control of Information Notebook Number 3* (1973), (104 Earl Hall, Columbia University), p. 9 ff.

air programs concerning the problem of security in large apartment
complexes.) Since in the past, the minimal requirements of the FCC
have become the maximum service offered by owners,[22] each cable
company has offered only one channel for public access. Because companies have been so careful to provide only the minimum, some have
spoken of public access as a "myth." [23]

(2) *The backgrounds of the commissioners have been frequently,
although not uniformly, related to industry-specific issues.*[24] In the
early days of radio, when the industry was concerned with the allocation of radio frequencies to stations, the commissioners tended to be
engineers. Until 1961—the last date at which the backgrounds of commissioners were examined in depth[25]—the commissioners had been
mostly recruited from the FCC staff, the military (particularly its communications branches), politics, or the broadcast industry. After leaving the commission, most commissioners have found an industry-
related job in which their FCC experience can be turned to their
employers' advantage. (This is also common in other regulatory agencies, such as the Federal Trade Commission and the Interstate Commerce Commission. Retired generals and admirals also frequently find
jobs tied to their previous military employment; for instance, working
for military contractors.[26])

(3) *The FCC has never taken away the three-year license of a television station on the grounds that it did not "serve the public interest."* In 1969 it was the courts that vacated the license of WLBT-TV
for not serving the public. Although it is difficult to define legally
what the public interest is, it is more difficult to believe that all but
one of the over 900 television stations in the United States served the
needs of both the majority and minority groups in their communities.
And these needs are just one facet of the present FCC definition of the
public interest, a definition which has varied considerably since 1934.
In over a twenty-year period, the FCC has refused to renew fewer
than 10 television licenses. Through 1969, only *seven* television stations
had their licensing application denied or their licenses revoked by the

22 The Network Project, *Control of Information.*
23 The Network Project (104 Earl Hall, Columbia University), *Cable Television
Notebook Number 5* (1973), pp. 21–27.
24 Lawrence Lichty, "Members of the Federal Radio Commission and Federal
Communications Commission: 1927–1961," *Journal of Broadcasting* 6 (1962), pp.
23–34; and Lichty, "The Impact of FRC and FCC Commissioners' Backgrounds
on the Regulation of Broadcasting," *Journal of Broadcasting 6*, pp. 97–110.
25 Lichty, "Members of the FRC and FCC: 1927–1961." Krasnow and Longley
state that subsequent commissioners have had prior experience in government and
politics (*The Politics of Broadcast Regulation*, p. 29), but they provide no further
details.
26 C. Wright Mills, *The Power Elite* (New York: Oxford University Press, reprinted 1968); pp. 240, 213 ff.

FCC:[27] One station didn't have the money or backing to be properly run, and the applicant failed to appear for the FCC hearing. Two other stations were abandoned. Two stations made misrepresentations to the commission in their license applications. Another station made misrepresentations and engaged in an unauthorized sale of its license. The last station, WHDH-TV in Boston, had its temporary license (subject to yearly review) awarded to a competing applicant because of the competitor's "superiority under diversification and integration criteria." (WHDH-TV had been under the ownership of a newspaper, that also held both AM and FM radio licenses. The competing applicant for the license did not have any mass media holdings, and it promised to hire more minority members and to present more "minority programming" than the previous owner had done.)

(4) *The case of WHDH-TV provides an additional example of the extent to which the FCC engages in symbolic politics and symbolic regulation.* Put bluntly, Boston is one of the five top markets* in the United States, and licenses to its VHF frequencies are very valuable commodities.[28] Moreover, in 1968, 27.2% of all television stations were owned by newspapers, WHDH-TV being included in this group.[29] As Wolf reported in 1971,

> In the top 50 markets taken as a single unit, 51 of the 158 stations in that unit were owned by firms publishing newspapers within that unit. Another way of stating this same fact is to say that some 30 percent of the stations serving a national audience in 50 cities were owned by papers serving that same audience. This national audience . . . constituted at least 75 percent of all television viewers in the country. Two additional top 50 stations were owned by newspapers published in cities not among the 50 largest markets. In total, then, there were, as on January 1, 1971, 53 stations in the 50 [top] markets that were owned by newspapers. This amounted to almost exactly one-third of such stations. . . . [In addition, there] was considerable concentration of ownership among these newspaper owned stations.[30]

*All signal areas in the country are ranked on two scales: the number of homes reached and the amount spent on television advertising. These ranked areas are called "markets." There is only one slight discrepancy between the two scales.

27 John D. Abel, Charles Clift, III and Fredric A. Weiss, "Station License Revocations and Denials of Renewal 1934–1969," *Journal of Broadcasting 14* (1970), pp. 411–21.

28 In 1971, WSAZ-TV was sold to Lee Enterprises for $18 million. It is located in Huntington, West Virginia, the market ranking number 48 of the 230 television markets. *Broadcasting*, "Two Big Ones Make a Record Year: Recap of '71 puts station sales near $400 million as trend toward shifting ownership gains strength," January 17, 1972, p. 27.

29 Christopher H. Sterling, "Newspaper Ownership of Broadcast Stations, 1920–68," *Journalism Quarterly 46* (1969), pp. 227–35, especially p. 234.

30 Frank Wolf, *Television Programming for News and Public Affairs: A Quantitative Analysis of Networks and Stations* (New York: Praeger, 1972), p. 21.

Given this national pattern, one wonders why the FCC took away WHDH-TV's license. The apparent answer is, *Boston is a top market. By denying WHDH's application for a permanent license, the FCC could appear to be engaging in the regulation of the industry on a grand scale.* And, because the Supreme Court had already refused to rule on the conviction of WHDH's owners for trying to influence illegally the FCC, WHDH seemed a good candidate for scapegoat. Actually, this is only another example of symbolic politics and symbolic regulation. In unusual circumstances, WHDH had already operated on a series of one-year temporary licences for almost twenty years, while it appealed both court convictions and FCC rulings. It is even possible that the FCC bothered to mention the existence of monopoly ownership of TV stations, because in the near future, TV stations will be a less important component of the telecommunications industry. The FCC has already "deregulated" radio. And, in a relatively short time the prime money-maker in telecommunications will be cable television.

This interpretation, stressing that the FCC divested the parent newspaper of WHDH-TV to appear to be active in regulating the industry, is supported by the history of the aborted merger between the American Broadcasting Company and International Telephone and Telegraph. Critics[31] and even Commissioners[32] Johnson and Cox questioned the wisdom of the merger, noting that IT&T was very active internationally and might well have an equally active interest in the manner in which ABC network news presented international items. Despite the likelihood that this merger might impinge upon the admittedly ill-defined "public's right to know," the FCC approved it. The merger did not take place, because the two conglomerates cancelled their plans after the Department of Justice instituted a suit against the FCC.

(5) *Peculiarly, despite its self-limitation to symbolic activity, the FCC is under attack by both the television industry and the Executive Branch, represented by the White House Office of Telecommunications Policy (OTP).* To use a loose analogy, it is as though one house-union (the OTP) is attacking another house-union (the FCC) for being too militant. Battle lines are drawn around both the First Amendment and the expanding power of the Executive Branch. Although regulating the television and radio industries is the task of

---

* Renamed by Nixon, the OTP is an outgrowth of White House liasons with the Department of Defense concerning communications policy. More communications bands are assigned to government than to industry.

31 For instance, Harry J. Skornia, *Television and Society: An Inquest and Agenda for Improvement* (New York: McGraw-Hill Book Company, 1965).

32 Nicholas Johnson, "The Media Barons and the Public Interest: An FCC Commissioner's Warning," *The Atlantic* 221 (June 1968), pp. 43–51.

Congress, which it invested in the FCC through the Communications Acts of 1934 and 1962, American presidents since Truman have shown an increasing concern with communications policy. To understand the debate, one must return to the history of the broadcasting industry, and pay particular attention to two things: the relationship between individual stations and television networks and the original mandate of the FCC.

NETWORKS, STATIONS, AND REGULATIONS

According to FCC Commissioners Johnson and Cox, the FCC originally intended the American television industry to be responsive to local needs.[33] They claim that a desire for a locally based television system prompted the licensing of "individual" stations around the country, rather than the development of centralized services—such as networks—that would dictate programming for all localities and all groups. But I have already argued that the shape of the television industry is a direct outgrowth of the pattern of ownership and regulation established for radio. Since there were already three well-developed radio networks by the time that the FCC was created, the claim laid down by Johnson and Cox appears a bit peculiar.

Legally, the FCC can only *directly* regulate television stations, because the television networks do not themselves broadcast on the public airwaves. Instead, they rent airtime from their affiliated stations to broadcast both advertisements and programs. (The affiliates retain the right to broadcast local advertisements at prespecified points during and between programs, generally on the hour and at the half-hour.) The networks deliver their programs to their affiliates via telephone wires, microwave, and messenger services, methods substantially different from direct use of the "public airwaves." Because the networks use procedures of this type, the FCC can only regulate the television networks indirectly, either by commenting upon the practices of their affiliated stations, by regulating the practices of the five affiliates owned and operated by each network, or by refusing approval of the rates AT&T charges the networks.[34]

The FCC does *not* monitor programs, since this would supposedly interfere with freedom of speech. It has promulgated the Fairness

[33] Kenneth A. Cox and Nicholas Johnson, "Broadcasting in America and the FCC's License Renewal Process: An Oklahoma Case Study" (n.d.g., mimeograph), p. 2.

[34] According to a network informant, the FCC and the networks maintain informal contacts. For instance, a network may ask the FCC how it would rule, if the network asked affiliates to carry out some directive that violated FCC regulations. The "five-station" limitation is a compromise. Some reformers favor forbidding the networks to own any stations. The networks would like to own more. Affiliates and independents would like to eliminate the networks' domination of broadcasting.

Doctrine, mandating the presentation of opposing sides of a political
issue, if that issue is to be discussed on the public airwaves. But, because the FCC does not monitor programs, it relies upon complaints
to learn whether the Fairness Doctrine has been violated. Most of
these complaints are routinely processed and filed away.[35] Similarly,
the FCC relies upon complaints to learn whether a station has violated the standards of good taste—an ill-defined concept—dominant
in the station's market, and whether a station is *not* serving the minority groups in its market. The understaffed FCC rarely initiates
actions against individual stations. Indeed, the only way a dissident
group can insure that its complaints against a station will be heard
is to challenge that station's right to maintain its license at renewal
time. The best way to capture a network's attention is to challenge
the license of one of its owned and operated stations, much as in
1972 the National Organization for Women challenged the license
of ABC's flagship station, WABC, to change the sexist depiction of
women by television and to increase the proportion of women in
responsible positions. (As of March, 1974, negotiations between N.O.W.
and WABC were continuing.)

The licensing procedure used by the FCC is a review of all stations
on a state-by-state basis in a rotation cycle lasting three years.[36] The
FCC renewal forms request such information as (a) the proportion
of programs originated by the station; (b) the proportion of programs
devoted to news and to public affairs; (c) the proportion of diverse
broadcasting hours, systematically categorized, devoted to commercial
advertisements and to public service announcements, such as re-
minders to immunize young children against rubella or to contribute
to the local Community Chest. This inquiry into the types of television content broadcast in the past and planned for the future is the
closest that the FCC comes to inquiring about the content of programs. The FCC can insist that a minimum proportion of broadcast
time is devoted to news and public affairs, but it does not ask what
topics were covered. In many cases, it automatically assumes that the
news programming obeyed the Fairness Doctrine, even if viewers wrote
to the FCC to complain about unfairness.[37]

35 Bradley C. Canon, "The FCC's Disposition of 'Fairness Doctrine' Complaints,"
Journal of Broadcasting 13 (1969), pp. 315–24.

36 For a description of the process, see Cox and Johnson, "Broadcasting in
America and the FCC's License Renewal Process."

37 The FCC has never refused to renew a license on the grounds that the
applicant had violated the Fairness Doctrine. See Abel, Clift and Weiss, "Station
License Revocations and Renewals 1934–1969." Canon ("The FCC's Disposition of
Fairness Doctrine Complaints," p. 319) finds that "More than 75% of the 'fairness' complaints emanate from private citizens. However, more than 75% of the
successful complaints come from sources other than private citizens." A successful
complaint is one that elicits a reprimand from the FCC.

This *pro forma* power almost insures that FCC regulations will be symbolic, as opposed to substantive. Other factors also guarantee the symbolism. The FCC is the creature of Congress, and individual Congressmen, especially those from sparsely populated areas, are dependent upon their local television stations for favorable news coverage. These Congressmen have been known to press the FCC to favor the stations in their districts.[38] (So many congressional districts fall within the signal area of television stations within densely populated markets that here the relationship between a Congressman and a station is not as close.) The FCC also tends to side with stations in their occasional battles with the networks over carrying or "clearing for" network news and public affairs programs. The "net effect" of FCC rules passed in 1940 "is to make it legally impossible for a network to force any affiliate to broadcast any program or series, *even if* the station has contracted to do so in advance." [39] More generally, the FCC's *pro forma* review and symbolic regulation enable both the stations and the networks to seek their own economic self-interest with little chance of agency interference.

In general, the economic interests of affiliated stations and of networks are in perfect harmony. Both parties are interested in maximizing the number of viewers who may watch a program in order to maximize the advertising revenues each receives, for frequently, a program that maximizes the rates of local stations also maximizes the rates that can be charged by the networks. If more people in Duluth watch a network program, the size of both the local and of the national audiences will be increased. All advertising rates, both those of individual stations and those of networks, are based upon a formula of x dollars per thousand viewers as measured by the Nielsen Rating Service. The significant exception to this general rule is provided by advertisers' recent concern with "demographics." [40] Some advertisers prefer a young (18–49 years old) and urban audience and are willing to pay a higher rate per thousand to reach this audience, much as the consumer pays more per pound for prime ribs of beef than for half of a cow. If a network is trying to sell a program at "prime rib rates" and the large Duluth audience is not young and urban, the interests of the station and of the network may conflict.

In sum, CBS, NBC, and ABC are dependent upon affiliates to carry their programs. The affiliates are dependent upon the networks to

---

38 See Krasnow and Longley, *The Politics of Broadcast Regulation*, p. 56.

39 Edward Jay Epstein, *News From Nowhere: Television and the News* (New York: Random House, 1973), p. 52.

40 Alan D. Fletcher, "Advertisers' Use of TV Ratings: Some Recent Changes, Implications." *Journalism Quarterly 48* (1971), pp. 261–68; *cf.* Les Brown, *Television: The Business Behind the Box* (New York: Harcourt, Brace and Jovanovich, 1971), p. 59 and *in passim*.

provide programs that their local viewers will watch in sufficient numbers for each affiliate to charge a high rate per thousand viewers. For
network purposes, the "best" program is one which appeals to the
taste of people scattered around the country. For purposes of the individual affiliates, the "best" program is one which appeals to the
taste of people in its market area. This system of economic exchange
and mutual interest encourages the networks to provide programs that
will appeal to the "lowest common national denominator." It also
discourages local stations from producing their own entertainment
programming; in the long run, it is cheaper for a station to "clear"
for network programs than it is to produce their own (unless, of
course, a specific national program would supposedly "offend" local
viewers). After all, in 1970, the networks spent from $100,000 to $250,-
000 per hour either to produce prime-time entertainment or to follow
the more common practice of buying prime-time entertainment from
independent production companies,[41] such as Universal. (The production companies are themselves multi-million dollar corporations.)
It is, to say the least, a far cry from this interlocking of economic interests to the local community-based broadcast system supposedly envisioned by Congress in 1934.

Prompted by now retired Commissioners Johnson and Cox, by
rare Congressional complaints about television, and by increased challenges to existing licenses, the FCC has recently sought to make individual stations more responsive to their local communities. A 1970
FCC ruling limited the amount of network programming that affiliates
could carry during prime-time, as of the 1971–72 television season.
Filling that "released time" with either locally produced programs or
with syndicated shows is not as profitable for the affiliates as is carrying network programs. (However, it is more profitable for non-affili-
ated stations who must always procure their own programs. The ruling gave them a better chance to compete for local viewers in the
7:30 to 8:00 P.M. time-slot.)

Furthermore, mainly because of court rulings, the FCC had to hear
license challenges from minority groups, such as blacks and Chicanos,
who claimed that the stations were not meeting their programming
interests and were discriminating against minorities in their hiring
practices. For the moment, it looked as though the courts and changing social practices might coerce the FCC into enforcing its own regulations. The watchdog agency might be forced to bite.

The broadcasting industry, accustomed to a placid regulatory
agency, was enraged. A license to broadcast might no longer be a
license to a self-perpetuating profit. This would be particularly true
if license holders could no longer sell their licenses with the assurance

41 Epstein, *News from Nowhere*, p. 127.

that the FCC would rubber-stamp the transaction—that is, if the FCC insisted that a hearing be held to meet challenges of minority groups before the proposed sale was ratified. And, court rulings seemed to be pushing the FCC to insist upon such hearings.

Within this context, a new "house-union" emerged to protect broadcasters from the supposed militance of the FCC, a militance foisted upon the FCC by the courts. Arguing that the FCC was interfering with the rights of local stations and using the First Amendment as a symbolic cover, the White House OTP entered the fray. In December, 1972, Clay Whitehead, OTP Director,

openly challenged the FCC's mandate to regulate broadcasting. Mr. Whitehead announced that the Administration was prepared to introduce broadcast license-renewal legislation that would virtually dissolve the FCC's authority in this area. The White House bill would extend the license duration from 3 to 5 years, abolish FCC requirements that stations devote airtime to specific categories of programs (e.g. news and public affairs), and adapt license-renewal procedures to eliminate practically all grounds for challenge.[42]

As the Network Project put it,

In return for this protection of the broadcasters' extremely valuable 'property' (. . . the license is technically a temporary franchise allowing the broadcaster to serve as steward of a community trust), the Administration bill would require local stations to monitor network news and public affairs programming, and challenge what Mr. Whitehead alleged to be its liberal and elitist bias.[43]

In addition, the Administration bill, as propounded by Whitehead, would substantially revise the admittedly imperfect Fairness Doctrine. Rather than having the responsibility to "present opposing spokesmen" on controversial issues, under the proposed legislation, individual stations would be required to "sell time" to groups wishing to present either a social or political issue.[44] That the economic resources with which to buy air-time are not equally distributed among elements of the population is an issue ignored by the OTP.

Rather, comparing television stations to newspapers, Whitehead insisted that the legislation proposed by the OTP embodied a better interpretation of the First Amendment than the Fairness Doctrine does. As he put it, the owners of television stations should have the same freedom of expression—the freedom to express their own views and to ignore those of their opponents—given to newspaper publish-

42 The Network Project, *OTP Notebook Number Four* (1973), p. 25.
43 *Ibid.*, p. 25.
44 *Ibid.*, p. 24.

ers.[45] Whitehead ignored the legal tradition that station owners hold a public franchise, since the airwaves are "public property." In contrast, the medium through which newspapers disseminate information —newsprint—is legally defined as private property.

In effect, the policy promulgated by the OTP would increase the sway of the profit motive in American broadcasting. The already symbolic powers of the FCC to control the industry would be even weaker. The FCC—the "watchdog agency" that refuses to bite—would be deprived of its power to bark at the industry it supposedly regulates, while the industry, newly allied with the OTP to hold the FCC in check, would gain virtually full control over its own actions.

STATIONS, NETWORKS, AND PROGRAMS

It is a far cry from saying that the industry's structure and its symbolic regulation reflect American economic and political structures to saying that this structure influences programming. Here the impact of this structure upon programming will be examined. Concentration on the *type* of programming presented will show that on both the network and the station level, economic factors dominate programming decisions.

Before beginning, let's review some basic terms and relationships:

A *network* is a corporation that seeks stations as its contractual affiliates. It contracts to lease airtime from affiliates in order to present programs which it prepares, and it sells segments of that leased time to advertisers for commercial use.

An *affiliate* is a station that has a contractual relationship with a network and promises to rent its airtime to the network. This rental is known as "clearing" for network programming. The affiliate retains the right to use segments of every hour for local commercial advertisements.

An *owned and operated station* is an affiliate that is owned and operated by a network. Each network owns and operates five VHF stations, the maximum permitted by the FCC.

An *independent station* is not affiliated with a network. It must either produce its own programs or purchase them from national syndicates. Independent stations mainly purchase programs from national syndicates.

A *group station* is owned and operated by a corporation that also owns and operates several other stations. The maximum number of VHF stations that may be grouped is five. A group station may or may not be affiliated with a network. However, it is more likely to be an affiliate than is a "single" station.

---

[45] Statement made by Whitehead on NET's "The Advocates," rerun in New York City the week of June 11, 1973.

A *single station* is a station that is not grouped. However a single station may be owned by a multi-media corporation. For instance, it may be owned by either a newspaper or a newspaper chain that has radio and cable television holdings.

A station may be a group station and an affiliate, a single station and an affiliate, an independent group station, or an independent single station. All "owned and operated" stations are affiliates.

The most complex organizational relationship is that of the network and the affiliate. Affiliates may refuse to "clear" for a network program, thereby decreasing the size of the audience upon which the network bases its advertising rate. For instance, in Spring, 1973, soon after the release of Americans captured in Vietnam, CBS cancelled "Sticks and Bones," an anti-war play, because too many affiliates argued that the program was in "questionable taste" and refused to "clear" for it. Affiliates may schedule a program for a time-slot disliked by the network. Many ABC affiliates scheduled "The Dick Cavett Show" for 1 A.M., and significantly cut down the size of that program's audience. Affiliates may also adamantly complain about specific programs at the annual "affiliates meeting," a convocation of network officials and executives of the affiliates; or demand that the network *institute* programming in a specific "time slot." In 1973, purportedly because they were losing money on local programming, ABC affiliates demanded that the network provide a program to compete with NBC's "Today Show" and CBS's "CBS News." [46]

Conversely, the networks can exert admittedly illegal pressures upon their affiliates. A network official may "informally" telephone an affiliate-official and inform him/her that unless the affiliate carries program "A," it will not be offered program "B." Instead, program "B" will be offered to a local competitor. Program "B" is always highly popular (that is, profitable) in that affiliate's market.[47] If the network has relatively few affiliates (ABC has substantially fewer than either NBC or CBS), the network has fewer weapons to wield against the affiliate. The weapon of last resort—cancelling the affiliate-network relationship and finding a new affiliate in that market—is often unsatisfactory, for many markets only have two or three VHF channels in operation, and each is tied to a network. Replacing an uncooperative VHF affiliate with a UHF affiliate is unsatisfactory, because many television sets are still not equipped for easy reception of the UHF frequencies. Since fewer people watch UHF channels, a UHF station cannot contribute to the network's national ratings as well as a VHF station can.

Given this economic interdependence, how does affiliation and ownership affect profits and programming?

[46] Reported in conversation with a network official.
[47] Reported in conversation with a network official and in another with the publicist for a network program beset by rating problems.

THE ECONOMICS OF PROGRAMMING: THE STATIONS

The most important economic asset any station may own—not counting its FCC license to broadcast—is a contract as a network affiliate. This, common industry folklore, may be teased out of a report by Anderson, Coe, and Saunders,[48] researchers closely allied to the broadcasting industry. Along with whether a station is part of a group or is independent, affiliate status explains both the proportion of news and public affairs programming presented by station in the top 50 markets, and the time-slot in which those programs are broadcast. But as explained by Wolf,[49] the relationship is a complex one, not simple and additive. Affiliate status and group or independent status influence programming through two intermediate issues: viable economic alternatives and economies of scale.*

In 1971, in the top 50 markets, network owned and operated stations devoted the most minutes of air-time in an average week to news and public affairs programming.[50] They were followed by "single" affiliates, group affiliates, group independents, and single independents respectively. The difference in the number of minutes presented by owned and operated stations (1042), group affiliates (982), and single affiliates (1036) is rather small—at least when compared to the independent stations. Group independents presented 380 minutes of news and public affairs, and single independents, 186 minutes.

Wolf associated this pattern with economic well-being in the top 50 markets.[51] Because affiliates are wealthier than independent stations, they can afford to present more news and public affairs. Since significantly fewer people watch news and public affairs than watch entertainment and sports events, non-affiliates—independents—need the additional advertising revenue derived from presenting entertainment.

Wolf finds two other programming patterns which show that economic factors influence programming practices. Although they broadcast less news and public affairs, independents are more likely to present what they do carry in prime time than are the affiliates.[52] The

---

* "Economies of scale" refers to the ability of broadcasting groups to buy programming wholesale, so to speak.

48 James A. Anderson, Robert L. Coe and James G. Saunders, "Economic Issues Relating to the FCC's Proposed 'One-to-a-Customer' Rule," *Journal of Broadcasting*, 13 (1969), pp. 241–52. The rule would forbid the sale of a television station to a corporation already owning a mass medium in that market. The Department of Justice would like the FCC to apply the rule as licenses come up for renewal. The National Association of Broadcasters has instituted a suit to block any application of the rule.

49 Wolf, *Television Programming for News and Public Affairs*, pp. 33–47.

50 *Ibid.*, p. 41.

51 *Ibid.*, p. 42 ff.

52 *Ibid.*, p. 63.

independents, Wolf explains, are trying to attract a "minority" audience—an audience not attracted to network offerings at that hour:

> Since the non-affiliates found it difficult to compete for audiences with network affiliates, they tend to engage in what is commonly called "counter-programming." This means that, when the network affiliates presented soap operas, the non-affiliates presented films or "talk shows"; when the affiliates presented entertainment programming, the non-affiliates offered cultural and news and public affairs programming . . . when the affiliates covered public events, such as national nominating conventions . . . , the non-affiliates presented entertainment programs.[53]

By presenting news and public affairs in prime time, the independent stations are not virtuously presenting a public service: they are "seeking their own economic well-being," [54] trying a ploy to raise their ratings and revenues.

Second, single affiliates are more likely to "clear" for network public affairs programming, such as documentaries or "60 Minutes," than are group affiliates.[55] Again, the motives are not virtuous: they carry public affairs programming for lack of better options. Group affiliates can substitute local commercial programming, with its larger revenues, because the owners may engage in economies of scale. Wolf reports:

> The owned and operated stations, despite their juridical and institutional "independence" from the network headquarters, were obviously most reluctant to resist the efforts of the networks that owned them to put on news and public affairs programming. The single . . . [affiliates], heavily dependent upon their network affiliations as a source of popular and lucrative programming, were also comparatively reluctant to resist the will of the networks. This reluctance was also a reflection of economies of scale, from [the expense of] procuring programs from other outside sources . . . [to the expense of] being less readily available to single . . . stations than to group . . . stations.[56]

In addition, unlike the owners of group affiliates, the owners of single affiliates have all their eggs (or assets) in one basket, so to speak. Because of this, they find resisting network pressure a greater risk than group owners do. This is especially true if an independent station shares a market with several other VHF stations.[57] As Wolf reminds us, group stations are clearly better equipped to resist network pressures.

Wolf's data indicate that economic factors—ownership and affiliation

[53] *Ibid.*, pp. 43, 45.
[54] *Ibid.*, p. 45.
[55] *Ibid.*, p. 52.
[56] *Ibid.*, pp. 52, 53.
[57] *Ibid.*, p. 56.

—directly affect stations' programming practices. Seeing the complete relationship is, to be sure, a matter of juggling diverse economic considerations that dictate what a station can or cannot afford to do. But, Wolf's findings have certainly upheld the expectations thus far derived from the "reflection hypothesis."

THE ECONOMICS OF PROGRAMMING: THE NETWORKS

It is more difficult to learn whether economic factors influence network programming, since direct evidence concerning the profits of individual stations is inaccessible to the researcher. These matters are highly classified industrial secrets. Most of the evidence that can be located again concerns news and public affairs, and it suggests that the networks present this programming when they can afford it and when they can force their affiliates to carry it.

Consider the relationship with the affiliates. ABC, the so-called third network, is less able to foist programming upon its affiliates than either CBS or NBC. It expanded its network news to a half-hour in 1967. The other two networks had done so in 1963. As one affiliate executive explained to Epstein, "the networks used their news programs as a wedge to expand prime time." [58] Epstein notes,

> The networks did, in fact, increase their share of evening advertising time by five minutes through the expansion of network news, with the affiliates losing a like amount of commercial time. Those extra minutes made network news profitable. For instance, the five minutes of commercial time on the CBS Evening News, which could be sold for upwards of $28,000 a minute in the peak season in 1969, brought in about $36 million a year in revenues for the network. At that time it cost the CBS network about $7 million a year to produce the Evening News program, $9 million in "compensation" paid to affiliates for carrying the program, and $5.4 million in rebates to advertising agencies (which receive 15 percent of the price advertisers pay the networks)—which left a profit of about $13 million a year.[59]

But, if a network is in economic trouble, it may not even be able to force its owned and operated stations to present its news and public affairs. In the late 1960's, though the ABC network was either operating at a deficit or barely breaking even, its owned and operated stations (a separate organizational division) were turning a fine profit.[60] Until the 1972–73 television season, ABC's "flagship station," WABC-TV in New York, did not carry a regularly scheduled public affairs program in prime time. According to *Variety,* the previous refusal had "reveal[ed] a corporate policy that evidently places the [owned and op-

58 Epstein, *News from Nowhere,* p. 87.
59 *Ibid.,* p. 88.
60 According to an informant.

erated stations] as a major profit source ahead of the network, regardless of the reduced 'image' impact of the ABC news that results." [61]

Qualitative evidence—reports issued for former reporters, former news executives, social critics, trade reporters, and academic researchers[62]—suggests that news and public affairs programming is directly related to profits. I shall concentrate upon the evidence presented by Fred Friendly,[63] drawn from his tenure as a producer and eventually as President of the CBS News Division.

Friendly relates that the network news division was pressed to limit its treatment of controversial issues. (Neither Friendly nor other sources have ever managed to explain how one identifies a controversy.) Ultimately, he suggests, he was pressured to assess news decisions in terms of their consequences upon the profits of both CBS and its affiliates. When he and Edward R. Murrow were broadcasting "See It Now" during the 1954–55 television season, they

did a two-part report of cigarettes and lung cancer, and both CBS and Alcoa [the sponsor] felt the pressures of the tobacco industry, which buys both airtime and aluminum foil. The attitude at CBS was: "Why does Murrow have to save the world every week." [64]

Friendly adds, as the season progressed,

"The pressure on Alcoa also mounted. Aluminum salesmen had difficulty explaining to their irate customers why their company felt it necessary to sponsor programs *against* McCarthy and *for* Oppenheimer, *against* cigarettes and *for* 'socialized medicine'—which is what some doctors thought our program on the Salk vaccine advocated." [65]

Finally, "See It Now" covered a "gigantic Texas land scandal involving high members of the state government . . . At that time, Alcoa was

[61] Robert MacNeil, *The People Machine: The Influence of Television on American Politics* (New York: Harper & Row, Publishers, 1968), p. 29.

[62] Examples include reporter Robert MacNeil, *The People Machine*; executive Fred Friendly, *Due to Circumstances Beyond Our Control* (New York: Random House, 1967); social critic Skornia, *Television and Society*; *Variety*'s Les Brown, *Television: The Business Behind the Box*; and researchers Edward Jay Epstein, *News from Nowhere*; and Herbert Gans, "Broadcaster and Audience Values in the Mass Media."

[63] In *Due to Circumstances Beyond Our Control*.

[64] *Ibid.*, p. 69. Entertainment programming cannot criticize corporations in general. Script writer David Gerrold reports (*The Trouble with Tribbles: The Birth, Sale, and Final Production of One Episode*. New York: Ballantine Books, 1973, p. 58) that he could not identify a corporation as "the villain" in a science-fiction script. The program's producer advised to build in drama by making "the conflict between two different planets" rather than between a new company and an established corporation.

[65] *Ibid.*, p. 75.

enlarging its installations in Texas, and the feedback [to Alcoa] was instantaneous. The pressure was just enough to tip the scales." [66] Alcoa withdrew its sponsorship. Simultaneously, the prime-time quiz-show craze emerged, making the half-hour "See It Now" occupied adjacent to "The $64,000 Question" too valuable to waste on the limited audience appeal of public affairs programming. The weekly half-hour program became a monthly hour special, telecast in varying time-slots so that its regular audience would have to search it out. In retrospect, Friendly believes

that the decision to change to irregular programming was primarily a business calculation to create more financial yield from the time period. That others in the company hoped that the weekly headaches would be eased to monthly ones was strictly their dividend.[67]

Similar considerations governed the CBS decision *not* to televise hearings on Vietnam, held by the Senate Foreign Relations Committee in 1966. Friendly reports assessing the news value of this story, while thinking,

Not running *I Love Lucy* at 10 A.M. would mean the loss of about $5000, and *The McCoys* at 10:30 about the same, but the cancellation of *The Dick Van Dyke Daytime Show,* another rerun scheduled for 11:30 A.M., would cost the network about $25,000 or $30,000.[68]

Friendly was told that preempting one day's programming cost the network about $175,000 and probably cost the affiliates a similar amount.[69] He claims that NBC continued to cover the hearings, while CBS discontinued preempting its regular programs, because of economic factors: "The programming they gave up during the morning cost them less than half of what it cost us." [70] At the time, CBS led in the daytime ratings race.

A similar economic pattern determines the planning of specific programs. At a public meeting, Gore Vidal described one encounter with the staff of "The Dick Cavett Show." [71] During the pre-interview re-

[66] *Ibid.,* p. 76.
[67] *Ibid.,* p. 78.
[68] *Ibid.,* p. 221.
[69] *Ibid.,* pp. 223, 258, 263. Whether a network runs daytime programming at a profit has a substantial effect upon its budget. In addition, daytime ratings are included in the evaluation of which network has led all ratings that year. Supposedly, this affects the ability of the networks to sell time to advertisers. As described in *Variety,* in 1971–72 CBS went through an executive shake-up, bringing in new personnel (some from NBC) and redesigning its soap operas, when NBC began to forge ahead in the daytime ratings.
[70] Friendly, *Due to Circumstances Beyond Our Control,* p. 222.
[71] At a panel of the [MORE] counter-convention, April, 1972.

quired before an appearance, he was warned not to discuss politics, since many found his left-leaning political views distasteful. The interviewer explained that the affiliates were in the process of renewing their contracts to carry the program, and his political views might decrease their willingness to renew. Similarly, Merle Miller reports on the "defenestration" of a programming idea.[72] Network officials feared that it was "too new"—too different—and so would be too great a ratings-risk. Brown outlines how ABC spent extra money to transform "The Johnny Cash Show" to a routine variety hour.[73] He explains that ABC preferred to spend extra for a routine program resembling those that glean good ratings rather than to spend less for a non-traditional program that might fail.

The pattern of the economic determination of programming is so clear that one wonders why the networks present any public affairs programming—the type of program for which affiliates are most apt to refuse clearance. Several answers, mainly concerning the economics of broadcasting, are available. Firstly, if the networks can design a suitable non-controversial documentary, the affiliates provide a built-in market. For, affiliates are required by the FCC to present a minimum of public affairs programming, and they are more likely to clear for non-controversial documentaries. Non-controversial documentaries are also easier to sell to spot advertisers, and thus the networks may pay the affiliates more for clearance.[74]

Secondly, the cost of producing documentaries is lower than the cost of producing or buying entertainment. In 1969, according to Epstein, NBC spent from $36,000 to $90,000 to produce a one-hour documentary. (The stated cost is higher—$60,000 to $150,000. The higher estimate includes such fixed costs as studio space, correspondents' salaries, and camera crews—in other words, costs that are covered by other budgets.)[75] *If* a documentary can be plugged into a weak spot in the week's ratings, and *if* the network can cancel the production of a future episode in the regularly scheduled entertainment program (eliminating its production cost), and *if* the network can line up a sponsor before the documentary is put into production—in short, *if* ideal conditions can be insured, then documentaries can even turn a modest profit. Frequently, the sponsors choose the topics of documentaries from a list submitted by the networks. This is yet another part of the attempt to insure a profit.[76]

Finally, the networks make the cost of preempting regular program-

[72] Merle Miller, *Only You Dick Daring: or How to Write One Television Script and Make $50,000,000* (New York: Sloan, 1964).
[73] Brown, *Televi$ion: The Business Behind the Box*, pp. 20–31.
[74] Implied in Epstein, *News from Nowhere*, p. 127, *cf.* p. 97.
[75] Epstein, *News from Nowhere*, p. 127.
[76] *Ibid.*, pp. 128, 129.

ming appear to be a good deal higher than it really is, to show how great a sacrifice they make in their dedication to "the public interest," and to still hostile social and Congressional critics. They inflate estimates of cost by ignoring both fixed costs and make-goods. Such estimates are based upon the assumption that advertisers who have contracted for a 30-second spot during an entertainment program will cancel their contract if public affairs programming is substituted. However, some advertisers do not cancel. Almost all of the others accept "make-goods," a promise that the commercial will be shown at the contracted hour on a future date. Since networks and stations seldom manage to sell all of the time they allocate for spot advertising (promoting their own programs or running public service announcements in the unsold slots), the "make-goods" rarely force out other paid advertisements, though this will vary with the season. (There is more unsold time in the summer, less just before Christmas. The most unsold time is found between Christmas and New Year's.) In addition, other advertisers make special arrangements by which they are contacted when regular programming will be preempted. They pay to be identified as sponsors for these programs.

Epstein provides a splendid example of how this works: the cost to NBC of covering Robert Kennedy's shooting, hospitalization, and funeral. The network announced that its coverage cost $800,000. Of this, $500,000 were fixed costs, such as correspondents' salaries and studio space, leaving a real cost of $300,000. To quote Epstein,

> Entertainment programming can easily cost $200,000 an hour, so, as a network vice-president pointed out, "We didn't exactly lose any money on the [Kennedy] funeral train." He explained that most, if not all, of the preempted commercial time was "made good" at later dates without unduly interfering with the network's sales schedule, and hundreds of thousands of dollars were saved in production costs by cancelling future segments of filmed series.[77]

As NBC's president put it, with slight understatement, "We don't throw away money profligately." [78]

In short, economic considerations dominate decisions both to present entertainment programming instead of public affairs, and to broadcast public affairs programming instead of entertainment.

ORGANIZATIONS, PROFESSIONS, AND HEGEMONY

Thus far, guided by the reflection hypothesis, I have argued that economic decisions concerning corporate well-being dominate broadcast-

---

[77] *Ibid.*, pp. 116, 117.
[78] Quoted in Epstein, *News from Nowhere*, p. 117.

ing's relationship with its regulators and also dominate decisions about programming. But, theorists of various persuasions concur that economic factors are not, by any means, the sole determinant of the content of a medium. They also cite political factors and personal associations, as well as characteristics of organizations and of professions.

POLITICAL INFLUENCE AND THE ORGANIZATIONAL HIERARCHY

Some researchers have shown that at the highest reaches of the networks, executives sustain strong ties to members of the military and governmental power elites. Schiller and others[79] cite both common memberships in organizations sponsored by the Department of Defense and public statements by network presidents that support defense activities. These researchers also note that RCA (owner of NBC), Westinghouse (owner of five television stations), and others active in the broadcast industry are important contractors to the Department of Defense.[80]

It is more than difficult to prove that these ties consistently influence programming, though, to be sure, there are examples that seem to indicate just that. It is known that either the President of the United States or his assistants have, on occasion, telephoned network officials to comment upon newscasts. It is known that a Democratic president asked CBS officials to remove Morley Safer from Vietnam, because his reports were anti-administration. In much the same vein, Friendly writes[81] that both he and Paley, Chairman of the Board of CBS, were sufficiently close to Dwight Eisenhower so that he initially interpreted a 1966 telephone call from the General as an attempt to patch up his argument with Paley. Of equal importance, Friendly notes that Eisenhower had called to discuss a potential documentary.

However, these contacts are not routinely significant in the day-to-day and hour-to-hour conduct of industry affairs. First, at times, high-placed network officials may disagree with one another about the importance of administrative contacts. Again, consider a report by Friendly:

Earlier during this meeting, [UN Ambassador Arthur] Goldberg had again chided me for neglecting to televise live [a] United Nations debate [about Vietnam]. I winced then, but cherish his wrath now; he was right, and his

---

[79] Herbert I. Schiller, *Mass Communications and American Empire* (New York: Augustus M. Kelley, 1969); The Network Project, *Directory of the Networks, Notebook Number Two. Cf.* Erik Barnouw, *The Image Empire: A History of Broadcasting in the United States, Volume 3* (New York: Oxford University Press, 1970), for an historical discussion of television and foreign affairs.

[80] Schiller, *Mass Communications and American Empire*, p. 60, provides a listing of industry contractors to the Department of Defense.

[81] Friendly, *Due to Circumstances Beyond Our Control*, p. 248.

criticism helped to condition me for the struggle over Vietnam air time that lay just ahead. Later, when I told [network President] Stanton about the dressing-down . . . , he seemed disturbed. "What right does a UN Ambassador have to concern himself about what we broadcast?" [82]

Secondly, contacts on these lofty levels frequently do not directly filter down to the reporters and programmers who make the daily decisions. The opinions of higher echelon officials may only be important when lower ranking personnel are divided on a course of action and request a consultation, as in an incident concerning the Vietnam war reported by MacNeil.[83] NBC had film showing American soldiers cutting off the ears of dead Vietnamese for souvenirs. Divided about presenting it, program personnel consulted a news department executive, and the film was not telecast.

Finally, program officials at individual stations may independently decide that broadcasting certain kinds of stories is not "in the public interest." For instance, in the late 1960's, the producer of one local news program, telecast at an independent affiliate, decided not to broadcast Stokely Carmichael making public statements.[84] He feared that Carmichael's charisma would draw sympathizers to his cause, whereas the supposedly neutral summary of his statements by an announcer would not, he believed, recruit more advocates of black power. Significantly, this producer did not fear that interviews with accused felons or their families would recruit more murderers and robbers. Instead, like other journalists, he worried that news coverage might prejudice a jury against the defendant.

In sum, although decisions bearing the largest economic consequences are made at the highest corporate level of the networks, and although corporate officers make policy recommendations to subordinates and receive requests for guidance from them, decisions about content are made on every organizational level. Patterns of association between corporate executives and other elite groups do not provide a sufficient explanation for the content of programs. Rather, other factors contribute to the creation of appropriate television fare.

ORGANIZATIONAL AND PROFESSIONAL FACTORS:
ENTERTAINMENT

Broadly speaking, economic factors define the limits of both acceptable programming and acceptable programs. Organizational factors—themselves dependent upon an economic rationale—further limit program possibilities. They define the format of programs and the gross classi-

---

[82] *Ibid.*, p. 223.
[83] MacNeil, *The People Machine*, p. 66.
[84] From field notes gathered for my dissertation "News, the Newsman's Reality" (Brandeis University, 1969).

fications through which television constructs its realities. And, within the broadcasting organizations, professional factors, such as an emphasis upon techniques, contribute to the dominance of the economic rationale. The professions' influence is facilitated by the selective self-recruitment of professionals[85] and by their socialization to organizational aims.[86] Together, all these factors inculcate hegemony. The remainder of this section will discuss organizational and professional factors that contribute to hegemony.

The effect of these factors is particularly clear in the case of entertainment programming. Making these programs involves integrating the work of both free-lance and line staff through a series of interdependent processes.[87] Consider just a few of the steps involved in making a program for a series shown on a network during prime-time.[88] Once hired, a free-lance writer is generally given six weeks to produce a script. Checked by the producer and other program personnel, the script is then submitted to the network censor who may delete scenes, advise that a specific cinematic technique be used to frame a shot, or order the entire script to be discarded. If the required changes are extensive, the writer may have to change the script without additional pay. Then, once all appropriate parties have approved it, the producer will hire a free-lance director, whose job is to turn the script into a film of prespecified length with one week of preparation and in six and a half days of shooting. Finally, the film must be edited in time to be previewed by the censors and distributed to both the network and its affiliates. In 1970, the cost of processing a 48-minute (hour) episode of an action-adventure series was $200,000.

The close synchronization involved in making the program and the high expenses prompt two inevitable outcomes. To insure future employment, free-lance personnel must please a producer. And, producers must minimize conflicts with the network. Together, these two methods of maintaining the production schedule frequently mandate self-censorship. If a censor rejects a script, the writer must rework it without payment; if the censor rejects a finished show, the production

[85] One recent discussion of this is Lee Sigelman, "Reporting the News: An Organizational Analysis," *American Journal of Sociology 79* (1973), pp. 132–51.

[86] See Warren Breed, "Social Control in the Newsroom: A Functional Analysis," *Social Forces* 33 (1955), pp. 326–35; Gaye Tuchman, "Objectivity as Strategic Ritual: An Examination of Newsmen's Notions of Objectivity," *American Journal of Sociology* 77 (1972), pp. 660–79; Epstein, *News from Nowhere*, pp. 205–20.

[87] James Thompson, *Organization in Action* (New York: McGraw-Hill, 1967), describes some ramifications of this form of organizing work.

[88] These processes are described in Muriel Cantor, *The Hollywood Producer* (New York: Basic Books, 1970) and Thomas F. Baldwin and Colby Lewis, "Violence in Television: The Industry Looks at Itself" in Surgeon General's Scientific Advisory Committee on Television and Social Behavior, *Television and Social Behavior Volume 1*, pp. 290–365 (Washington, D.C.: U.S. Government Printing Office, 1972).

company may have to pay $200,000 to replace it. According to Baldwin
and Lewis,[89] to avoid either of these·

When the producer hires a writer, he is not necessarily looking for a creative
genius. As one respondent observed, "A script by a genius may contain a
scene twenty-five minutes long that can't be edited" [to fit between commercials in the conventional teaser–three-acts–epilogue format]. Instead, "the
producer looks for a writer who can meet deadlines and give him material
that he can shoot in six and a half days, within his budget, and without any
trouble." By "trouble" the speaker meant chiefly objections from the network
censors.

The organization of work even redefines what we may think of as good
and bad writers. As Baldwin and Lewis put it, producers insist that
"good writers do not get unacceptable ideas";[90] that is, ideas that will
be rejected by the censors.

Militating against the introduction of new, innovative, unusual, or
controversial ideas, the structure of work has a decisive impact upon
the finished entertainment program. In addition, it encourages professional producers to pay only lip service to the notion of professional
autonomy, or to find a new job. For, according to Cantor,[91] a producer's
career aims and his past employment, in other words his orientation to
the organization of work, help to determine the extent to which producers combat network pressures.

Although Cantor does not discuss self-censorship, she identifies three
types of producers: *Film-makers* (primarily concerned with using their
television employment to perfect technical skills and to obtain jobs producing feature films); *Old-Line Producers* (those who have been working in either movies or television for some time); and *Writer-Producers*
(recruited to producing from free-lance writing). Each career pattern
is associated with an orientation to professional work that affects relationships with network officials. According to Cantor, Film-makers are
more concerned with techniques than with ideas and yield to network
pressures regarding ideas for programs. Old-Line Producers tend to
subscribe to the old-Hollywood view that the measure of entertainment's worth is its box-office or ratings success. Viewing themselves as
employees of organizations rather than as independent professionals,
they kowtow to the network's concerns. Cantor claims only Writer-Producers subscribe to the notion of professional autonomy, which arises
out of their past unwillingness to have their ideas censored.

Needless to say, given the proclivity of writers to engage in self-

89 Baldwin and Lewis, "Violence in Television," p. 362.
90 *Ibid.*, p. 362.
91 Muriel Cantor, "Television Producers and Network Control," a paper presented
at the meetings of the American Sociological Association, Washington, D.C., 1970.

censorship reported by Baldwin and Lewis, these battles for ideas do not concern weighty intellectual matters. The ideas for which the Writer-Producer may fight may differ only marginally from existing programs. For instance, Cantor reports the complaint of a producer who had "envisioned a series with forensic psychiatry as its main theme." He told her,

> I had to change it from a forensic psychiatry series to a general psychiatry series. Network X had bought it, and they told me in no uncertain terms that I change it into a general kind of psychiatry with general kinds of stories. They said that no one had ever heard of forensic psychiatry, but I thought the combination of courtroom drama with psychiatric themes would be interesting and different.[92]

Apparently, Cantor's informant did not ask himself, "How is this combination different? Is it merely a new twist within which existing values may be perpetuated?" Indeed, feeling that he "fights for ideas" more than other producers and ignoring the existence of self-censorship, Cantor's informant may be able to ignore the extent to which the structure of work transforms him into a technician and a *de facto* employee of the networks, producing supposedly neutral and apolitical entertainment.

Indeed, as will be seen later, marginal differentiation and belief in apolitical entertainment blind television personnel to aspects of American life that they take for granted. To cite a seemingly minor example now, taking for granted the use of cars by heroes and villains may help encourage viewers to think of cars as a romantic necessity rather than as a drain upon natural resources and a pollutant of the urban environment. In this sense, the process of making an entertainment program and the pressures associated with getting the work done may ultimately encourage hegemony.

ORGANIZATIONAL AND PROFESSIONAL
FACTORS: NEWS

It is more difficult to outline the ways in which the structure of newswork ultimately encourages hegemony, mainly because the influence of network officials is not felt as directly in newswork as it is in producing entertainment. Nonetheless, the organizational structure of newswork sets the frame in which news personnel cover or create news stories, helps to establish a professional ideology that insists upon the political neutrality of TV newswork, and ultimately encourages hegemony.

The relationship between a network and its affiliates, central to an understanding of newswork, influences the *shape* of network news

---

[92] Cantor, "Television Producers and Network Control."

stories. Epstein, as we will see in Chapter 1, explains that the network-
affiliate relationship helps to set the budget of news programs, and
budgetary restrictions become a tool with which personnel shape the
news. Because of budgetary factors, events occurring in New York,
Washington, D.C., and Chicago are presented as news of immediate importance, while events originating in other cities or other countries
are cast in terms of general issues. Significantly, news personnel's
handling of the content of stories, including the extent to which they
believe they must maintain an image of objectivity, varies according to
whether an event is deemed important for its immediacy or for its
illustration of a general theme.

As I have argued elsewhere,[93] a similar process occurs in the local
television newsroom. Like all organizations, local news operations must
schedule work, cope with a specific technology, and predict the kind of
newswork to be accomplished in both the immediate and the not-so-
immediate future. Without the ability to perform these tasks, local
television newsrooms would be at the mercy of events and would not
be routinely capable of processing information about events, of transforming events into news.

The ways in which local television news personnel sort out reality
to transform events into news are directly related to solving organizational tasks. For instance, newsmen deem events that confront them
with immediacy to be "hard news." They develop special procedures
and organizational structures to anticipate the possibility of covering
them, including such relatively simple procedures as keeping tuned to
the police radio. Events that do not require immediate coverage and
dissemination are termed "soft news" and enable news organizations to
allocate personnel in a more flexible manner. Significantly, in describing these stories that require differing organizational arrangements, the
news staff invokes different professional standards. The most relevant
of these standards is "objectivity," supposedly a professional requisite
in the treatment of hard news, but not in the treatment of soft news.

According to newsmen, the practice of objectivity—the professional
dictum to give both sides of a story formalized in the Fairness Doctrine
by the FCC—maintains the political neutrality of news presentations.[94]
Actually, to get their work done and to meet the future exigencies presented by potential hard news stories, newsmen, in practice, mean by
objectivity that one must interview an opponent and a proponent of
any controversial measure. Since the opponents and proponents whom
they identify are those persons with whom they are most frequently in

[93] Gaye Tuchman, "Making News by Doing Work: Routinizing the Unexpected,"
American Journal of Sociology 79 (1973), pp. 110–31.

[94] Gaye Tuchman, "Objectivity as Strategic Ritual: An Examination of Newsmen's Notions of Objectivity," *American Journal of Sociology* 77 (1972), pp. 660–80.

routine contact,[95] this means by and large that newspersons interview officials, for interaction between reporters and officials is routine.[96] Reporters are, as a result, more dependent upon established officials for daily information than they are upon those who challenge government authority.[97] As Molotch and Lester argue,[98] the newspersons' routines are based upon political work accomplished by the corporate and governmental elite.

The insistence upon balance, then, maintains the organizational structure and minimizes the importance of those who challenge government authority. Balance means in practice that Republicans may rebut Democrats and *vice versa,* that Congressmen may rebut members of the Executive Branch and *vice versa,* that established governmental and bureaucratic authorities may rebut the so-called "illegitimate" challenge of social movements. But, these supposedly illegitimate challengers are never offered the opportunity to criticize governmental statements with the same frequency. Instead, reporters will search for a partisan critic, an "establishment critic" such as a "maverick Senator" or for a "responsible spokesman" whom they have themselves created or promoted to a position of prominence. The nomination of Kate Millett and Germaine Greer as "spokesmen" for the women's movement, accomplished soon after the publication of their respective books, provides a particularly clear example of this. (Not that these women not active in the women's movement; rather, the media, not a group of women, made them "leaders.")

As Elliott emphasizes in Chapter 4, this tendency is also pronounced in preparing public affairs programming. He studied all the steps, from the inception of the idea to the actual broadcast, in the production of a BBC series about prejudice. To make the series, the producer needed an assortment of information. Both the producer and the researchers that were hired found that people whom they could personally contact and could ask either to help or to appear were more apt to cooperate. These people were contacted through professional networks (chains of

[95] Dan Nimmo, *Newsgathering in Washington* (New York: Atherton Press, 1964); The American Institute for Political Communication, *The Federal Government— Daily Press Relationship* (Washington, D.C., 1967); *cf.* Leo Rosten, *The Washington Correspondents* (New York: Harcourt, Brace and Company, 1937).

[96] See Douglass Cater, *The Fourth Branch of Government* (Boston: Houghton Mifflin Company, 1959).

[97] William L. Rivers, *The Opinion Makers: The Washington Press Corps* (Boston: Beacon Press, 1965) does not even discuss the relationship between journalists and the social movements.

[98] Harvey Molotch and Marilyn Lester, "Accidental News: The Great Oil Spill" (Mimeo: University of California at Santa Barbara, 1973) presents content analyses concerning the coverage of governmental views and views of the ecology movement after the Santa Barbara Oil Spill.

professional contacts and professional friendships), and through personal friends. However, using this method meant that the program's staff could locate ideas with broad currency, but not ideas that challenged dominant views. Indeed, some preliminary research[99] indicates that those who are well integrated into professional networks (or chains to use Elliott's term) are *least* apt to adopt new ideas and new techniques. Although contacting people in this manner insured that the work would be done and that the program would be politically "neutral," it also insured that the series would perpetuate trite ideas.

As with entertainment programming, the attempt to meet technical standards of professional competence may also maintain the organizational structure, and ignore the assumptions built into the techniques. Elliott argues that the programs' theme, prejudice, was dissipated by adopting them to accepted visual techniques that would fit within the allocated budget, and that the staff paid more attention to the ritualistic satisfaction of technical standards than to ideas. Similarly, as I have said elsewhere,[100] news teams take ritualistic visual conventions for granted in order to achieve "cinematic objectivity." For instance, in framing the head of a newsmaker as though he were engaging is a friendly business communication, they will not notice that this technique lends authority to his ideas.

Enabling the news personnel to meet organizational requirements, these professional practices maintain only the aura of neutrality. Both Miliband[101] and Molotch and Lester[102] claim that news practices such as these perpetuate hegemony, "an order in which a certain way of thought and life is dominant, in which one concept of reality is diffused throughout society . . . informing with its spirit . . . all social relations, particularly in their moral and intellectual connotations." [103] Like Lazarsfeld and Merton,[104] Miliband stresses that the mass media are central agencies in the legitimation of authority. Upholding the importance of civic order, news accounts pay more attention to the administrative version of reality than to the attempts of a social movement to discuss a story. Seeming politically "indeterminate"—to use Epstein's term[105]—the media take for granted both the centrality of Republicans and Democrats and the need to use cars. They assume, for objectivity's sake, that criticism of the medical profession on a

99 Mark S. Granovetter, "The Strength of Weak Ties," *American Journal of Sociology* 78 (1973), pp. 1360–80.

100 Gaye Tuchman, "The Technology of Objectivity: Doing Objective Television News," *Urban Life and Culture* 2 (1973), pp. 3–26.

101 Miliband, *The State in Capitalist Society.*

102 Molotch and Lester, Chapter 2 in this book.

103 Williams quoted in Miliband, *The State in Capitalist Society*, p. 130.

104 Paul Lazarsfeld and Robert Merton, "Mass Communication, Popular Taste and Society Action."

105 Epstein, *News from Nowhere*, p. 227.

news program requires a response from the ever-lobbying American Medical Association. But, they view the many entertainment programs emphasizing the skill and concern of doctors as neutral and apolitical, rather than as propaganda against socialized medicine. In essence, these professional practices only seem objective and neutral, while they promulgate accepted values.

Let us review the basic points:

The structure of the broadcasting industry resembles American corporate structures and reflects a corporate economy.

Like other industries, television's corporate owners greatly influence their supposed regulators.

As a result, decisions governing both the types of programs to be broadcast and the content of specific programs are primarily influenced by the industry's economic motives.

And, rather than mitigating this economic influence, organizational and professional factors adapt to it and perpetrate a myth of neutrality.

Two final questions remain: Why does this matter? What is the long-range of television? To answer these questions, we must turn more directly to the notion of hegemony.

HEGEMONY: A LONG-RANGE EFFECT

Ellul notes that in the United States, ideological hegemony—which he terms "sociological propaganda"—is a "natural result of the fundamental elements of American life . . . Mass production requires mass consumption, but there cannot be mass consumption without widespread identical views as to what the necessities of life are." [106] Ellul thinks that media personnel, as propagandists, do not deliberately introduce sociological propaganda, "though many practice it unwittingly, and tend in this direction without realizing it." [107] Instead, he suggests,

When an American producer makes a film, he has certain ideas he wants to express, which are not intended to be propaganda. Rather the propaganda element is the American way of life with which he is permeated and which he expresses in his film without realizing it.[108]

The long-range effect of such propaganda is to solidify American social and political institutions.

[106] Jacques Ellul, *Propaganda* (New York: Alfred A. Knopf, 1966), p. 68.
[107] *Ibid.*, p. 64.
[108] *Ibid.*, p. 64.

From a very different theoretical perspective, Lazarsfeld and Merton made similar statements during radio's heyday.[109] Writing of the effect of the mass media upon individuals, they argued that the mass media "ethicize" audience members (teaching them appropriate social values by conferring status and legitimating persons, policies, groups, and institutions) and also enforce social norms by "exposing deviations from these norms to public view." Additionally, they suggest, the media serve a "narcotizing dysfunction" that militates against the formation of both individual and group action:

> The individual . . . takes his secondary [media] contact with the world of political reality, his reading and listening and thinking, as a vicarious performance. He comes to mistake *knowing* about problems of the day for *doing* something about them. His social conscience remains spotlessly clean. He is concerned. He is informed . . . But, after he has gotten through his dinner and after he has listened to his favored radio programs and after he has read his second newspaper of the day, it is time for bed.[110]

Unfortunately, these theoretical notions are notoriously difficult to test empirically. Some attempts have been made to measure apathy, passivity, anomie, and their relationship to mass media consumption,[111] but these do not measure changes in the same individuals over a period of time.[112] Nor do they control for the possibility of reinforcing effects from the environment. More important, these studies do not truly operationalize the "narcotizing dysfunction." Ellul's somewhat more sophisticated treatment of sociological propaganda as ideological hegemony with structural consequences is impossible to measure.

Only short-term effects of the mass media can be subjected to rigorous empirical analysis at this time. For instance, one may measure persons' attitudes, expose them to media messages, and then remeasure their attitudes to discover the presence or absence of change. Such a procedure is frequently used in controlled experimental situations.[113] However, individuals do not normally receive media messages in experimental situations, and this technique involves some peculiar prob-

109 Lazarsfeld and Merton, "Mass Communication, Popular Taste, and Social Action," pp. 461–65.

110 Lazarsfeld and Merton, "Mass Communication, Popular Taste and Social Action," p. 464, emphasis in original.

111 These are discussed by Otto Larsen, "Social Effects of Mass Communication," in R. E. Faris, ed., *The Handbook of Modern Sociology* (Chicago: Rand-McNally and Company, 1964).

112 Chapter 8 of this book, a study by Harold Wilensky on the relationship between mass society and mass culture, tackles these issues.

113 An early example is Carl I. Hovland, Irving L. Janis, and Harold H. Kelley, *Communication and Persuasion* (New Haven: Yale University Press, 1953).

lems in coding the subjects' responses.[114] It is also well established that the social context in which individuals experience the media influences their effect upon them. Because of this, sampling techniques that mark individuals for study, rather than contexts and groups, fail to tap at least one vital dimension of the problem.[115] As a consequence, large-scale surveys of the effects of the mass media tend to be theoretically sterile. At their best, they tell us the kinds of "needs" the different media are reported to fulfill.[116] But even here, serious problems exist. For instance, some research distinguishes between information- versus escape-needs, or the reality versus the fantasy function of the mass media. Books are identified with reality, as are newspapers. Television entertainment is thought to be synonymous with escape. What about novels? More important, what about television news? The day Robert F. Kennedy died, television broadcast what amounted to re-runs of his shooting, much as they had previously "rerun" the death of Lee Harvey Oswald at the hands of Jack Ruby. Supposedly, news is classified as informational and reality-oriented. Do these "informational re-runs" cross the line to fantasy?

Consider an example that illustrates some of these problems. Suppose one wanted to study the effect of television violence upon children, a question with which a national commission was greatly concerned. One cannot control the television watching of a sample to insure that one group watches violent programs and the other does not. One cannot be positive that the children really watched the programs they report they have viewed. Nor, realizing that parents have more of an influence upon children than television does, can one control for the effects of parental behavior, peer behavior, and school. Certainly, one can take steps to minimize these considerable problems. For instance, one can study several classes of children in one school over a period of years, trying to adjust for the extent to which children inaccurately report which programs they watch and trying to minimize the problems associated with the drop-out rate from this kind of panel study.

Both NBC researchers[117] and researchers commissioned by the Sur-

---

114 Some aspects are discussed in Kathleen Crittenden and Richard J. Hill, "Coding Reliability and Interview Data," *American Sociological Review* 36 (1971), pp. 1073–80.

115 Eliot Freidson, "Communications Research and the Concept of the Mass," reprinted in Wilbur Schramm, ed., *The Process and Effects of Mass Communication* (Urbana: University of Illinois Press, 1954), pp. 380–88.

116 Elihu Katz, Michael Gurevitch, and Hadassah Haas, "On the Use of the Mass Media for Important Things," *American Sociological Review* 38 (1973), pp. 164–81.

117 J. Ronald Milavsky and Berton Pekowsky with Thomas E. Coffin and Sam Tuchman, "Exposure to TV Violence and Aggressive Behavior in Boys," paper presented at the annual meetings of the American Sociological Association, New Orleans, 1972.

geon General's Scientific Advisory Committee on Television and Social
Behavior[118] tried a variant of this approach. Each used a different statistical method to analyze the data. The NBC researchers found that
television does not have a causal relationship to violence; the Commission researchers traced a causal chain.

One could indefinitely catalogue the methodological questions and
answers flung at and by researchers attempting to assess statistically the
effects of the mass media. *The debate is primarily a methodological one.*
Although it centers around some questions of theoretical interest to
social psychologists (such as imitative learning), it eschews any serious theoretical questions regarding the social structure. Indeed, the
important questions cannot be approached statistically at the present
time. For instance, Leo Bogart, a researcher that NBC, ABC, and the
National Association of Broadcasters had blackballed from being a
member of the Surgeon General Advisory Committee on Television and
Social Behavior, notes: "Suppose social scientists had been asked in
1960 to measure the effects of treating Negroes as 'non-persons' on
television . . . It would have been even more difficult to demonstrate
the effects of this treatment on the attitudes of the white majority" [119]
than it is to prove that violence on television causes violent behavior
in children.

Bogart reminds us that the networks used to claim that they had to
treat blacks as non-persons in order to sell audiences to advertisers.[120]
(Additionally, many Southern stations refused to "clear" for programs
that had black actors in prominent roles.) With the re-introduction of
this crucial sale, this argument swings full circle: harnessed to sales,
television content ultimately reflects the American status quo.

American television perpetuates the American way. Symbolically
regulated by a "watchdog agency" that may lose its power to bark, the
industry is run for the profit of monopolies and conglomerates who sell
viewers to advertisers like cattle on the hoof. Due to the cost of advertising, the price of consumer goods increases, even if the non-Nielsen
family turns off its television set in disgust. Programs are designed to
appeal to the lowest common national denominator and to turn the
largest possible profits for both the networks and the stations. Organizational and professional influences do not necessarily serve as a corrective; they may even exacerbate the problem.

[118] Monroe M. Lefkowitz, Leonard D. Eron, Leopold W. Walder, and L. Rowell
Huesmann, "Television Violence and Child Aggression: A Follow-up Study," in
Surgeon General's Scientific Advisory Committee on Television and Social Behavior,
Television and Social Behavior, Volume 3 (Washington, D.C.: Government Printing
Office, 1972), pp. 35–135.
[119] Leo Bogart, "Warning: The Surgeon General Has Determined That TV
Violence Is Moderately Dangerous to Your Child's Mental Health," *Public Opinion
Quarterly* (1973), pp. 491–521, quotation on p. 518.
[120] *Ibid.,* p. 518 fn.

Barnouw claims, "If such a system had been outlined in 1927 or 1934, when our basic broadcasting laws were written, it would . . . have been rejected." [121] I doubt it, for clear omens of this system, the existence of networks and the use of advertising, already existed. But, it is fruitless to guess what might have happened, if American legislators had understood the full implications of establishing a system of broadcasting dominated by laissez-faire.

For, what ultimately counts is the long-range effect of the broadcasting system that we do have. And that effect is clear: American television perpetuates hegemony; it adumbrates political and intellectual discourse. It not only buries dissent; it buries the possibility that new ideas may emerge. The conditions under which the broadcasting industry flourishes makes a farce of the notion that the United States encourages a free marketplace of ideas.

[121] Barnouw, *The Image Empire,* p. 336.

I

Making news

It is obvious that corporations aim to make a profit. In the first chapter of this section, Edward Jay Epstein goes beyond that: he describes economic logic as the basis of network news coverage.

Earlier in *News from Nowhere*, from which this selection is taken, Epstein described the "logic of audience maintenance" for network news programs to which network executives subscribe. According to this logic, the size of the audience and, necessarily, the size of the ratings and of advertising rates are dependent upon two factors: the number of affiliates clearing for the network news and "audience flow." To encourage affiliates to clear for the network news, it must appear to be nationally oriented. But, according to the theory of audience flow, coverage of this type does not necessarily attract audiences. Rather, viewers tune in to watch local weather, sports, and news, and then stay tuned to watch the network news.

The logic of audience maintenance makes it foolhardy to dispense reporter-technician teams around the country to cover breaking stories, if the network can give the appearance of national coverage by spending less money. After all, individual viewers are not attracted by either the breadth or depth of the network news. In the selection printed here, Epstein describes the way the networks simulate national and world coverage. They cover breaking news events occurring in cities that are linked to New York by permanently rented cables. But, they avoid dealing with breaking events in cities that are not constantly linked, because to cover them, the networks would have to rent cables to New York or to buy time on a domestic satellite, and both alternatives are expensive. To counteract the correct impression that almost all filmed stories about breaking news originate in either New York, Washington, or Chicago, the networks develop feature stories. Pegged to discuss a general issue without timely references to specific events, these may be filmed anywhere and shipped by plane, a reasonably priced procedure. Epstein argues that this type of cost-accounting determines what the networks select as news.

Epstein's data indicate, as Molotch and Lester argue in the second selection, that news does not exist apart from the people and organizations that process it. Rather, news is a constructed reality. Molotch and Lester take the process of construction back further than Epstein does. Discussing the ways in which issues come to the attention of newsmen and then to the public, Molotch and Lester claim that the processes of construction reveal the use of power and the nature of politics in America today.

Under routine conditions, political and economic elites maintain the ability to peddle their version of reality as truth. However, when accidents and scandals occur, the links between interest and power and between big business and government regulators may stand naked. For these to be revealed, though, the federal government and economic forces extraneous to a local community must interfere with that community's economic well-being. As an example, Molotch and Lester discuss the accidental oil spill in the Santa Barbara Channel. Both the city government and citizens' groups opposed the drilling. The city did not receive tax revenue from it; and clean beaches were essential to maintaining tourist revenues. Fighting to remove drilling after the accident, the residents "discovered" the existence of a power structure that made decisions about their welfare without consulting them.

Molotch and Lester suggest that *when accidents and scandals occur, the powerful work to make them over into routine events.* For instance, they claim that governmental actions against the newspapers which had published the Pentagon Papers—revealing a national scandal—successfully diverted attention from the revelations contained in the documents. They say activities, such as making a scandal into a routine event, lead to the creation and management of news in the largest political sense.

Mindy Nix's discussion of the "Meet the Press Game," the next selection, supports Molotch and Lester's views. Nix reviews the people interviewed on "Meet the Press," "Face the Nation," and "Issues and Answers" and the kinds of questions they are asked. She argues that these programs are pro-administration, regardless of who is formally in power. Furthermore, Nix notes, the programs rarely recruit the leaders of social movements, even if they are based in Washington or nearby New York. (New Yorkers can be transported to Washington television studios with a minimum of expense.) Like the material supplied by Molotch and Lester, Nix's article suggests that programming expenses do not provide an adequate explanation of the relationship between television and the newsmaker. Rather, doing television and making news are inherently political activities.

The final selection, Philip Elliott's case study of the making of a BBC documentary series, adds some information about how public affairs programs may perpetuate existing ideas. Although the BBC is run by the state, as opposed to a conglomerate, Elliott notes that the production team wanted to maximize the size of the audience, suggesting that the processes Elliott describes might be applicable to some American television.

Elliott describes seven stages in the making of this documentary series on prejudice. He argues that in defining the subjects to be covered, deciding how they were to be presented, and gathering materials for presentation, the production team paradoxically ignored what should be said about prejudice. Further, he claims, the range of materials that could be included was limited, because the team contacted people to whom they had ready access, rather than searching for new ideas. Selecting material, writing the scripts, and recording the programs are viewed as additional limitations on the subject matter to be broadcast. Elliott explains that adopting a position of supposed neutrality, the producer left the "conclusion" to emerge from the programs, resulting in cross-comments without intellectual substance. Indeed, Elliott implies that much of the program's subject matter could be described as platitudes.

Elliott's description of the preparation of this program indicates that "professionalization" and "ritualism" may dominate the preparation of documentaries. Concerned with meeting technical standards and getting programs on the air, communicators may go through the motions of dealing with substantive issues, but they actually fail to analyze them. In this regard, Elliott's article fills in the gaps between activities occurring in the social world and activities that are telecast. If applicable to the United States (and the programming concerns appear similar to those found in America), his data indicate that these ritualistic production methods may perpetuate the status quo by limiting the ideas to be presented and then by over-simplifying them.

Taken together, the articles suggest how news and public affairs programs construct reality. Working within strict budgetary limits that define what can be presented as news (Epstein), using set production procedures that limit the ideas to be presented (Elliott), falling into the easy acceptance of versions of reality offered by the power elite under routine conditions (Molotch and Lester), and even favoring the governmental elite by bowing to its power (Nix), the programs cater to the status quo.

c h a p t e r   o n e

News from nowhere

EDWARD JAY EPSTEIN

THE LOGIC OF A NETWORK
NEWS OPERATION

While it might make economic sense for a newspaper to invest resources in increased news coverage on the assumption that it would produce exclusive and sensational stories which in turn would lead to a higher newsstand circulation, it does not make economic sense for a network to maintain anything more than the minimum number of camera crews necessary to fill the available news-programing time if one accepts the prevailing theories about audience. Additional

From *News from Nowhere: Television and the News*, by Edward Jay Epstein, pp. 100–111. © 1973 by Edward Jay Epstein. Reprinted by permission of Random House, Inc., and the author.

camera crews might well improve the quality of the news coverage, but they would not, at least according to the assumptions of network executives, significantly increase the Nielsen ratings of network news or the advertising revenues derived from it.

The costs for gathering and producing news programing is controlled mainly by the deployment of camera crews and correspondents. Aside from costing about $100,000 a year to maintain in salaries and overtime, each camera crew generates a prodigious amount of film— about twenty times as much as is used in final stories—and this has to be transported, processed, edited and narrated. NBC accountants, in using a rule-of-thumb gauge of $14 in service cost for every foot of film used in the final story (or $504 a minute), have estimated that in 1968 each film crew accounted for about $500,000 annually of the budget of NBC News. In other words, if NBC decided to hire another twenty camera crews, it would add roughly $10 million in salaries, film costs, editorial services, and so forth, to the total budget. Of course, a minimum number of crews is necessary to provide enough news film to fill the networks' news-programing time. But aside from this bare minimum, the actual number of film crews deployed, and their whereabouts, is not only a critical budgetary decision but one which defines the scope of the entire news-gathering operation. "The news you present is actually the news you cover," a network news vice-president said; "the question is how far do you fling your net."

From a journalistic point of view, the more camera crews deployed, the better, since the more news beats and potential happenings that can be covered by camera crews, the greater the chances are to capture the significant news of the day. A large number of film accounts might also lead to a more interesting program, since the producer would have more stories from which to select. But even if it produced a program with greater appeal to viewers, a wide-flung net of camera crews would make little sense from an economic point of view, given the paradox of audience flow, since it is not the appeal of the program that mainly garners the audience.

Answering his own question somewhat circuitously, the vice-president continued: "We use practically everything . . . everything that's done results in practically some use," and added, "There aren't enough crews, so we can only cover the top stories." In other words, the number of crews deployed is expected by network executives to be related to the number of hours of programing rather than the number of possible news events. Reuven Frank noted this as one of the main budgetary controls on the news division: "Like everyone else my indices are money, but my goals aren't money. . . . I'm asked questions [by network executives] like why it is [that] with no increase in total hours [of news programing] the use of film stock is up 15 percent from last year."

In fact, NBC relies mainly on only ten regular camera crews in the five cities where it owns television stations (New York, Chicago, Los Angeles, Washington and Cleveland), and three staff cameramen (who can assemble camera crews) in Boston, Houston and Dallas, to cover the entire country. In 1968, more than 80 percent of all domestic stories shown on the NBC Evening News were produced by the ten NBC camera crews and three staff cameramen. (In comparison, to cover the news of *one* city, Los Angeles, NBC's local news operation used twelve camera crews, according to their news director, to fill local news-programing needs, which ran two hours.) CBS used a similar number of crews—located at its own stations in New York, Chicago and Los Angeles, as well as in Atlanta and Washington—for the bulk of its domestic news stories. ABC, which had considerably less news programing in 1968 because it produced no morning news, was able to get most of its national news stories from eight full-time crews, in New York, Chicago, Los Angeles, Washington, Atlanta and Miami. All three networks also maintained regular camera crews in nine cities overseas, including London, Paris, Bonn, Rome, Tokyo, Saigon and Hong Kong.

To be sure, in the event of a momentous news happening, the networks can quickly mobilize additional crews regularly assigned to news documentaries, sports and local news at network stations, or the camera crews of affiliated stations. But the net which is cast for national news on a day-to-day basis is essentially defined by the ten or so crews that are routinely available for network assignments, a number which proceeds directly from the economic logic of news coverage.

THE LOGIC OF NETWORK
NEWS PRODUCTION

Even though the scope of news coverage is not assumed to be important in attracting an audience for network news programs, the appearance of a truly national news service must be projected for two independent reasons. First, affiliates clear network news . . . not only for economic reasons but also because it is presumed to be in the "public interest" (as defined by the FCC) to carry national as well as local news. However, if network news were perceived to be no more than local news from a handful of cities, affiliates would have a less compelling reason to yield some of their most valuable time for it, especially when the time could be used for its own news and advertising sales. Second, to hold the maximum possible audience throughout the program, producers work on the theory that each story should have some "national" appeal.

Network news producers thus have the problem of creating the illusion of truly national coverage, a world literally ringed with news cameras, and of "national stories," which are of interest everywhere, with the reality of a minimal number of film crews based in a few cities. To meet this demand, network producers have adopted the strategy of commissioning the national, or trend, stories they need well in advance of the actual happening (very much in the same way that magazines commission timely articles), so that they can attain the maximum use out of the available camera crews. Av Westin summed up this policy in a memorandum to correspondents when he took over as executive producer of the ABC Evening News in 1969: "I am operating on the theory that a producer should be aggressive and 'produce' a broadcast, not waiting for news to happen in order to scramble after it. Anticipating events is most important." For example, he asked correspondents the next week for the "future production" of stories on "medical, consumer, geriatric and pediatric reports, as well as ombudsman reports"—subjects which he subsequently explained to me were "chosen with an eye towards the demographics of the news audience."

Westin also applied the policy of "anticipating events" to overseas news, explaining it in some detail to correspondents:

I want to point out to correspondents and Bureaus, particularly overseas, that the same pre-thought which we are engaging in here, before sending a cabled assignment, ought to be exhibited where you are. A specific example. Rote assignments to cover May Day in *every* capital. Unnecessary. They arrive too late for air, and unless there is major news anticipated, I am willing to take the risk and not cover. The off-chance that some "beleaguered" Berliners, Diffident Englishmen, Unemotional Japanese, or War-weary flower children in Saigon will do something is not enough reason to spend your time, Bureau energy, and our money on coverage. . . .

It is possible that in previous years, no one in New York ever expressed these thoughts and since no one ever said "Do Not Cover," the tradition of blanket coverage has grown up. Please consult New York before you assign these "annual" stories. Stringers and crews cost money. And I'd rather spend these funds on having Dunsmore in Beirut, when the Lebanese Government fell [and other stories]. . . . In short, we're spending correspondent's time and crew resources where it counts, and not for some two-day late electronic feed. I am not trying to usurp correspondent's prerogatives to assign coverage of news stories in their areas, but I am suggesting a re-evaluation of judgments based on the criteria now operative on the evening news.

This strategy of preselecting stories was well adumbrated for network news by Reuven Frank, who wrote in 1963 when NBC expanded the evening news from fifteen minutes to a half-hour:

The picture of the producer frustrated at what he has to leave out is less accurate than the picture of the producer canvassing the nooks and crannies of the cutting room for 45 seconds more [film]. We cannot do the same for

fifteen more minutes. . . . Except for those rare days when other material
becomes available, the gap will be filled by planned and prepared film
stories, and we are assuming the availability of two each night.

The deficit in day-to-day news coverage can thus be compensated
for by producers anticipating and "producing" the desirable stories,
which would be free of daily news contingencies. "We simply couldn't
find the type stories we need for balance and pacing," an NBC producer pointed out, "if we had to rely on the news film that comes from
general coverage every day." To implement this strategy, the CBS
Evening News divided the responsibility between two producers. One
is in charge of daily news stories; the other is responsible for commissioning and developing film stories, called "enterprise pieces" or
"magazine stories," for future use. The latter explained that "local
news, which has much less area to cover, can set up a camera at City
Hall, and whatever it records is shown that night. We have the whole
country to cover, and we can't just set up cameras and wait for news
to happen somewhere. We have to plan it out in advance." For example, the Charles Kuralt "On the Road" series he produces "covers
the nostalgia of smalltown life in America" which "could never be
found in day-to-day news coverage."

However necessary it may be to project an image of a national news
service, the process by which the networks "produce news" involves
more than simply "mirroring" news events: decisions must be made
about which stories will be "anticipated" and sought out.

THE GEOGRAPHY OF NEWS

The quest of attaining the appearance of truly national news programs is further complicated by the simple but intriguing fact that it
costs a good deal more to transmit stories from some places than it
does from others.

While the fixed costs and overhead of the news operation, such as
salaries of camera crews, correspondents and executives, are subsumed
in the general budget of the news division at each network, the more
incremental costs that news programs add to the general overhead are
charged directly against their budgets. At the beginning of each year,
the network allocates each news program a budget to which the producer is expected to conform (unless it is subsequently adjusted because of extraordinary events, such as the invasion of Czechoslovakia
in 1968). The single most flexible item, and one which comprises from
30 to 40 percent of the total program's budget, is the outlay for transmitting stories over telephone cables from "remote" locations—that is,
any place outside the networks' facilities in New York and Washington—to the networks' broadcasting centers in New York City. The

closed-circuit lines that interconnect networks with their affiliates across the country normally can only be used to transmit programs in one direction: from the network's nerve center in New York to affiliates. Therefore, to transmit news reports electronically from any "remote" location to the network for rebroadcast, a news program must order special "long lines," or closed-circuit connection, between the two points from the American Telephone & Telegraph Company. In 1969 the charge for the "remote" was $1.60 per mile for up to an hour's use of the long lines, and from $800 to $1,500 for the "loop," which is what the package of electronic equipment that connects the transmission point (usually an affiliated station) with the AT&T's long lines is called. Such costs make a considerable dent in the producers' budgets.

Although the NBC Evening News had a total budget of about $160,-000 a week in 1969, and the CBS Evening News one of about $100,-000 a week for seven nightly half-hour programs, most of the budget was actually committed in advance for the salaries and expenses of the producers, editors, writers, and other members of the unit, and for the studio and other overhead costs which were automatically billed to the program. (The difference in these accounting charges is responsible for most of the difference in the budgets of the NBC and CBS Evening News.) Only about $49,000 a week, or $7,000 a program, was left over in the budget for "remotes." Since a news program needs six to eight film stories a night, and some remote charges can be as high as $5,000 apiece, the budget in effect limits the number of "remote" stories that can be transmitted each week or month. Indeed, as Fred W. Friendly, former president of CBS News, wrote: "The cost of long lines is so high that often television fails to take advantage of one of its greatest assets."

In weighing the value of individual stories against the costs of transporting them to New York, producers must consider such questions as: Is the story a "mandatory" one, which will be on competing programs (and thus seen by both network and affiliate executives who "use the competition as a scorecard")? Can the story be delayed and the film shipped by airplane (which might involve a few days if the film is from Vietnam), without "dating" the material? Is the program running ahead or behind its budgetary schedule?

While mandatory stories—those stories of moment in all the headlines—are rarely eliminated from the program, "optional" stories, which are defined by one producer as "stories which will never be missed" by the executives or the audience, are not infrequently dropped to save the long-line costs, especially when the budget is "running tight." For example, when an NBC executive unexpectedly inquired why a news story about the unveiling of a new Boeing 707 passenger plane was not carried on the NBC Evening News, a producer replied, "I just didn't think it was worth four thousand dollars [for a long line] to go to Seattle." He later explained to me that the unveiling would probably have been included on the program if it had occurred in New York City instead of Seattle. The budget officer added that "there were enough other good stories to choose from without ordering a special [long line] to Seattle when we are running over budget."

While news stories from some cities like Seattle are relatively expensive for network news programs to obtain, news stories from a few cities are "free" (at least in terms of the bookkeeping charges) because they can be fed to New York over permanently leased network cables that connect Chicago and Washington, as well as cities en route, to New York, during the hour between 5:30 and 6:30 P.M. EST when these closed-circuit lines are not otherwise being used by the network to transmit programs to affiliates. Thus at NBC a news story can be fed from Chicago during this time period over the "round robin," as the circuit is called, at no cost to the program's budget, and to get stories from points farther west, a producer need only pay out of his budget for a special long line from the remote location to Chicago (or Washington, or any other point on the round robin), from where it can be relayed to New York "free." Furthermore, the networks themselves maintain permanent loops connecting stations they themselves own to the AT&T transmission point, which means that network news programs can send stories from these stations without having the cost of renting loops from the telephone company charged against their budget. This leads to some sharp variations in the cost of obtaining news in different parts of the country.

Because of these cost differences, producers have a positive incentive to take news stories, at least "nonmandatory" ones, from some cities rather than others, especially if their budget is strained for other reasons. The fact that networks base most of their camera crews and correspondents in New York, Washington, Chicago and Los Angeles further reinforces the advantage of using news stories from these cities . . . so it is not surprising that most of the film stories shown on the national news originate from these cities, according to an analysis of film logs in 1968–1969. Although the geographical distribution of film stories varies greatly from day to day, over any sustained period of time it leans in the direction of these few large cities. This also means that certain types of stories that occur in these areas are more likely to be covered by network news. For example, the business manager of NBC news pointed out that "civil rights is very expensive" to cover in the South because it is an "out-of-town story," meaning that loops and long lines had to be installed.

On the other hand, covering confrontations between black militants and police in cities connected by the round robin is much less expensive for network news. It is therefore economically more efficient to consign news of small town America and remote cities to such timeless features as the CBS series "On the Road with Charles Kuralt." This suggests that if network news tends to focus on the problems of a few large urban centers, it is not because, as [former] Vice-President Agnew argued, that an "enclosed fraternity" of "commentators and producers live and work in the geographical and intellectual confines of Washington, D.C., or New York City" and "draw their political and social views from the same sources," but because the fundamental economic structure compels producers to select a large share of their film stories from a few locations.

The high cost of transmitting stories electronically also affects the distribution of stories over time as well as space. Since none of the network news programs are given sufficient budgetary allocations to transmit film stories regularly back to New York from overseas bureaus by satellite relays, all but momentous foreign news stories must be shipped back by airplane, which means that they seldom can be shown to an American audience on the day they happen. Because of the almost certain delay on foreign news, producers are virtually compelled to commission timeless stories from overseas bureaus, especially ones that can easily be "pegged" to likely future news bulletins. And if the satellite costs are to be avoided, stories that are tied to a definite news happening, such as a battle in Vietnam or civil disturbance in some country, must be detached from the dated event and recast, through editing and narration, in vaguer terms. For example, NBC News obtained "excellent footage" from the BBC of a riot that flared up between Protestants and Catholics in Northern Ireland in late September 1968, but since there was not time to ship the film to New York by plane while the event was still in the headlines, the producer of the Evening News requested his London bureau to do a "backgrounder" on the confrontation in which the BBC film could be used. The next week an NBC film crew went to Londonderry and shot footage of boarded-up windows, riot damage and a protest march, which was edited together as "a civil rights story," ending with, as the script describes it, "various shots of cops and kids sitting down in the street" and the narrator concluding: "Still, youth may break down the cruel walls separating Ulster's two communities." Since the story described a general phenomena (youth resolving conflict), rather than a specific one (that is, a riot in Londonderry), it could be shown more than a month later without appearing to be dated.

Moreover, Fred Friendly claims that the "excessive charges" for relaying stories electronically back to New York substantially "discourage competition and are responsible for the networks' use of the 'pool' system on space stories and other big news events." Confronted with an extraordinary news event overseas, such as a President's visit to Europe, which is expected to be broadcast on the same day as it occurs, a network producer can defray part of the expense of sending the story via satellite by entering into a "pool" with one or both of the other networks. The programs in the pool get the same footage, though they may edit it differently, but divide the satellite charges between themselves. President Nixon's trip to Europe in 1968 was handled this way. Occasionally a pool arrangement can also make a satellite transmission unnecessary, since it guarantees that a story will not be shown first by a competing network, and thus can be shipped by plane. For instance, when the Soviet press agency Tass made film available in March 1969 depicting the fighting between Soviet and Chinese troops on the Ussabi River frontier in the Far East, an NBC producer called his counterparts at CBS and ABC and arranged a pool for the film, which CBS at least up to that time was considering relaying back to New York by satellite. But the pool made such an expenditure unnecessary, since the film would not be shown on any other network before CBS had access to it, and it was shipped back by airplane and shown the next day. However, such arrangements tend to be relatively infrequent, if only because there are not many stories from overseas that producers consider to be worth the cost of covering as a major event.

To be sure, one can find sufficient incidents in which network news covered costly events that could have been avoided without any repercussions in terms of a diminished audience or executive disapproval to make it clear that news decisions cannot be entirely explained in terms of weighing immediate costs, benefits and budgetary pressures. The argument given here is not, however, that individual news decisions are made with a budget in hand, but that the economic logic— which effectively denies that any benefits in revenue will come from an increase in the quality of the news content of newscasts, yet at the same time demands that the illusion of national coverage be maintained—affects the news operation in very fundamental ways. . . .

c h a p t e r t w o

Accidents, scandals, and routines: resources for insurgent methodology

HARVEY MOLOTCH AND MARILYN LESTER

News is the information which people receive second-hand about worlds which are not available to their own experience. Out of a vast "glut of occurrences," a relatively few happenings are translated by mass media into things "fit to print," i.e., *the* important things worthy of constituting our conceptions of the community, state, nation, and world in which we live. News, and the process through which it is produced, determines the experience of publics; it is an important source of whatever ideological hegemony exists in a given society; those who make the news are crucial actors in making publics what they are.

The power of the media to create experience rests on what we'll term the "objectivity assumption," to which almost everyone pledges allegiance. This assumption has it that there is indeed a world "out there" and that an account of a given event reflects that world, or a piece of it, with some degree of accuracy. The "objectivity assumption" states not that the media are objective, but that there is a world out there to be objective about. Operating on the "objectivity assumption," lay people read a newspaper or listen to a news broadcast with the aim in mind of finding out about the world which is described in the produced account. People, in other words, read newspapers to find out about an assumed objective state of the world. Sociologists in their work on power, on the media, and in their methods of content analysis, usually do much the same thing.

"Accidents, Scandals, and Routines: Resources for Insurgent Methodology," by Harvey Molotch and Marilyn Lester. From *The Insurgent Sociologist* 3 (1973), pp. 1–11. Reprinted by permission of the publisher.

This essay was originally prepared for presentation at the annual meetings of the American Sociological Association, New Orleans, 1972. The authors are grateful for the encouragement of T. R. Young and Timothy Lehman, as well as for critical comments from Richard Flacks, Hugh Mehan, Milton Mankoff, Milton Ohlin, Charles Perrow, Michael Schwartz, David Street, Gaye Tuchman, Eugene Weinstein, and Don Zimmerman.

It's all very reasonable, to be sure, but there is an alternative possibility. Newspapers, instead of reflecting a world out there, might reflect the practices of those who have the power to determine the experience of others. Harold Garfinkel [1] has made a similar point about clinical records which he investigated. Rather than viewing an institution's records as standing for something which happened, as sociologists typically do, Garfinkel saw in those records the practices of people who make records: the hedges they play, the short-cuts they take, the theories in their heads, the purposes-at-hand with which they must deal. In other words, there are "good organizational reasons for bad clinical records." And those "good reasons" spell out the social organization of the clinic.

We think that mass media should similarly be viewed as one big, bad clinical record. Our present interest, however, does not lay in an opportunity for name-calling criticism, but rather in a possibility for understanding how the product comes to look as it does. We want to study media in order to see in them the methods through which the powerful come to determine the experience of publics. We look for the methods which accomplish ideological hegemony by examining the records which are produced.

We conceive of people doing news as people who are guided by a purpose at hand. In trying to explain what news is, we must meet the challenge of explaining how it is that certain phenomena are included as news while an infinite array of other phenomena are ignored. The traditional view, held by those who rely on the "objectivity assumption," inevitably falls back on the notion that some things are just more *important* than others. This, of course, begs the question: what determines what is or is not important? For our own answer, we begin by invoking the concept of selective perception from psychology. Selective perception teaches that individuals, when faced with a glut of stimuli in perceptible space, confront an analogous challenge in terms of discriminating the important from the trivial. The creation of a meaningful field of perception requires that this selection be accomplished. That accomplishment is carried out through *purposiveness*. We discriminate chairs from other surrounding matter because of the recurrent need to sit. Carpenters discriminate among woods and eskimoes among snows. In all instances, the motive for discrimination and for meaning creation is present need. And since needs and purposes are not the same from one individual or culture to another, so it is that the meaningful worlds of individuals and cultures differ.

A sense of history, of community, of nation is created in the same

1 Harold Garfinkel, "Good Organizational Reasons for Bad Clinic Records," Chapter 6 in *Studies in Ethnomethodology* (Englewood Cliffs: Prentice-Hall, 1967).

way: purposes at hand carve up the *temporal dimension* of the perceptible field in order to make certain occurrences more important than others. When something happens which a given observer thinks is so important that *others* should hear it, he spreads the word—and that means there is *news*. We thus make news because *we* think something is important.

The summary of all this is that what is or is not news depends upon what we want others to think; and what we want others to think is guided by what we anticipate the consequences will be to our purposes. Thus, the newspaper and TV newscast are the results of purposive activities of certain actors who are trying to determine the experience of others. This purposiveness may be crude and transparently "selfish," or it may be absolutely unconsciously purposive and be viewed as "objective," without bias, and so forth. But all such newsmaking must emerge in some way from certain practical goals, simply because there is no other viable explanatory mechanism for the production of creative meanings.

We have inventoried three separate kinds of news events: Routine Events, Accidents, and Scandals. These differ in the ways in which the purposes of some people function to get them across on the printed page and in the news broadcast. We want to describe them here in order to help provide some alternative imageries which insurgent scholars and citizens can use to see the social system in the news. We will take up each in turn.

ROUTINE EVENTS[2]

Definition: Routine Events are deliberately promoted occurrences which were originally deliberately accomplished by the promoter.

During the Santa Barbara oil spill in late January, 1969, President Nixon made an inspection tour of certain beaches and subsequently announced to the nation that the damage caused by the blow-out had been repaired. He did not announce that the stretch of beach he inspected had been especially cleaned for his arrival, while miles north and south of him remained hopelessly blackened. Let's take another example, drawn from the other side of the world: The supposed Gulf of Tonkin attack of 1964 by the North Vietnamese was promoted as a

---

2 Following Molotch ("Oil in Santa Barbara and Power in America," *Sociological Inquiry* 40 (1970), pp. 131–44), Roger Manela ("The Classification of Events in Formal Organizations," Ann Arbor Institute for Labor and Industrial Relations: mimeo, 1971) has developed a typology of events using similar terminology. Manela treats events as objective phenomena which are typed according to how well they fit or fail to fit established routines of formal organizations. Our treatment and purposes are distinct from Manela's, although certain intriguing parallels exist.

public event through news releases, press conferences, briefings, and speeches; it served to legitimize the escalation of American involvement in the Vietnam War.

These are examples of *routine events*, which partake of the most managed features of news-making. An individual or group promotes one or more of its activities as newsworthy because it is useful for them to do so. If that news is subsequently adopted by the media, we must assume then that they, also, have a use for publishing it. We learn from these events what others intend for us to learn: nothing hostile to the purposes of the event-makers, nothing useful to groups with conflicting purposes and interests. Public politics, public events, and what we read in the newspaper is in large part dominated by this type of event. Murray Edelman[3] (1964) describes the dominance of routine events as the "symbolic use of politics":

> Basic to the recognition of symbolic forms in the political process is a distinction between politics as a spectator sport and political activity as utilized by organized groups to get quite specific tangible benefits for themselves. For most men most of the time politics is a series of pictures in the mind placed there by television news, newspapers, magazines, and discussions. The pictures create a moving panorama taking place in a world the mass public never quite touches, yet one its members come to fear or cheer. They are told of legislatures passing laws, foreign political figures threatening or offering trade agreements, wars starting and ending, candidates for public office losing or winning, decisions made to spend unimaginable sums of money to go to the moon. . . . Politics is for most of us a passing parade of abstract symbols.

Not only is routine event-making the standard fare of the mass media; it also provides the "data" for sociologists investigating the social structure. Edward Banfield,[4] for example, in his classic study of community power, employs a decisional case study method in endeavoring to discover who influenced the outcomes of six "key" issues in Chicago. He selects the issues which received the widest coverage in the media and assumes these to be synonymous with "key" political issues, uncritically letting the organized ways in which events get done determine his subjects of study. Consequently, the very "issues" Banfield studies are issues simply because his respondents made them such by promoting them as routine events, as material to fill the media's "news hole" and the public's mind. No contrast is made between routine events in the news and those events which Edelman considers to constitute the nonsymbolic political sector where tangible

---

[3] Murray Edelman, *The Symbolic Uses of Politics* (Urbana: University of Illinois Press, 1964).
[4] Edward Banfield, *Political Influence* (New York: Free Press, 1962).

resources are actually distributed by and among members of the elites. No suggestion is made that what is published is done so for purposes that might have nothing to do with any "objective" importance or newsworthiness, if seen from other possible standpoints. Lost in this type of research are the ways in which powerful event makers are able to have their public agendas adopted by the media through their organized promotional activities.[5] Lost also is what Bachrach and Baratz[6] term the "second face of power," the ability to create an event or public issue and the ability to prevent other options, activities, decisions, etc. from being publicly debated.

It is certainly not by chance that the kinds of issues to which we typically have access are of the sort which Banfield studies; e.g., where to locate the next branch of the University of Illinois or the next convention center. These are the kinds of issues which are deemed safe for public consumption, the kinds which will not significantly upset, challenge, or change the larger contextual basis of political life in America. They constitute, for the most part, all the news that's fit to print.

A routine public issue might best be described as *an event about which the elites divide,* where there is an agreement to disagree, because the stakes—although possibly important to some people—do not involve any critical restructuring of the social system and thus represent no threat to existing orders of power and privilege. When there exist competing definitions of events among powerful parties, or when an event can serve competing purposes, there is an *issue.* Since members of the elite disproportionately have the power to make all events, they also have disproportionate access to creating issues. The surfacing of public issues, especially through routine events, should thus be seen by the critical content analyst or newspaper reader as inherently trivial, useful only as an index of splits among the routinely powerful.

Less powerful groups can have radically different uses for events; and they too try to cause issues to surface on the basis of positions, which if taken seriously, question basic socio-political structures. But by virtue of their lack of power, they must typically assemble themselves in an inappropriate place at an inappropriate time in order to be deemed "newsworthy." The fact that they are forced to resort to spectacular displays, e.g., sit-ins, allows those with easy access to the media to respond to the "inappropriate" display rather than to the questions which underlie it.

Thus, routine events are planned as events by those who have both

[5] Daniel Boorstin, *The Image: A Guide to Pseudo Events in America* (New York: Harper, 1961).

[6] Peter Bachrach and Morton Baratz, "The Two Faces of Power," *American Political Science Review* 57 (1962), pp. 947–52.

a use for them and the ability to promote them as public. To select the media's "key events" for study is to employ a consensus methodology;[7] the researcher uncritically adopts a sample of events which fits the publicity needs of some small groups of people as his study topic.

ACCIDENTS

Definition: Accidents are unplanned occurrences which are promoted by a party other than the agent who inadvertently caused the underlying occurrence.

Accidents—occasions in which miscalculation or mistake leads to a breakdown in our conception of order—are specifically antithetical to the interests which produce routine event-making practices. Accidents are embarrassing; an accident occurs when those who were parties to an occurrence never intended to have that occurrence become a public event. Oil companies never intended, in drilling for oil, to cause a huge blow-out at Santa Barbara; those who designed our emergency alert system never intended for that system's total incompetence to be demonstrated through a false alert; those who built and deployed hydrogen bombs never intended for several to be "lost" in the Spanish countryside. At least in their early stages, accidents transcend and render inoperative the managed and contrived nature of routines. Nobody who ordinarily makes news is ready; the stories aren't straight; powerful people screw up. The accident's inherent features present many problems for those who ordinarily make public events; their capacity to define the public agenda to serve their own interests and purposes is inhibited.

Moreover, the very appearance of accidents and the fact that large numbers of people often witness their direct consequences (oil on beaches, dead sheep strewn across two Utah valleys) demand that the media provide some minimal event-coverage. If they did not, censorship would be blatantly obvious. This would be inimical to the media's aura of objectivity which it needs to maintain and to its role definition as a mere reporter of what's "really happening," rather than as an active participant in the generation of news. Thus, in the case of accidents, the media become an ally, though often a reluctant one, and a resource for groups with competing uses for events (including sociologists seeking a radical perspective on the structure of American society).

The accident, quite unlike the routine event, provides access to normally obfuscated political structures—to decision-makers, to decision-

---

[7] T. R. Young and Timothy Lehman, "Conflict Methodology," paper presented at the meetings of the American Sociological Association, New Orleans, August, 1972.

making processes, and often to the private domains of individuals (e.g., Ted Kennedy at Chappaquiddick Island) which in everyday life are kept far removed from the public events sector. The accident can serve as a high-powered microscope, a resource for generating information typically prevented from public consideration. If Banfield had selected his "key issues" on the basis of news surfacing as accidents, he (or some more reputable scholar) might have come away with other conclusions about power in American society.

Thus, as Molotch[8] has described in a previous paper, we gain from the Santa Barbara oil spill a rare view of the oil companies' marriage to the federal government and the effects of that marriage upon local communities. We see how the latter come to be dominated by private decision-making in corporation board rooms and in the office of the Department of the Interior. As upper-middle and upper-class Santa Barbarans struggled to be heard, to gain access to key decision makers, they gained even more direct information about power in America and about the inefficacy of local protest. The discrepancy between pronouncement and practice on the part of corporate and federal officials was poignantly illustrated. Though the goal of getting oil out of Santa Barbara was thwarted, the President of the United States, heads of government departments, and corporations magnates stood naked before both investigators and citizens, and to a much lesser extent, before the country as a whole.

Similarly, we have been assured for years about the effectiveness of our early warning defense system. And yet, at the North American Air Defense Command located in Colorado Springs, Colorado, on February 21, 1971, an accident occurred which exposed the irrelevance of public assurances. Two IBM tapes hang on the wall there, one tape containing the code word for a real alert, the other a test tape. Twice each week the test tape is put on the teletype which automatically assumes control of the AP and UPI wire services. At 6:30 A.M. on that day, the operator mistakenly grabbed the tape for a real emergency alert. Since no procedure had ever been established to handle a false alert, a full forty minutes passed between the beginning and the end of the alert. The error was compounded at the local level: for example, in one place, paper was jammed in the teletype ticker, so the message was never received; in another, the broadcaster said he "just couldn't summon the courage to tell everybody there was a national emergency" and the message was not broadcast; in another, where the ticker is located in the basement, no one checked the wires until five hours after the alert had passed.

Were that to have been a real alert, it would have failed. Without

8 Harvey Molotch, "Oil in Santa Barbara and Power in America."

the accident, no one would have realized how "unsafe" we all are, despite the rhetoric of public officials. The accident provided a view that contrasted sharply with previous speeches, press releases, and pronouncements.

A final example of the accident may be instructive. Dugway Proving Ground, located near Denver and Salt Lake City, spans one million acres. It is one of six military chemical and biological warfare installations where several different kinds of chemical and biological warfare weapons are tested, ranging from nerve gas and defoliants to synthetic versions of rattlesnake venom and Bubonic plague.

On March 13, 1968, a test involving the spraying of nerve gas "VX" from a jet airplane at a height of 150 feet was done. The objective was to determine "how the gas distributes itself in down winds between 5 and 25 miles per hour." [9] As one of the planes zoomed up after a trial run, a valve on the two high explosive dispensers failed to snap firmly shut. The gas poured out, was picked up by winds, and was carried as far as 45 miles from the target area.

Within the next week 6400 sheep were dead. Two veterinarians called to the scene to assist ranchers suffered temporary illness. Although there were no other known effects on humans (the falling night snow of March 13 brought the gas to the earth and the combination of the hour and inclement weather kept exposed populations indoors), dead carcasses were clearly visible to citizens, reporters, Army personnel, and investigators; and the pictures which appeared in the press could not be obliterated with a slogan eliciting symbolic support against the "Reds." It was clear to all that chemical and biological warfare weapons could accidentally affect U.S. citizens as well as purposely destroy Communists.

These examples point out that, for social scientists, accidents provide a convenient resource for gaining entrance into unstudied and often hidden features of politics in America. Especially in the earliest stages of an accident, we have found few prohibiting factors to research save the ability to get to a scene when an accident abruptly occurs. By virtue of the accident's internal characteristics, we can employ a case study technique which here becomes an insurgent methodology. That is, we now have access to an array of events and issues which defy the programmed character of routine events.

The situation changes, however, after the initial event, as those in power—e.g., the oil companies in the case of the oil spill, the defense department in the case of the false alert—seek to regain control of the event-making process.

---

[9] Seymour Hirsch, "On Uncovering the Great Nerve Gas Cover-Up," *Ramparts* 3 (July 1969), pp. 12–18.

One of the most important routinizing tactics is the deliberate complication of the issue so that final responsibility for the cause of the event is ambiguous. This was the strategy in the nerve gas case. For several months after the sheep carcasses were found, the Department of Defense, the U.S. Public Health Service, Utah State Departments of Health and Agriculture, as well as local scientists, conducted tests to discern the cause of death. The local scientists were positive that nerve gas "VX," sprayed accidentally from the plane, was responsible. But the other agencies first suggested that there was only an accidental correlation between the gas tests and sheep deaths; they searched for other causes—in poisonous plants, pesticides, and diseases, to name a few. When these tests proved negative, the Army advanced a multi-cause theory. They said that a variety of reasons were probably responsible, of which the nerve gas may have been one.

In routine events it is at best difficult, at worst highly arbitrary, to try to separate key background decision making from the cloaking activities of the elite; that whole scene has been neatly packaged for public consumption. With accidents, on the other hand, because the perpetrators are caught off guard, routinizing can occur only after the event and must be superimposed upon the consequences which have already been felt. Thus, we can directly observe endeavors to normalize the accident and to recapture hegemony on the part of the powerful. We can isolate, study, and publicize them for what they are: attempts to cover over the possible long-range ramifications of the accidents' revelations.

We can also use this understanding to study the way in which information is controlled in the first place. The tactics which actors use to normalize troublesome events are just more transparent examples of the everyday procedures of creating routine news.

In the accidents we have studied so far, one of the more exciting findings is that citizens are able to make connections between interest and power, between big business and governmental regulators. From these connections they can critically understand the discrepancy between public and private politics, an understanding heretofore restricted to the "insider." What citizens seem to lack, however, is the ability to move from what they learn from a specific accident to a more general conceptualization about how the entire society works. That linking activity is the work of the sociologist. Thus, the accident is a potential mobilizing force for publics which, after more work on the sociologist's part, might develop into a blueprint for change. As one Santa Barbara resident remarked:

We, the people, can protest and protest and it means nothing because the industrial and military junta are the country. They tell us, the people, what is good for the oil companies is good for the people. To that I say "like hell". . . .

Contrary to popular belief everyday people who have access to the necessary information are all too willing and able to draw the logical connections and to act on the basis of that knowledge. It is not that the issues are too complex for "mundane minds"; rather, the issues themselves are strategically complicated, and the thesis of the "dumb citizen" is itself an ideology for keeping publics at a distance.

Of course, accidents do not always mobilize vast groups of people for mass action. But they do provide some insight into the conditions under which a population can be roused. The fact that people do not overtly confront the perpetrators of an accident is an event in itself and should be contrasted with its opposite—where groups seize upon the accident's mobilizing potential. Such a contrast can pinpoint some of the obstacles which must be faced in trying to summon a mass movement for social change in the society.

For example, unlike Santa Barbarans, Utah citizens did not undertake an overt struggle against the Defense Department. While local elites in Santa Barbara were deeply involved in promoting the spill as a national public event and issue, local Utah elites were at best ambivalent in their response. The difference in attitude is to be found in the economic circumstances of the respective areas: Santa Barbara reaps few benefits from oil drilling in the channel; but the Utah economy is dependent on the Department of Defense and its hundreds of millions of dollars. Utah local elites could not afford to promote the occurrence as a public event; the local citizens had no difficulty in comprehending the predicament—that their lives are daily endangered by the hand which feeds them.

SCANDALS

Definition: A scandal involves a deliberately planned occurrence which is promoted by a party different from the occurrence's agent.

The third type of event, the scandal is a kind of mixed case in our typology. Here are a few examples:

On May 1, 1971, an announcer at a local California radio station reported that Governor Ronald Reagan paid no state income taxes the previous year. The information was revealed through a "leak" in the confidential files of the Franchise Tax Board. For the next several days, this story was widely discussed, by newspapers and other media, by political opponents of Reagan, and by those on the left. It was a paradoxical revelation since the Governor was constantly on the warpath against cheats, rip-offs, hippie students, welfare recipients, and since he had opposed income tax withholding because, he said, "Taxes should hurt."

On the national level a similar type of event occurred on June 15, 1971, when *The New York Times* published an excerpt from the 47 volume secret study of the origins of the Vietnam war. In the next three weeks eight more excerpts were printed. Shortly after the publications began, however, the stories on the Pentagon Papers were in part overshadowed by the complex court battles which were taking place over the fact that a leak had occurred, over the right of the newspaper to print such government documents, and over the possible danger to national security posed by the publications. As typically occurs with accidents, the powerful were attempting to routinize the event by transforming the issue into one more compatible with their own purposes and fitting their own perspective on what is newsworthy, interesting, important, i.e., on what is "news."

Like the routine event, but unlike the accident, a scandal is planned, not by the central party involved, however, but by an informer— usually some sort of insider. Like the consequences of accidents, scandals can also be embarrassing: they provide insight into normally protected structures and activities. Reagan lost, at least temporarily, some of his support as a result of the publication of his tax status; and from the publication of the Pentagon Papers, U.S. involvement in Vietnam became suspect. The scandal also allowed for issues to be raised concerning classification of government documents, freedom of the press, and private decision making in the execution of national policy.

What makes the scandal a type of event in its own right is the way in which it becomes a public event. Scandals involve persons who have at least some access to private sectors and who, for one reason or another, provide out-groups with information about that private sector. Scandals require "leakers" or "informants"; thus, they are contingent upon some dispute or disagreement among persons who are supposed to operate in substantial harmony. The scandal can only emerge when some insider is pissed-off or when some insurgent manages to be placed inside; and it can occur only if the media is willing to be a party to the exposure. The amazing thing about the Pentagon Papers, then, is not that Presidents tell lies, but that *The New York Times* was willing to expose that fact.

Nevertheless, scandals provide many of the same resources and research advantages as do accidents. We suggest a similar program of study: use scandals to accumulate otherwise obfuscated data about individuals, groups, and decision-making activities; attempt to pull together information gained from many scandals; try to draw profiles about the typical scandal, where it occurs, how it runs its course; make the resultant material and analysis available to groups who typically

are unable to gain a foothold into the private political arena and who
are working to contrast routine events with alternate conceptions.[10]

DISCUSSION

We can summarize: News is a constructed reality; newsmaking is
political work. There does not exist "out there" a set of objectively
important events waiting to be picked up by the mass media. Rather,
newsmaking is a process whereby certain actors are able to create and
thus to manage the news—"manage" in the largest sense. That is, individuals and groups do many things; those in powerful positions make
many decisions. Only a small part of those are done with the intention
of making news. Typically, activities are promoted as public events
because they serve the actors' purposes or goals, while simultaneously
these actors prevent any activity which would be inimical to their
purposes from becoming a public event.

"Important" events are totally contingent on the makers' purposes
at the time. Activities which are not promoted as events are *important*
for keeping private although other groups may, of course, have use for
those activities as events. Importance or "fitness," then, is conditioned
and constituted by the relative positions of the actors; there are as
many versions of "important" as there are variations in actors and
actors' situations. When there are inconsistent versions among those
with sufficient power to have media access, there is a public issue.

Similarly, the media is not an objective reporter of events but an
active player in the constitution of events. Through their selection,
they help to create public events. Their goals—profit, image, power—
lead them to constitute events for news coverage. If they habitually
cover the same kinds of events, made by the same small groups of
actors, it is not because the latter are intrinsically more newsworthy.
Rather, coverage is given to those actors whose goals and purposes
correspond with those of the media. For newsmen, objectivity is, as
Tuchman[11] notes, "strategic ritual."

This work of selection and transformation by the actors and media,

---

[10] There is a fourth type of event which logically flows from our schema: the
serendipity event which takes place when a non-deliberate occurrence is deliberately
promoted by the occurrence's agent. Put in informal language, a serendipity
event involves making hay out of what was accomplished accidentally, but without
admission that there ever was an accident. Unfortunately, because of the very
fact that a serendipity event is deliberately promoted in ways identical to the
routine event, it is usually impossible to know in a given case whether or not the
precipitating occurrence was accomplished purposively. It is for the reason of its
invisibility that we treat serendipity events as a residual category, largely un-
retrievable to investigation.

[11] Gaye Tuchman, "Objectivity as Strategic Ritual," *American Journal of Sociology* 77 (1972), pp. 660–79.

respectively, should be viewed as two levels of creative filtering which determines what becomes news and thus what we, as readers and researchers, have access to. Events and information hostile to the status quo are structurally blocked. To read the newspaper as a catalogue of the important happenings of the day, or to use the newspaper for selecting subjects of study, is to be duped into accepting as reality the political work by which events are constituted. Only by the accident and the scandal is that political work transcended, allowing access to "other" information and thus to a basis for practical action which is directly hostile to those groups who typically manage the public political stage.

A corresponding research activity involves investigations of how we as insurgent sociologists and as people seeking a radical transformation in society can best use accidents, scandals, and routines for our purposes. At least we have a new way to read papers and hear news broadcasts, as well as a new way to select research topics and do content analyses. More ambitiously, following T. R. Young[12] and activists like Jerry Rubin, we suggest the possibility of the sociologist as methodological promoter of accidents and scandals—someone who does what can be done to upset routine news-making, simultaneously contributing to social reconstruction and gathering data on the impediments to such reconstruction.

[12] Young and Lehman, "Conflict Methodology."

chapter three

The meet the press game

BY MINDY NIX

The National Broadcasting Company threw a big party at the Statler-Hilton in Washington last month to celebrate the twenty-fifth anniversary of "Meet The Press." Actually, the date was last Nov. 6, but Congress was not in town at the time so NBC decided to hold off until Jan. 17, when not only Congress but almost Everyone Else was on hand for the Inauguration. Indeed, most of official Washington was invited to the fête, as was every guest and reporter who had ever appeared on the program. And no less than 1,500 showed up for the buffet reception. James Farley, the first guest back in 1947, was there. So were Hubert Humphrey, the record-holding politician with 22 shots, and Richard Wilson, the *Des Moines Register & Tribune* columnist who has cross-examined the mighty on 174 occasions. A quick sample of the crowd also included Melvin Laird, Katharine Graham, Edward M. Kennedy, Peter Lisagor, Roy Cohn, David Broder, John Erlichmann, Clifton Daniel, Edmund Muskie, James J. Kilpatrick, J. W. Fulbright, David Kraslow and Mrs. Ferdinand Marcos, standing in for her husband who sent his regrets. To further note the anniversary, NBC took out full-page advertisements in *The New York Times* and *The Washington Post* offering an heroic sketch of Grand Old Inquisitor Lawrence E. Spivak over the observation that "Meet The Press" has "examined every significant issue that has arisen during its long life, and in the most cogent way—by questioning the leaders most concerned. Thus what happens during 'Meet The Press' on Sunday is often front-page news on Monday."

As an advertising pitch, that's not half bad. The "cogent" business is, of course, nonsense, as regular viewing quickly demonstrates. But the whole exercise is, indeed, aimed at landing on page one. Twenty-seven years ago, Spivak dreamed up "Meet The Press" as a radio promotion for Mencken's *American Mercury* magazine. The publication is long gone, but MTP and its offspring—CBS' "Face The Nation"

"The Meet the Press Game," by Mindy Nix. From [*MORE*] *A Journalism Review* (P. O. Box 2971, Grand Central Station, New York, N.Y. 10021) (February 1973), pp. 12–14. Reprinted by permission of the publisher.

and ABC's "Issues and Answers"—continue in that promotional tradition. Their major corporate purpose is to produce a story, with
appropriate credit for the network, in Monday's newspapers. To help
assure this, every Sunday afternoon the programs' staffs rush scores of
transcripts of that day's programs to the desk of every newspaper with
a Washington bureau. Sunday's a slow news day, and this ready-made
"news" can come in handy when a bureau or wire service reporter is
scratching around for a lead story. Many network affiliates, too, splice
portions of the programs into their Sunday evening news shows, thus
picking up both some free material and some public-service points to
display before the FCC come license renewal time.

No one at the networks seems at all bashful about any of this. "We
love to make news on Sunday instead of just talking about it," says
Sylvia Westerman, co-producer of "Face The Nation." NBC press releases boast that Spivak's "challenging questions continue to make
headlines in the record-breaking interviews with national and international leaders." I&A and FTN keep bulging scrapbooks full of the
newspaper articles that mention them; Spivak stores MTP's in file cases
kept in a bathtub in his Washington home. "Issues And Answers"
producer Peggy Whedon agrees with her counterparts that Monday
morning newsmaking is "an important reason for the existence of the
show—it matters a lot." But she goes on to say something more about
the relationship between the program and its guests in government.
"We court the guests the way they court us. Agnew knows that by appearing he's going to get publicity for himself in the next morning's
New York Times, and we know we'll be mentioned, too. That way we
do him a favor and we do ourselves a favor."

Just how much of a favor was indicated on ABC last fall. There
was Frank Reynolds, moderator of I&A, peering over his glasses and
the scrap of copy paper in his hands, looking at Sen. George McGovern,
guest for Oct. 22, just two weeks before the elections. "You have
likened President Nixon to Adolf Hitler," said Reynolds, glancing
down at the paper, ". . . how do you reconcile this with your position
that issues should be rationally discussed and that rhetoric is counter-
productive?" Reynolds' question was one of several prepared by Herb
Klein's White House Office of Communications, a sort of do-it-yourself
needle kit courtesy of the opposition. Klein's office shot the list across
town to ABC the day before the show and followed up with a not-too-
subtle telephone inquiry to I&A's Whedon later in the day. Had the
list arrived? Oh yes, the list had arrived.

That the White House had dared attempt using a news program to
put its opposition on the spot—and that it had succeeded—astonished
many who either saw the program or read about it later. It shouldn't
have. For the three Sunday news conference programs have always
served primarily as conduits for communicating Administration posi-

tions and points of view, no matter who was in power. NBC, for example, says in its MTP press releases that the show brings its audience "a continuing roster of prominent people discussing significant issues of the day." Further, "outstanding persons in the news are interviewed by a panel of newsmen in a live, unrehearsed press conference." Both statements are true; both are part of the problem. That "roster of prominent people" is composed almost entirely of Washington's elected and appointed officials, along with an occasional foreign head of state. The "discussion of significant issues" flows from the questions of a select handful of the Washington press corps—men like Wilson, Lisagor and Broder and such middle-ground columnists as Clark Mollenhoff and Carl Rowan. These men are hardly fools, but rarely do they or their colleagues who appear on FTN or I&A ask truly penetrating questions. Reporters on all three shows, in fact, less often ask questions than simply afford opportunities for the guest to reply any way he wants. Here, for example, is an exchange on MTP (Jan. 14) between NBC's Robert McCormick and Rep. Gerald Ford, Republican leader of the House of Representatives:

MCCORMICK: Congressman Ford, you are undoubtedly more aware than I am of the discontent in Congress among Republicans as well as Democrats— some of them at least. What will happen in Congress if we do not get a peace settlement in time? Will the President have any control left over Congress at all?

FORD: Mr. McCormick, I would prefer to look at the situation from the optimistic point of view that there will be some meaningful results. I think it would be unwise in this very critical, crucial stage, to speculate on what might come if things didn't turn out well. I think we ought to be hopeful. We ought to look at it optimistically and not make plans for something that might be unfortunate.

Over at "Issues and Answers" that same Sunday the questions were somewhat better, but hardly difficult. ABC correspondents Ted Koppel and Howard Tuckner were interviewing Sen. Nguyen Van Ngai, leader of the South Vietnamese delegation to the U.S., who said at one point:

You have to cling to . . . the right to self-determination of South Vietnamese people . . . the South Vietnamese people should be entitled to choose freely their own way of life . . . through democratic process without any threat of repression. And we think that the Republic of Vietnam must be given a free choice and we are determined not to effect any prefabricated formula, impose an arbitrary formula on the South Vietnamese people.

Neither Koppel nor Tuckner thought it worth asking the senator to what degree he thought the Thieu regime was "democratic" and represented the South Vietnamese people.

On "Face The Nation" that day, the questions were slightly better still (as they often are), but CBS correspondents George Herman and Roger Mudd nevertheless did little more in their talk with Senate Democratic leader Mike Mansfield than confirm what everyone already knows: that Congress is impotent.

MUDD: How does that happen, Senator, that a third branch of government, the Congress, gives away its powers?

MANSFIELD: Well, since the time of Franklin D. Roosevelt, on occasions we've bowed to the Executive, and in so doing we've allowed the transference of some of our powers under the Constitution to the Executive Branch.

MUDD: But I mean why do you bow? Is it just easier to bow than to fight the President?

MANSFIELD: Easier in some instances, not knowing the full facts and details in others. A number of factors had to be considered.

Doubtless the participants on the three programs Jan. 14 will argue that the above excerpts don't give the full dimensions of the interviews. And it's true, they don't. But a careful reading of the three transcripts suggests that no great unfairness has been perpetrated. For even granting an occasional stinger question, all three exercises resemble nothing so much as a dusty civics text—gray, superficial and unimaginative. Part of the problem, of course, is in the way the programs are structured, which would frustrate even the most determined journalist (particularly on MTP, where five reporters share 30 minutes, minus commercial breaks). And yet, a public official by his very appearance may leave much of the audience (an estimated 15 million for the three programs) with the impression he is not hiding. After all, he has submitted to questioning by the elite of the Washington press corps on nationwide television. Who would dare accuse James R. Schlesinger, head of the Atomic Energy Commission, of hiding in such a public forum? John Finney of *The New York Times* Washington bureau might have, but he didn't. On "Meet The Press" Dec. 17 he asked Schlesinger if he had been offered the job of director of the Central Intelligence Agency. "No sir," replied Schlesinger, whose appointment was announced a few days later.

All three programs live up to their billings, to be sure, but their very intentions contain powerful, unspoken assumptions about how society works. The most obvious is, of course, that Washington is the mover and everywhere else the moved. This parochialism would be laughable except that NBC is probably correct in proclaiming MTP "television's most authoritative and influential public affairs program." All three define the issues and confine the debate through their choice of guests. MTP, for instance, has interviewed leaders who run the gamut from O'Brien (Larry) to Dole (Robert), Bundy (McGeorge) to Ball (George), Heller (Walter) to Schulz (George), Nixon (old) to Nixon (new). Other regulars include Hugh Scott and Melvin Laird. Humphrey, besides meeting the press a record 22 times, has appeared on I&A 14 times in the last six years and faced the nation four times since mid-1971. The programs' world view is also revealed by looking at who was *not* picked as an "outstanding person in the news." Going back to 1966, MTP chose not to interview Malcolm X, Bobby Baker, Adam Clayton Powell, Saul Alinsky, Rap Brown, Nicholas Johnson, Dick Gregory, any leader of the Women's Movement, any leader of the National Welfare Rights Movement, or any oil company president.

"If this were the 'Today' show we could bring on people from the full spectrum, but with just a half an hour a week you really can't wing it with someone who may not turn out to be interesting or articulate or representative," says ABC's Whedon. "Anyway, there are enough representative people around. We've had the North, the South, the black, the white, the Europeans, the Latins, the glamor gals and the glamor men, prisoners too." Prisoners? Well, Jimmy Hoffa did appear just after his release from Lewisburg but no other ex-inmates or prison reform spokesmen appear on the guest lists of this or the other two programs.

Of the three programs, MTP has adopted the most insular approach. Blacks, white ethnics, and women haven't fared very well there. Black "regulars" on the three programs range all the way from Roy Wilkins to Ron Dellums (after he became a Congressman). FTN did have David Hilliard of the Black Panther Party; also Michael Klonsky when he was National Secretary of SDS; Father James Groppi the Milwaukee priest; and Navajo Nation Chairman Peter MacDonald. I&A presented Gloria Steinem and Betty Friedan but that's about it. Whedon says she has had some "far out" guests—Hoffa, Bernadette Devlin, Maurice Chevalier, and the Apollo 17 astronauts.

Sometimes, not ranking among "the representative" can make a difference to political candidates. That's what Shirley Chisholm argued when I&A did not originally include her in its debate between California primary front-runners Humphrey and McGovern. The FCC agreed and ordered the network to include her. MTP found itself under similar attack, only this time the network wasn't tagging front-runners, just deciding who was and who was not a bonafide "Democratic hopeful." NBC thought former Governor Terry Sanford and Representative Wilbur Mills were not. Sylvia Westerman, co-producer of CBS's FTN—which has strayed farthest from the Establishment for its guests—says it's more a matter of priorities. "We'd like to get into the world of ideas but there's always some screaming news story that we care more about. And there are only so many Sundays." Still another explanation comes from columnist Robert Novak, a frequent panelist on MTP. "If you had Muskie or Mel Laird one week, Abbie Rubin [sic] the next week, and a guy from the American Nazi Party or a Gay Liberationist the next, why I think that would be a distortion. To overemphasize the extremes would be a mistake." But extremists are not really the issue. The question is why the thinking of leaders all along the spectrum goes unrepresented on the programs just because they are not big names in Washington, D.C.

The shows' fascination with Washington movers and shakers and visiting prime ministers or princes wouldn't be half as bad if that narrowness of vision did not extend to their choice of reporters. Many of them are network newsmen, on the whole a group not exactly known for tough questioning. I&A uses only ABC reporters—two of them each week. FTN uses two of CBS' own and one from the outside. MTP uses Spivak, an NBC reporter, and "big name" guest panelists like Novak. Every so often Pauline Frederick appears—usually when the guest is a woman (Indira Gandhi and Golda Meir in 1971). Carl Rowan is often called in when the subject is race or the cities. FTN's Westerman says "We do as much talent-scouting for panel members as we do for guests. This is a fast-moving program where you have to get a lot of questions in. Someone may be a great reporter but not a very good questioner." Both qualities, of course, can be found in, among others, I. F. Stone, William Rusher, Carey McWilliams, Hunter Thompson, Mary Perot Nichols, and David Halberstam. None has appeared on any of the programs. Even Mollenhoff, a former Nixon staff man now Washington correspondent of the *Des Moines Register & Tribune*, and a frequent panelist and great fan of MTP, concedes there is "some posturing, some concession to the guest."

Richard Nixon once wrote Lawrence Spivak to tell him that "the type of sharp incisive questioning that your panel and you in particular have always done is precisely the kind of national service that the Fathers meant to guarantee when they wrote 'freedom of the press' into the First Amendment." John Kennedy met the press eight times and described the program as the "fifty-first state." Hubert Humphrey called MTP "honest and courageous." Barry Goldwater wrote that it "has consistently met the highest standards of fair and penetrating news coverage." Doubtless "Issues And Answers" and "Face The Nation" would win similar accolades. No news programs that draw such praise from the men they question can be all that good.

chapter four

Selection and communication in a television production—a case study

PHILIP ELLIOTT

THE RESEARCH IDEA
AND METHOD

The case study reported in this paper was designed as part of an exploratory project to fill a gap in mass communication research and theory.[1] The intention was to supplement a survey of audience reactions to a television documentary series, with an analysis of the way these programmes were produced. Most mass communication research has started with the output of the medium as given and then gone on to assess audience effect.[2] This study was designed to investigate the processes of selection and decision through which the programmes passed before they reached the viewer.

The programmes were a series of seven half-hour documentaries, titled 'The Nature of Prejudice', and originally transmitted on consecutive Sunday afternoons. The series was in production for just over fifteen weeks and throughout that time the activities of the production team were observed and recorded.[3] The observation was non-partici-

"Selection and Communication in a Television Production—A Case Study," by Philip Elliott. From *Media Sociology: A Reader,* ed. by Jeremy Tunstall (Urbana: University of Illinois Press, 1970), pp. 221–38, 517–20, and (London: Constable and Company Ltd., 1970). Reprinted by permission of the University of Illinois Press and A D Peters and Company.

[1] The project was designed and supervised by J. D. Halloran, Director of the Centre for Mass Communication Research. A survey of audience reactions was carried out by R. L. Brown. A full report is in preparation.

[2] Apart from the study of the feature film, *The Red Badge of Courage,* by Lillian Ross, exceptions to this generalization have generally been studies of journalists and of decision making within newspapers, and a few autobiographical accounts. See L. Ross, *Picture* (London: Gollanez, 1953), and for an autobiographical account of a television production M. Miller and E. Rhodes, *Only You Dick Daring* (New York: Wm Sloane Assocs, 1964).

[3] The author would like to acknowledge the great debt which this study owes to the producer and his team and others in the television organization for their help and cooperation throughout the research.

pant and loosely structured. Each day's notes were ordered into a prepared schedule summarizing the main activities and the part played by each member of the production team. Observation was guided by the general aim of the study. In summary this was to analyse the process of production to show the range of material included, the way this was shaped into programme form, the intentions of the different production personnel involved in this, and the way in which other factors, of a social, cultural or organizational nature, impinged upon the whole process.

There is a sense in which 'The Nature of Prejudice' series was both 'typical' and 'unique'. It was a typical documentary series in production. But each series has a different subject and a different production team. Rather than simply describe the work of the individuals who made up this team, attention has been directed towards factors in the situation which are likely to be similar for all productions. Nevertheless, allowance must be made for personal factors. In assessing the conclusions of this paper, it must be remembered that they are based on only one case. They are put forward as starting points rather than final assertions.

Although there has been considerable argument over the precise nature of the relationship, it has been a common assumption in sociology that literature and art 'reflect society'.[4] It is one of the aims of this paper to illustrate one aspect of the relationship for this programme series, by analysing the collection and selection of programme material. Because of the way these processes were organized, the eventual programme content may be described as a sample of the 'conventional wisdom' current in society on this particular subject.[5]

The second aim of this paper is to question a model of mass communication which is based on an analogy with interpersonal communication.[6] According to this model the relationship between television production and the audience is a circle of communication and feedback. The model is comparable to the two person interaction models of social psychology. In particular it stresses the communication intended by the production personnel as an important factor in pro-

---

4 An analysis of some of the different forms which this relationship has been given may be found in M. C. Albrecht, 'The Relationship of Literature and Society', *American Journal of Sociology*, Vol. 59 (1954), pp. 425–36.

5 'Conventional wisdom' is borrowed from J. K. Galbraith's analysis of contemporary economic theories to draw attention to the diffuse, anecdotal and largely unanalysed nature of opinions about phenomena which are widely disseminated in society. It is not intended as a pejorative term. See J. K. Galbraith, *The Affluent Society* (London: Hamish Hamilton, 1958).

6 One of the most explicit statements of the analogy is to be found in D. McQuail, 'Uncertainty about the Audience and the Organization of Mass Communications' *Sociological Review Monograph* No. 13, 1969, pp. 75–84.

gramme production.[7] It is easy to show that one link in the model—the feedback from audience to production—is tenuous, except on the point of audience size.[8] This paper takes up the question of the other link—the communication from production to audience—and seeks to show that, in the case of these programmes at least, 'communication' —defined as the attempt to transmit particular knowledge and ideas— is not an appropriate term. In contrast, the model of television production suggested by this study is of a relatively self-contained process following established technical and occupational routines.

THE PRODUCTION
OF THE PROGRAMMES

Diagram I shows, in summary form, the production stages through which the programmes passed. Each stage included different activities, but all were part of the same interdependent process. The diagram is only an analytic device. There was considerable temporal overlap be-

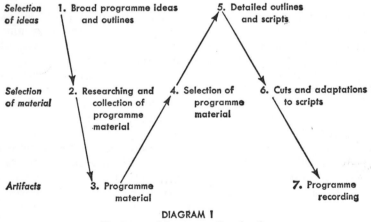

DIAGRAM I
The Stages of Programme Broadcasting

tween one stage and another, and the production personnel themselves used the technical names for their activities. These do not necessarily coincide with the names given to the analytic stages.

The diagram shows the way in which the production process moved twice from the level of ideas to the level of actual programme material.

---

[7] See, for example, H. J. Gans, 'The Greater Audience Relationship in the Mass Media', in B. Rosenberg and D. M. White (eds.), *Mass Culture* (Glencoe: Free Press, 1959).

[8] Indeed this forms the starting point for McQuail's argument, *op. cit.*

Stages two, three and four were all dependent on the broad ideas for subject areas developed in the first stage. Further ideas were developed at stage five, but these depended heavily on the material collected in the previous stages. This is the aspect of the production process upon which this paper will concentrate. Some attention will also be given to the final stage because additional factors appeared at that point which further inhibited 'communication'.

STAGE 1: PROGRAMME IDEAS AND OUTLINES

The idea for a series of programmes on prejudice had been under discussion in the television organization for some time. The associate head of the department dealing with documentary programmes eventually arranged transmission time for the series and he contracted a producer and a director to handle the production.[9] As executive producer, he had overall responsibility for the series within the organization. But the practice in this department was to leave the programme producer a relatively free hand. This was especially the case with 'The Nature of Prejudice', because the programme producer was a man of considerable experience and reputation, and well known to the executive producer. On appointment, the only direction on content which the programme producer received was that the series should not concentrate exclusively on problems of race and colour. It was felt that these had already been sufficiently covered on television, whereas an examination of the whole phenomenon of prejudice would break new ground.[10]

The programme producer actively disliked prejudice in all its forms.[11] However, he did not intend to make the programmes a direct assault on the problem by using either an emotional or a didactic approach. He thought the first better done through dramatic presentation in a play or a film. The second he regarded as a misuse of the medium because it would inevitably result in a decrease in the size of the audience. Instead the producer expressed his programme philosophy in terms of 'evidence' and 'conclusions'. He saw his task as collecting 'evidence' about the subject, from which both he, and the guests invited into the studio to appear on the programme, would be

9 Although this paragraph sets the situation of the production team within the organization it must be remembered that the study was limited to the level of programme production. It cannot, for example, answer questions about the general planning of programmes and output.

10 The executive producer did intervene in the production of the last two programmes in the series. This intervention does not affect the present argument and is outside the scope of the present paper.

11 This paragraph is based on a pre-production interview with the producer.

able to draw 'conclusions'. In the same way some of the audience might draw the same 'conclusions', or at least be inspired to think about the subject anew.

Thus two forms of direct 'communication', aiming at attitude change, were ruled out from the start.[12] Nevertheless the theory of 'evidence' and 'conclusions' did suggest that the programmes would arrive at a new statement about the phenomenon. The producer assumed that at least some of the audience would react to this statement in the same way that he did. The description of the programme materials as 'evidence' makes it especially important to analyse the methods and sources through which they were obtained.

In the first meetings of the production team, the producer outlined his general ideas for the programmes. The series was to move from an opening survey of the wide variety of prejudices to be found in society, to a concluding discussion, in which a panel of guests in the studio would be invited to sum up the phenomenon. In between, the programmes were to cover a number of different prejudices—race and colour, religious, social, inter-generational, inter-sexual, and national. Except the last, these all reflected the producer's assessment of the most important types of prejudice current in society.

Even at this stage, however, the producer wondered whether enough material could be found to make a series of programmes, each devoted to a prejudice of a particular type, without also making the programmes very repetitious. Drawing on the conversations he had had with a few academics and on some background reading,[13] the producer moved away from a topic-based, to a concept-based approach.

Most of the concepts which eventually provided the basis for different programmes in the series were explicitly mentioned in the early production discussions. These were the origins of prejudice, 'in-groups' and 'out-groups', stereotypes and methods of combating prejudice. These were partly the areas which the producer thought the most important, and partly areas suggested by the visual possibilities of programme ideas and material found in the researching stage (Stage 2).

Initially the topic-based approach ran side-by-side with the concept-based approach, but gradually the latter began to predominate in guiding the researching activities. Most of the researching was com-

---

12 It must be emphasized that the term 'communication' is not intended to include just a socially purposive message, but any ideas and information about the subject.

13 This included especially a general survey of the field, G. W. Allport, *The Nature of Prejudice* (New York: Addison-Wesley, 1954), and reference to the work on the authoritarian personality as an important controversy in the field. T. W. Adorno, E. Frenkel-Brunswick, D. J. Levinson, and R. N. Sanford, *The Authoritarian Personality* (New York: Harper, 1950).

pleted, however, before the producer finally decided how the concepts would divide up into individual programmes. Both the topics and the concepts mentioned above, functioned throughout the researching stage as general headings under which programme material was organized.

STAGE 2: RESEARCHING
FOR PROGRAMME MATERIAL

The process of researching may be conceptualized in terms of three separate chains. These chains represent both three separate ways through which programme ideas were generated, as well as describing the three necessary conditions which any programme material had to meet to qualify for inclusion.

THE SUBJECT CHAIN

The Subject Chain was an extension of the broad subject headings discussed in the previous section. The producer played a key part in deciding which of these headings would form the basis for the series. They derived from his own ideas and experience, supplemented by some background reading and two contacts with academics interested in the subject. These broad subject areas then themselves led on to specific ideas for illustrative programme material. For example, the heading of stereotyping was developed because it obviously lent itself to visual illustration. Nevertheless the fact that initially a criterion of importance played as great a part as a criterion of visual possibility, is shown by the example of social prejudice. The producer repeatedly referred to this, even though there was some doubt among the production team as to whether it was still applicable, and few ideas were forthcoming on how to make it visual. Thus little reference to social prejudice was included in the eventual programmes because it failed to satisfy the other two necessary conditions. The Subject Chain is illustrated in Diagram II.

THE PRESENTATION CHAIN

At the start of the production, the series was allocated a budget. This allocation provided one basis for the second chain—the Presentation Chain. The programmes were to be shown in an 'off-peak' time-slot. Attached to that time-slot there was a recognised 'normal' budget figure. Both time-slot and budget figure were associated with production in a particular style, involving little use of film and based on studio presentation.

In their initial discussion of the series the producer and director planned within this accepted production style. Much of the programme time was to be devoted to discussions in the studio between

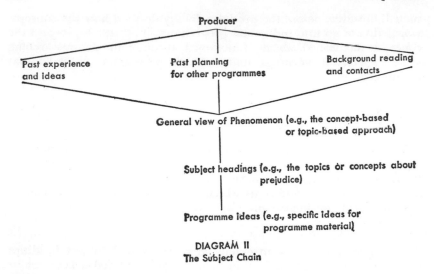

DIAGRAM II
The Subject Chain

panels of expert guests. These would be led by a presenter, who would also link the other visual material which could be worked into the basic format. This consisted mainly of stills, a small amount of archive film and film specially shot for the series.[14]

Planning followed the accepted style, even though the budget figure initially suggested by the executive producer was considerably higher than the norm (by 25%), which suggests the importance of production routines accepted by those working in the medium. In this case plans for the series were not constrained or limited by the budget figure, but structured by the production style associated with budget and time-slot.

The one adjustment which was made by the producer when he found he was well within the budget figure, was to increase the amount allowed for original filming. The final budget estimate allowed for ten days' hire of film crew, instead of four. The power of the accepted

[14] Figures for the use of different visual techniques in all the programmes of the series taken together were:

		%
Studio discussions		53
Original film	Individual interviews	23.5
	'Vox Pop' interviews	1.4
	Research experiments and school locations	4.4
Archive film		3.9
Presenter's links		13.8

The use of stills is not counted separately. They are included with the presenter as they usually illustrated his links.

production style is demonstrated again however by the fact that in the end only five of these days were used.

Nevertheless, for a combination of reasons, both the producer and the director thought it desirable to obtain original film for the series. Because film is the most expensive production technique, it has a scarcity value; its use marks a programme out from others. Film is a very flexible medium which can be cut and edited by producer and director to meet their requirements. It is easier to capture dramatic action on film than in a studio and so film is believed to have greater impact.

Most of the film eventually shot for 'The Nature of Prejudice' was of 'talking head' interviews. It is particularly interesting that the above arguments applied to the film material in this case. This was despite the fact that the content of the film was mainly 'talking heads', the usual content of studio production. For example, in deciding how to employ a film unit for the time available, one subject suggested was 'Vox Pop' interviews. These were justified on the grounds that they could be easily arranged to fill the film unit's time, and they would provide original film with 'actuality' impact.

These 'Vox Pop' sequences are one example of an idea thrown up by the Presentation Chain, shown in Diagram III. Programme ideas

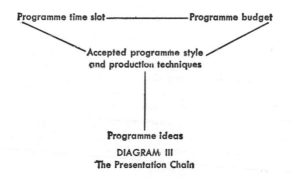

DIAGRAM III
The Presentation Chain

suggested themselves, or were confirmed, because they were particularly suitable for one of the methods of presentation within the accepted production style.

THE CONTACT CHAIN

The Contact Chain, shown in Diagram IV, is an elaboration of the very simple point that, to qualify for use, a subject had to be known to the production team. One example of the operation of this principle resulted in the inclusion not merely of a new programme idea, but also of another broad subject heading—national prejudice. The producer was put in touch with a psychologist who had recently com-

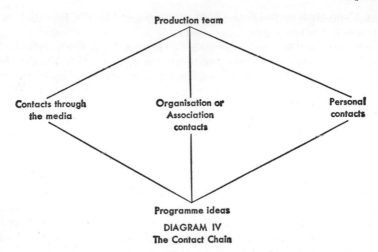

Production team

Contacts through the media

Organisation or Association contacts

Personal contacts

Programme ideas

DIAGRAM IV
The Contact Chain

pleted a series of experiments investigating the development of national stereotypes in children. National prejudice was added to the list of subject areas because the techniques used in this experiment could be re-enacted on film. (Thus the idea was confirmed by the Presentation Chain.)

The Contact Chain was especially important during the first few weeks of researching. Indeed the role of the researcher can be seen as an attempt to institutionalize contact mechanisms within the production team.[15] The researcher's task was to search out programme material within guidelines laid down by the producer. To do this she needed a good knowledge of possible sources.

One of the first requirements was to find interview subjects for the film sessions. The producer wanted to recruit examples of both prejudiced people, who would be prepared to state their views on film, and of the victims of prejudice, who had their own case stories to tell. The interview subjects were eventually recruited from three main sources: first stories in the press published during the researching period, second organizations and associations representing people who were a likely target for prejudice, third contacts personally known to a member of the production team. These were the three basic contact mechanisms which applied to all forms of material, with the variation of

[15] The core production team consisted of the producer, the director, the researcher, the production assistant and the presenter. In formal terms, the producer was responsible for the content of the programmes; the director for their appearance; the researcher collected programme material for the producer; the production assistant handled the administration and the presenter, in addition to appearing on the screen, played a part in script writing especially by reviewing the pieces written as his links.

course that other material involved other organizations, specializing in the relevant subject.

These mechanisms were relatively productive of examples of 'victim' of prejudice, but not of 'prejudiced' people.[16] The eventual lack of 'prejudiced' interviewees is a good example of the way the production team depended on the three mechanisms. Three 'prejudiced' interview subjects were thrown up by stories in the press, but two of these were vicars whose statements to camera were too theological to be very useful. In addition the producer asked the people he stopped in the street for the 'Vox Pop' interviews, to confess their prejudices. This method was also largely unsuccessful in obtaining statements of prejudice on film. Out of 40 'Vox Pop' interviewees, 32 denied having any prejudices themselves, and only four admitted feeling prejudiced on specific subjects.

Two of the other interviewees had recently completed research projects in an area of race relations. Again stories in the press were the contact mechanism which brought them to the attention of the production team. Two other pieces of research were re-enacted on film for inclusion in the programme. One of these was the investigation of the development of national stereotypes, mentioned above; the other was a study of the development of colour preferences among children. The producer was put in touch with both psychologists through personal contacts and, in both cases, he found that the research was eminently suitable for film presentation. Apart from the guests invited into the studio, discussed below, these four pieces of programme material were all the academic research included in the programme. It can be seen that this sample of research was drawn through the Contact Chain, reinforced by the Presentation and Subject Chains.

Although the way the individual interviewees were recruited illustrates most points about the Contact Chain, the mechanism of personal contact did play a more important part in the selection of some of the other types of material. There were a number of reasons why the production team tried to use personal contacts wherever possible, especially in preference to formal approaches through bureaucratic machinery. Indeed put together with the personal basis of selection for employment within the organization, and the use made of personalized, quasi-charismatic relationships at work, it appears as if personal, particularist relationships are uniquely important in the organizational system of television production.[17]

---

16 In research generally it seems to have been difficult to make people admit that they themselves hold prejudices. See for example W. W. Daniel, *Racial Discrimination in Britain* (Harmondsworth: Penguin, 1968).

17 This appears to have important implications for such questions as the accommodation of creativity in organizational structures but these cannot be developed in this paper.

The reasons for using personal contact mechanisms in researching may be divided into four main groups. First, personal contacts were believed to be more productive—the producer could detail his own requirements and short-circuit cumbersome formal procedures. For example, permission to film in a multi-racial school was initially refused by the local authority. Eventually qualified permission was obtained by a direct approach to a member of the authority, known to the producer.

Second, personal contacts gave the producer greater control over the source of the material—he was more likely to see the full range of material and so was better able to assess its quality. For example, direct approaches were made to the film librarians for archive film in the hope of making full use of their personal knowledge of their libraries' contents.

Third, personal contact tended to result in greater co-operation from the subjects. While recruiting the interview subjects, the researcher approached a social worker with whom she had previously worked on another programme. This social worker provided not only six examples of 'victims' of prejudice for interview, but also a location in which the filming could take place.

Fourth, the ability to produce personal contacts at appropriate moments reflected on the status and expertise of the production personnel. The ability to produce such contacts was part of the formal role requirements placed upon the researcher, but others in the team also felt it incumbent upon them to suggest contacts. For example, in the course of a vain pursuit of some American educational film, a telephone call was made to a contact in New York on the off-chance that it might prove fruitful.

These reasons all contributed to the stress on personal contact which, together with the press and the organization mechanisms, played an important part in structuring the range of material available to the producer at the next stage.

DISCUSSION OF THE
THREE CHAINS

In introducing the three chains, it was mentioned that each was both capable of generating programme ideas, and a necessary condition which each programme idea had to satisfy. Thus programme ideas had to fall within one of the broadly defined subject areas—though as we saw in the case of national prejudice there was scope for re-alignment of the areas if an idea was strongly supported by the other two chains. Second, programme ideas had to be suitable for presentation by one of the accepted techniques. Third, programme ideas had to be visible to the production team through a narrow range of contact mechanisms.

In many ways the criteria which were missing at this point are as interesting as the three which were present. In particular there was very little reference to the substantive content or meaning of programme ideas. For example none of the four pieces of academic research was included primarily for its findings. The Subject Chain itself simply defined the broad headings under which programme material was to be collected. It did not suggest what should be said about any particular area. At this stage, programme material was collected through well-developed production routines and not as contributions to any particular 'communication'. Moreover, the range of material visible to the production team was very limited, especially by the action of the Contact Chain.

STAGE 4: THE SELECTION
OF PROGRAMME MATERIAL
STAGE 5: THE WRITING
OF PROGRAMME SCRIPTS

These two stages will be considered together. The producer preferred to write the scripts around the programme material once it had been collected. But after the material had passed two initial selection criteria, the variety available to the producer was limited, so that he had little scope in compiling the programmes.

Most of the programmes in the series were divided into two parts. In the first part the presenter linked together statements taken from the filmed interviews and occasionally other types of inserted material. The second part was usually devoted to a studio discussion between the presenter and one or more expert guests. The first, and the last two programmes, varied from this format. Programme 1 contained no studio discussion [18] while both the last two programmes were almost entirely produced in the studio.

The material from the individual interviewees could only be selected for its substantive content once it had already passed two initial tests. These were for coherence and authenticity. Interviewee statements had to be reasonably complete, coherent and concise, because any used had to stand alone in the programmes without support. The interviewer's questions, for example, were not included. This was a special problem with the 'victims' of prejudice. Several of these were taxed beyond the limits of their verbal skills by the interview situation.

[18] Programme 1 also included most of the archive film because this was believed to have special impact to attract an audience for the series.

The second criterion also affected the 'victims' more than any other group. Some asserted prejudice or discrimination against themselves without providing sufficient circumstantial evidence to convince the producer that their claims were completely authentic. Table I shows

TABLE I: THE USE OF THE FILMED INTERVIEWS

Type of Interviewee	No. Unusable	No. Usable	Average No. of Usages in Series
'Victims'	6	10	2.2
'Prejudiced'	1	2	—*
'Experienced'	0	3	3.3
'Representatives'	0	3	4.7
'Researchers'	0	2	—*

* In both cases a mean figure would be misleading as one interviewee was used four times and the other only once.

the number of complete interviews which were ruled out as unusable by these two criteria. These figures understate the ratio of unusable material because they show only the rejection of complete interviews. Several interviews, counted as usable, only yielded one or two short statements.

Two types of interviewee, the 'representatives' and the 'experienced', were the most productive of coherent, authentic statements. This is suggested in the table by the figures for average use. The 'representatives' were three men who held leadership positions within different minority groups. The 'experienced' were people who worked in different multi-racial situations and who were invited to comment on their experiences. The use made of the 'representatives' seems an especially interesting point for future work to follow, particularly because organizations and associations were an important contact mechanism at the researching stage.[19]

In terms of the producer's original production philosophy, set out above, the interview statements, and the other material, went into the programmes as 'evidence'. But the list of different types of interviewees shows that there was some variation in the authority which they had for giving 'evidence'. One use made of the interviewee material was

19 Again the implications are outside the scope of the present paper but it is interesting to relate this point to such work as Selznick's study of the Tennessee Valley Authority and Kornhauser's theory that in mass society voluntary associations tend to disappear, leaving the mass available to the élite through the media. The suggestion here is that the media themselves need voluntary organizations as a source of material. This also suggests another reason why the media devote attention to leadership figures, apart from the assured appeal of personalizations. See P. Selznick, TVA and the Grass Roots (Berkeley: University of California Press, 1952); W. Kornhauser, The Politics of Mass Society (London: Routledge and Kegan Paul, 1960).

to provide statements of a series of different points of view. Little attempt, however, was made to differentiate between the different arguments contained in these statements, or to show the viewer their relative merits.

This point is well illustrated by the use made of some statements by one of the 'prejudiced' interviewees. It so happened that he was a lecturer in social psychology. In one statement, for example, he alleged that different coloured rats exterminated each other and concluded that such colour differences were biologically important. The producer regarded this as an inaccurate and prejudiced statement, but the only clue he provided for the viewer, to counteract the authoritative impression already given by the interviewee's caption—'Lecturer in Social Psychology'—was the presenter's next words: 'Well, possibly. But there are surely a lot of flaws in that argument. Even if black and brown rats are as hostile to each other as is claimed, what about black and white and brown rabbits?' This is a particularly good example of what appeared to be a general lack of concern with both the 'communicative' effect and the authoritative basis of the statements included in the programmes.

But although the interviewees varied in the authority they had for making their statements, they were all questioned in a similar way to elicit a series of personal opinions. This applied even to the 'researchers' and the 'experienced'. For example only one of the former was questioned directly on the findings of the research.

Thus the scripts, written around the results of the researching and selection stages, included simply a sample of the personal opinions current in society about the topic of prejudice. The statements were 'evidence' of the 'conventional wisdom' available in society. Nevertheless, according to the producer's production philosophy, the 'evidence' was to lead to 'conclusions', especially in the studio discussion sections of the programmes, analysed in the next section.

STAGE 7: PROGRAMME RECORDING

The very fact that the producer left the 'conclusions' to emerge from the expert guests in the studio discussions, meant that he could play less part in deciding their content. This was partly because the guests had expert status and so were expected to be responsible for their own opinions, and partly because this production stage involved another member of the production team, the presenter, who not only led the 'live' discussion, but also played an important part in deciding its content.

The guests themselves were selected through similar channels to the contact mechanisms described in the researching stage. One difference however was that, in place of the press, previous appearances on television not only brought different experts to the attention of the production team, but also enabled them to judge their televisual competence. What any given expert would say appeared to be a far less important selection criterion than his ability to say something in a presentable way. The producer did provide the guests with outlines of the programme material and of the part which he expected the studio discussion to play in the programme, but except for the first discussion, in Programme 2, the studio sections were not extensively prepared or rehearsed. This exception is examined more closely below because, on this occasion, the producer did start with the intention of 'communicating' particular ideas. He was largely prevented by the operation of other factors in the process.

One important intervening factor was the nature of the studio discussion itself. This was an uneasy compromise between two possible modes—a spontaneous conversation and an information channel. The ideal of a spontaneous conversation was most clearly expressed in planning for the final programme, which was to provide the 'conclusions' for the whole series. Conversational ability was the main criterion for selecting guests for that programme. They were to be 'global thinkers' who were able to 'get out of the box and into the living-room'.[20] That is they were expected to sustain a smooth and erudite conversation, in which the viewer would feel he was present.[21]

In contrast the producer's initial plans for the discussion in Programme 2, were for a series of exchanges which would contain the information—the 'conclusions'—which he wanted put across. These exchanges were planned and rehearsed with the two guests involved. The conversational ideal was present however in both the dress rehearsal and the final 'take'. It inhibited the use of the discussion as an information channel, particularly by the making of conversational points. For example one of the guests emphasized the influence of British colonial experience on racial attitudes. The presenter took this up by suggesting that physical differences must be more important because most people alive now had not participated in the Empire. While this was a perfectly good point to make, it does illustrate the way in which the format of the discussions tended to reproduce the series of contradictory statements and questions contained in the rest of the programme material. Conversational points tended to be of a

20 The production of the programme followed a series of controversial Reith Lectures which had the effect of elevating the Reith lecturer into the select company of 'global thinkers'. These criteria were apparently also in use in other productions. The lecturer turned down a request to come on the programme, because he had already been inundated by other such invitations.

21 The ideal seems to approximate to the image of conversation in an Oxbridge Senior Common Room or an exclusive London Club. In this context it is interesting to compare the style of such early BBC–TV productions as *The Brains Trust*.

contradictory or critical nature and often moved the discussion away from the main theme. An example of this occurred in the discussion of the findings of the second piece of research, recorded on film. The presenter questioned the psychologist about his use of the categories 'English/Not-English' instead of 'British/Not-British', in order to make the point that the research appeared prejudiced against the Welsh and the Scottish. The result was that no findings from the research were elicited by the discussion.

It will be apparent from these examples that the use of the conversational mode was to some extent a result of the style adopted by the presenter.[22] Other aspects of the presenter's role also inhibited the use of the discussions as information channels. Thus, in Programme 2, the producer particularly wanted to include a discussion of the theory of the 'authoritarian personality', and of the principles of sampling to justify scientific method. Both these were dropped, at the presenter's instigation, because he argued they would cause the viewer to lose interest by over-complicating the issue. It was particularly noticeable that in the discussions immediately prior to programme recording, the presenter would 'take the role of the viewer' and use such phrases as 'what I and the viewer want to see is . . .'.

His situation differed in important ways from that of the rest of the production team.[23] He was able to take an outsider's perspective because he came to the programme material fresh on the recording day, whereas the production team had been working with it for some weeks. Moreover he was the only member of the production team actually to appear on the screen. It was accepted that this made the series to some extent 'his', so far as the viewers were concerned.[24] He had originally been picked for the 'weight' of his public personality, and he knew that his future work opportunities depended on the public personality which he presented, or was believed to present, to the viewer. In this context it is important that one aspect of 'weight' was the ability to conduct and participate in conversations on any subject.

Thus the presenter had more reason than others in the production team to attend to the viewer's reactions. He did this largely by simplifying the material to what he believed was the viewer's level of interest,

22 Another source for the discussion style adopted by the presenter was the interview style used in current affairs programmes. This lays particular stress on the journalist's responsibilities to ask the critical questions which might occur to the viewer, and, if necessary, to play the 'devil's advocate'.

23 The presenter's claim to represent the audience within the production team can be seen as an instance of a general occupational phenomenon. Members of occupations tend to claim special expertise which explicitly or implicitly rejects interference in their work by others who might want to control them. See especially E. C. Hughes, *Men and Their Work* (Glencoe: Free Press, 1958).

24 In this context it is interesting that many of the letters received from viewers after the transmission of the programmes were 'fan letters' for the presenter.

and occasionally by suggesting re-orderings of material for greater
dramatic effect. In the studio discussions, the presenter's concern with
simplification was reflected in his use of simple analogies and sum-
maries to illustrate the guest's argument. As these were made, 'off the
cuff', in the course of the conversation, it was not surprising that
several were denied by the guests as inaccurate or misleading. Even
those which were substantially correct further contributed to the impression of programme content as a series of bald statements of different points of view.

A third factor which contributed to the general inability to 'communicate' 'conclusions' through the guests in the studio, was the lack
of preparation given to these sections after Programme 2. This lack
of preparation was itself partly a deliberate policy, because the meticu-
lous rehearsal of the discussions in Programme 2 had prevented the
presenter from using some of his conversational points. Nevertheless
one consequence was illustrated by the discussion in the following
programme. The presenter's scripted introduction to the discussion
ended with a series of questions, which it was implied the guest would
answer. But the guest, struck by the statements made on film by the
'prejudiced' interviewee, the lecturer in social psychology, whom she
had just heard for the first time, devoted her attention to demolishing
his arguments. The fact that the lecturer in social psychology had been
included simply as an example of prejudice, was not explained to the
guest nor clear to her from an initial viewing of the programme.[25]

Thus situational factors in the final production stage further demonstrate the inapplicability of a 'communication' model. These factors
even impeded the attempt, which the producer did make in the second
programme, to 'communicate' specific ideas. Nevertheless the analysis
of this stage does show references being made to the audience, especially by the presenter. These references were specifically concerned
with audience *reaction,* however, and not with 'communication'. The
question was how to keep the viewer interested, not how to ensure he
assimilated, or even was presented with, particular items of information. This concern was mirrored at earlier stages in the process by, for
example, the argument that film had impact for an audience.

This distinction between *reaction* and 'communication' or effect, is
one of considerable importance, if only to prevent an extreme (and
empirically unjustifiable) extension of the argument of this paper. This
extension would be that the production team paid no attention at all
to their potential audience. They did pay attention but largely in
terms of *reaction,* not in terms of 'communication'. The production
team's principal concern about their audience was to prevent them

---

25 In fact at the instigation of the guest, not the producer, this discussion was
later re-recorded. The guest was afraid that she had devoted too much time to
what might appear simply as a dispute between academics.

switching off by trying to hold their interest and attention. One accepted way of doing this was to keep the substance of the programme moving, which suggests another reason why the programme content consisted of a series of different, briefly developed, points of view.

CONCLUSION

This paper has attempted to show the way in which the processes of selection and decision behind a series of television documentaries, followed a number of accepted production routines, which resulted in a relatively fortuitous sample of what has been termed, 'conventional wisdom' appearing on the screen. Because of the influence of the conversational mode in the studio discussions, these sections of the programme also produced little more than 'conventional wisdom', albeit from people speaking with the authority of experts, unlike those whose views were recorded on film. Throughout, the producer, and others in the production team, attempted to allow for possible audience reactions, but not to 'communicate' specific ideas or information to the audience.

In the space of this paper it is not possible to do more than suggest some of the possible wider implications of these conclusions. Indeed the conclusions themselves cannot be said to have been substantiated on the basis of this single case study. Nevertheless, it is interesting to relate them to the structural situation of the broadcast media; especially the need to avoid control by sectional interests which has resulted in a stress on such policies as balance, fairness and the lack of an editorial view.[26]

Another structural feature of the broadcast media is the divorce from direct contact with their audience. McQuail has argued that this divorce, coupled with the need to know how to communicate with the audience, results in such adaptations as 'professionalization' and 'ritualism' within the production organizations.[27] These are akin to the accepted production routines outlined in this paper, but the suggestion of this study is that these routines are explicable without reference to attempts to 'communicate' with the audience.

[26] For an introductory survey of such factors see, for example, J. Scupham, *Broadcasting and the Community* (London: Watts, 1967).
[27] D. McQuail, op. cit., pp. 80–1.

II
Finding the entertainment audience

All three chapters in this section concern the audience for entertainment programming. They indicate that producers and staff members are concerned with pleasing the network and affiliates, and network executives are primarily concerned with pleasing advertisers. Viewers, all three articles agree, have no direct effect upon programming decisions, and their indirect influence is frequently minor.

Brown's article emphasizes the influence of economic criteria upon programming decisions. He stresses that the networks sell audiences to advertisers, and that when advertisers change their policies in respect to buying, the networks change theirs in respect to programming. For instance, Brown notes, when Madison Avenue "discovered" demographics—ratings data specifying which age groups are watching which programs—and decided to aim advertisements for certain products at a young audience, the networks cancelled previously successful programs, programs that had been directed at older folk. The networks could charge higher rates for the young "prime" audience. Similarly, Brown charges, the emphasis upon likely consumers as the product sold by television has meant that blacks were underrepresented in the sample upon which the Nielsen ratings are based.

Since Brown wrote, the television business has flourished. In 1970, the networks charged $2.50 per thousand viewers (bulk) delivered to advertisers. According to the August 18, 1973 issue of *Business Week,* the rate for the 1973–74 season was to be $4.80, and an average prime-time advertising minute would cost $59,000. In 1973, ABC charged as much as $79,000 for a minute of prime-time during one of its films. With lower ratings for their prime-time movies, CBS and NBC charged $46,000 and up to $56,000, respectively. The gain of a single prime-time rating point could add $13.5 million to a network's profit before taxes. Balanced against this, the networks might spend $250,000 to develop a new half-hour series, and a contract agreeing to buy 13 episodes of a series can run $1.5 million or higher. Weighing considerations like these, and aiming to sell viewers at a profit, it is not surprising that the networks gear programs to attract the audiences that advertisers want to buy.

Nor is it surprising that, as Cantor reports in the second selection, the networks hold the final say on all production questions. Cantor's article about the producers of children's programs asks, Who is the audience, the viewers or the networks? She claims that just as the networks aim to please advertisers, so too the production companies must please the networks to make money. At best, the influence of the viewing audience is indirect. Not only are many series completed before they are broadcast, thus eliminating any prospect of viewer influence, but also the inexact ratings are ignored. Instead, producers pay attention to their own children and to those of their friends and relatives, a highly atypical and wealthy group. The rare viewer who writes to the producer is defined by him as either atypical or as a crank.

When producers do pay attention to the viewers, their concern resembles that of their primary audience—the networks. Using ratings that suggest what type of program content appeals to boys and what to girls, the producers gear the program to the needs of the projected sponsor. Thus, if the program is to be sponsored by toys for girls, it has different content than a program to be sponsored by boys' toys. Furthermore, Cantor reports, most of the producers considered what effect their programs have on children to be the responsibility of either the networks or parents. Their job was to make programs that the networks found suitable to broadcast.

Like Cantor's selection, my article concerns program production. Noting the importance of ratings and that staff members know little, if anything, about their audience, the paper examines the way guests are prepared for the program, including staff members' beliefs about their celebrity-guests and techniques used to assemble lively shows. This article asks whether the talk-show format lends itself to introducing new ideas. By describing the concerns and typifications of the staff members—concerns based upon economic pressures and typifications based upon participation in professional networks—it finds that controversial materials are severely limited, that controversy is "controlled," so to speak. Similarly, some of the ways in which staff members characterize guests resemble stereotypes found in the general culture. In this respect, this article, like Cantor's, and Elliott's from the preceding section, reports that television perpetuates existing and acceptable ideas. As in Cantor's selection, many of the examples involve sex roles. Like Elliott, I suggest that participation in professional networks may discourage the introduction of innovations. Indeed, if innovations are to be introduced, they are more likely to arise among those who are marginal to the professional networks of show business and the television industry.

c h a p t e r   f i v e

Televi$ion: the business
behind the box

LES BROWN

. . . During the chill weeks between the middle of January and the end of February, more network program decisions are made than in all the rest of the year; for this is deadline time on series options—do the performers and production unit stay together for another season or does the company disband?—and the networks must, in this period, make their determination of what is expendable for the next fall season and what, for competitive purposes, should be continued.

In a feverish five weeks at the three [networks], rating histories are scrutinized and analyzed, while pilot programs representing prospective

"Televi$ion: The Business Behind the Box." From *Televi$ion: The Business Behind the Box*, by Les Brown. © 1971 by Lester L. Brown. Reprinted by permission of Harcourt, Brace Jovanovich, Inc.

new series are screened by committees, tested, studied, and rescreened. Network committees in daily meetings debate the merits of the potential program supply for September, choosing finally what the consensus—or a leader—decides will best gain the network a larger share of the audience, and consequently of the market, than it had the previous year. In the dead of winter television programs are born and die.

They die, almost without exception, from rating anemia. For a program series to be worthy of a network berth it must earn numbers suitable for the prime-time economy and, at the same time, make a contribution to the over-all strength of the schedule. Quality may make its argument, but it is rarely persuasive in a competitive arena in which more than $500 million is staked annually by the three networks for program fare, against the $1.3 billion that advertisers aggregately spend.

Programs come into being to attract an audience. Not to feed their minds, or to elevate them morally or spiritually, but to deliver them to an advertiser. Just as it understandably costs more to rent a billboard on a busy street than on one where the traffic is light, so it costs more to buy a minute of television time in a program that dependably draws more viewers to the set than the programs opposite it. The difference between billboards and TV is that television shows can generate traffic while the billboard cannot.

The importance of winning the ratings (*i.e.,* beating the competition) is why—to the embarrassment of latter-day executives who want the business to appear more businesslike—television in America resembles a game.

In game terms, programs must be eliminated that do not perform adequately for the team, either by not holding up at their assigned positions or by not performing at the economic requirements. As baseball teams cut players from their rosters and bring up new ones in a constant rebuilding process, so the television networks reposition and replace their shows as a means of gaining a larger share of the advertising market.

A network that is far ahead of its rivals in popularity numbers will make sizable profits, one that lags too far behind will lose money, and if all three are at approximately the same rating level, all three, in a robust economy, should make money. But as in any business, the heads of the organizations are measured by their ability to show larger profits every year, and a chief whose profit center shrinks rather than expands will be replaced faster than a low-rated show. Thus, network administrations do not play the game casually, and network presidents and their lieutenants have too much at stake personally to be good sports. There have been exceptions, but the average tenure for a network president is three years; and at CBS the turnover in recent years has been even more rapid—five presidents within five years—but that was partly an effect of the parent corporation's haste in overhauling the management cadre to saturate the second echelon with young men.

Given the consequences of a program schedule that loses rather than gains ground for the network, the decisions made in January and February are momentous for an administration, for they involve not just its own alterations but those of its rivals as well. There is no improvement unless it is at a competitor's expense, and program schedules are blocked out with a mind to winning in each half-hour period, or at least to diminishing a rival's long-held dominance. Decisions, therefore, are based partly on what may be known or surmised of a competitor's plans, and adding to the frenzy of the moment are the intelligence reports, real or rumored, of rival strategies, transmitted usually by the advertising executives, television agents, or studio executives encamped on Television Row throughout the ordeal of schedule-making.

In January 1970, eight programs that had premiered with the rest of the field the previous September were either already off the air (having been replaced at mid-season) or had received notice of cancellation. Thirty-one others were in danger of being terminated, most of them on the borderline of the survival standard, their prospects for renewal depending in most cases on a marked uptrend or downtrend in the few remaining rating reports until deadline. New shows which premiered in January, as replacements, had only three or four weeks to prove themselves.

It calls for no special expertise to sort out the winners and losers at the extreme ends of the rating scale, but it is the programs in the gray area between which pose the difficulty and require analysis. A series that has been high on the popularity scale for many years may be showing clear signs of attrition, indicating it may flop if renewed one more season. Conversely, careful study of rating histories may reveal that certain program series which performed indifferently during the season had the potential of becoming hits if placed on a different evening, or at a different hour.

Each evening of the week, as well as each half hour of the evening, has its own peculiar audience characteristics.

In earlier years, it was all but automatic that a program whose season average was under a 30 share was canceled. But as rating analysis grew more sophisticated, it was perceived that certain shows with shares of 28 were building audiences while others with shares of 32 were slipping. More important, in a time when the advertising community prized a young audience, a 28-share program series with favorable demographics might be of more benefit to a network than a 32-share show that appealed to viewers who were too young or too old to interest Madison Avenue . . .

. . . [S]ales were becoming increasingly difficult in some of CBS's highest-rated series, because with every year of their continuance their audiences grew a year older. Although they were winning their time periods in total audience, they were not delivering enough viewers in the 18–49 age range to command the rates for hit programs. With its long-running series, CBS was beginning to fall victim to its own success and was developing a reputation as an old person's network. In a time of demographic consciousness on Madison Avenue, NBC's salesmen were making the most of CBS's deficiencies in the youth market.

Two of the hardest programs for CBS to sell during the 1969–70 television season were Red Skelton and Jackie Gleason. A few seasons earlier, when only the mass viewers counted, both were among the first to sell out completely for the year. Conscious now of the quality of audience—on age, income, and education levels—the media buyers of advertising agencies considered the two CBS comedians overpriced for the kinds of people they delivered.

It was traditional to grant raises of approximately 8 per cent to the star every year that a series was renewed. Thus, on a compound-interest basis, old programs in general are far more expensive than new ones. So, paradoxically, as a series grows older and costs more for a network to maintain, its attractiveness to advertisers diminishes. Red Skelton, on a $4 million program investment by CBS, returned a profit for the network in the 1969–70 season of only $25,000. Jackie Gleason represented a loss of $300,000 . . .

. . . Nielsen's numbers are not about television shows but the people who watch them and it is they who are the real product of the wonderful electronic picture machine.

Under the camouflage, the viewer is not the customer but only the consumer of television. He is what the advertiser buys like herds of cattle—$2.50 per thousand bulk, $4 to $8 per thousand select (young men, young women, teenagers, depending on the product marketed).

One of the myths about American television is that it operates as a cultural democracy, wholly responsible to the will of the viewing majority in terms of the programs that survive or fade. More aptly, in the area of entertainment mainly, it is a cultural oligarchy, ruled by a consensus of the advertising community. As it happens, television's largest advertisers—the manufacturers of foodstuffs, drugs, beverages, household products, automobiles, cosmetics and, until 1971, cigarettes, among others—have from the first desired great circulation among the middle classes, so that the density of viewers has become the most important criterion in the evaluation of programs. This emphasis on the popularity of shows has made television appear to be democratic in its principles of program selection. In truth, programs of great popularity go off the air, without regard for the viewers' bereavement, if the kinds of people it reaches are not attractive to advertisers.

It was not through oversight that the networks, and local stations, did not for years produce programs of specific interest to the black population. The ghetto Negro was not a target audience for most advertisers because, generally speaking, he was a low-income citizen with scant buying power. It was not that advertisers did not want to reach Negroes but that they did not want to reach them *especially,* and it was assumed that the poor black, as a heavy viewer of television, would be part of the audience composition of programs aimed at other segments of the audience.

So little valued has been the black man as a consumer of nationally advertised products that he was not properly represented in the Nielsen sample of the American television audience. Although this was generally known in the television and advertising industries there was no outcry, no move to set it right, no show of conscience that the ghetto black did not have a representative "vote" as a member of the viewing masses. The Nielsen Company, as well as the other, lesser, rating services, explained that it was difficult to place their hardware in ghetto homes, difficult to get representative families to keep viewing diaries adequately because of the high rate of illiteracy, and even a problem in the telephone methods of audience research because of the shortage of telephone homes in the ghetto.

This sound explanation, given conventional advertising priorities, seemed fair enough to everyone until it became desirable to count the audience for *Sesame Street,* the non-commercial children's show which had been designed for the culturally underprivileged of the ghettos. The real success of *Sesame* was not to be told in the total number of persons reached but specifically in the total number of slum children reached.

At approximately the same time, moreover, station WTOP-TV in Washington, D.C., complained that its black-oriented programing in a city whose population was predominantly black was receiving no advertising support because the rating numbers were slight for them, and they were slight, the station charged, because black households were not adequately represented in the rating samples. Thus, it became a matter of one station's economic interest and one conspicuous program's social value that the ghettos be adequately surveyed, and so far as is known corrective action then began to be taken.

No one created the American television system. It evolved in a series of patchwork progressions, affected variously by government regulations, corporate aims, technological advances, advertising and marketing requirements, and to some degree by public reaction. It probably did not start out to put commerce before communication, but if that was the inevitable result of the medium's great penetration into American life, its sweeping embrace of rural and urban households everywhere, the industry calmly accepted it. Product salesmen, who would be turned away at the door, were admitted into every household through the small electronic screen; and the world of business came to know that nothing could sell as well as television.

There was so much money to be made in television that a network or a station was remiss if it did not make the most of it. The industry's present system of values is descended from that pattern of easy affluence.

American television is a business before it is anything else, and within the broadcast companies the sales function is pre-eminent. That is as true at the local station level as at the networks and is indicated, if in no other way, by the top sales executive having a voice in the design of the program schedule, comparable perhaps to a sales manager taking part in the editorial decisions of a newspaper or magazine. Often, at the local stations, it is the sales director and not the program director who buys the syndicated programs and, at one network, NBC, the head of sales controls the selection of specials, rarely accepting one that is not already presold to a sponsor. A good program schedule is not a critic's schedule but a salesman's—one that will sell rapidly at the prices asked.

If that smacks of avarice, consider the problems inherent in the system. The television networks and a large number of the stations they serve are subsidiaries of public corporations and as such have obligations to their stockholders. And since stockholders in a broadcast corporation do not ask for better programs every year but rather for larger profits, it becomes clear where the priorities must be.

There is no other course but for broadcast managements to dedicate themselves to profit growth; their executive survival depends upon it. They must at the same time convey the impression of being stable and sturdy in the face of the speculative and volatile nature of show business, and so to whatever extent possible they divorce themselves from the impresario risks and behave as companies engaged in the manufacture of goods. They deal, therefore, in programs that will be instantly accepted by the audience, rejecting new and experimental forms that might take weeks or months to catch on, if at all. . . .

. . . Consumer groups, citizens committees, critics, the Federal Communications Commission, and idealists working in the industry have all tried to change television in their separate ways, but no institution has really succeeded except the advertising industry. Sooner or later, through its economic power, its will is accommodated.

Although he is no longer the sponsor who, as in the past, selected and paid for a show and thereby assumed the right to exercise creative and editorial control over its production, the advertiser still creates a favorable or unfavorable climate for types of programs and plays a direct part in the kinds of audiences the networks choose to pursue.

When by consensus, advertisers determine that Saturday morning is a cheaper and more efficient way to reach young children than by investing money in early prime time, the juvenile-slanted shows vanish from 7:30 P.M., which had been the children's hour since the start of television. When the advertiser's need is to set his fall budgets six or seven months ahead of the season, the networks adjust their fall planning accordingly. When advertisers manifest an interest in sports, they proliferate on the home screen; an aversion to serious original plays, they evaporate. And when the advertisers spurn the viewers who are past the age of fifty and assert a preference for young married couples, the networks obediently disfranchise the older audience and go full tilt in pursuit of the young.

Golf receives more television exposure than some more popular sports, although its limited audience defies the usual economic criteria. Partly, one suspects, this is due to its being a favorite recreational activity of TV executives, agency men, and their clients. Here they are their own rating service. Since golf matters to them and to nearly everyone else they are associated with, it seems to follow that golf reaches quality viewers, the *right* people. This recalls the possibly apocryphal story of the sponsor who, in the early days of television, berated his advertising agency for buying Sunday afternoon programs. "No one watches television on Sundays," he argued. "They're all at the polo matches."

There are also, apparently, sporting events for the wrong people. The advertising manager of a major company instructed his agency to spend most of the advertising budget for 1969 on televised sports, but he ruled out basketball. That sport, he felt, appealed to elements of society with which it was probably best not to associate his product. He meant, the agency man told me with a helpless shrug, blacks.

Sponsorship—advertiser identification with specific programs—has been a passing thing in television and scarcely exists today outside of specials and sports, although Kraft Foods still controlled the Wednesday night *Music Hall* and Procter & Gamble the half hour between *Walt Disney* and *Bonanza* on NBC, occupied in 1970 by *The Bill Cosby Show*.

Until the early sixties the practice, carried over from radio, had been for advertisers to control time periods at the networks, to fully underwrite the shows presented there, and in many cases to own the properties. This gave them the authority over subject matter and intellectual content, and allowed advertisers to impose their standards of production upon the show. The network was no more than a conveyance. Chevrolet, as a sponsor, once scratched "fording a stream" from dialogue because the phrase spoke the name of its competitor. The American Gas Company blipped out of a drama the reference to the means by which Jews were exterminated by Nazis in the concentration camps. A curious example of sponsor sensitivity; the gas, after all, was not guilty of genocide, the Nazis were. Numerous acts of advertiser censorship were less petty.

Obviously unhealthy, the system gave way to one in which the network had full control over programming and sold the advertiser one-minute spots, just as magazines maintain an editorial independence while selling advertisers full or partial pages. ABC, running third in the ratings, initiated it as a way to compete for advertising dollars, and the Madison Avenue consensus found it such a comfortable arrangement that the other networks were given no choice but to adopt it.

As the magazine concept solved one problem, it created another: overcommercialization. When the advertiser was sponsor it behooved him to be sensitive to the frequency and length of his program interruptions. As a buyer of minute *packages* which disperse his message over an assortment of programs on various nights of the week, he is unburdened of that aesthetic decency as well as other responsibilities.

There are no half-hour programs on television. Most are filmed or taped in twenty-six-minute lengths, including titles, plugs for next week's show, and credits. The hour show has an approximate running time of fifty-two minutes, give or take a few seconds for extra-program matters. What remains is the real goods of television, time for sale—six minutes to the hour for the network, slightly less than two minutes for the local station.

To the viewer, prime time is three and one-half hours long, but to the keeper of the network books, it is twenty-one salable minutes per night.

If the commercial breaks sell for $60,000 a minute and the program costs the network $200,000 per one-hour episode, obviously there's quite a profit when all six minutes are sold. But if the ratings are such that the minutes fetch only $25,000 apiece and the expenses are at the same $200,000 level, the loss is substantial. Each network has some of the latter and some of the former in its prime-time inventory, and the successful network is the one with a preponderance of profitable shows.

The function of the television program is to make the commercial breaks valuable. A good show is one that is important enough to the advertiser so that he will pay a premium for the minute breaks within; a bad show is one that sells at distress prices. Accordingly, the system thrives on *The Beverly Hillbillies* and will not support a *Playhouse 90*.

Against the industry's code of ten commercial minutes an hour in prime time, the networks' allocation of six an hour seems almost civilized. Yet any viewer who has spent a full evening before the set will be certain that someone has cheated, for he will have been subjected to many more than six sponsor messages in any sixty-minute period.

This is because the minutes are fractioned by advertisers into thirty-, twenty-, ten-, and even five-second "announcements," so that the three breaks in a half-hour program and the station's local minute following the show could add up to nine different commercials. In addition there may be "billboards" at the opening or close ("Tonight's episode is brought to you by—") and inevitably other brief nonprogrammatic material such as station identification slides (some stations even sell that to sponsors), the network color logos, public service spots, network promotion, station promotion, program titles, and program credits (required by the unions), all of which are recognized by the industry as irritating clutter to the viewer.

Not just the quantity of "sell" but the maddeningly intensive imperative of the commercials (*buy . . . pick up . . . be sure to . . . you'll want . . . ask your grocer . . . get . . . pamper yourself . . . hurry*) serve to make an evening at the set insufferable. Aware of this as an abuse of the viewer even before advertisers found it possible to produce "drama" in thirty seconds, the heads of the networks nevertheless, after a feeble show of resistance, allowed Madison Avenue to subdivide its minutes so that two commercials could be had for the price of one, doubling the assault on the public and compounding the problem.

The networks capitulated because the management apparatus is designed for short-range decisions. Each had to make its yearly quota of sales or face the consequences, and each was aware that the first network to accept the double-thirty minute would enjoy a flush of business. There was no suspense. The two-for-one commercial (called variously the *piggyback,* the *split-thirty* or *matched thirty,* depending on whether the two companion products were pitched contiguously or in separate commercial breaks) quickly became the standard. The networks, however, issued word that they would hold the line against the *triggyback*—three twenty-second commercials.

And how much did Madison Avenue appreciate the accommodation of the double-thirty?

In April 1970, at a seminar of the Association of National Advertisers in Absecon, New Jersey, the president of Grey Advertising, Edward H. Meyer, noted that there was a slight but discernible disaffection with television by national advertisers, and one of the reasons for it was the tremendous increase in clutter resulting from the thirty-second commercial, which was producing negative results.

To dramatize what he termed "the debasement of commercial television today," Meyer ran off a seven-minute film, an air check of a network, which spanned the actual end of one network show and the start of another. "That film," he said to fellow ad men, "is a dramatic example of where your television commercial is today. Allow me to do the counting for you. There were thirty-seven different messages during that brief seven-minute period. Is it any wonder that consumers are complaining and advertisers are restless?"

He cited *recall* research (noting how clearly TV consumers remember the advertiscments they were bombarded with during an evening) which showed a significant drop from recall levels of previous years. "If we want to get the same number of homes recalling commercials in 1969 as we did in 1965," he said, "we have to pay a cost per thousand increase of 45 per cent over 1965."

There was one other interesting bit of comparative research in his presentation. During the early sixties surveys indicated that sponsors were losing 15 to 18 per cent of the audience during commercial breaks. The figure was now up to 50 per cent. . . .

c h a p t e r   s i x

Producing television for children

MURIEL G. CANTOR

To find out how producers of series filmed for children (ages two to eleven) select content for their shows, I interviewed twenty producers and four writers who had shows in production in Los Angeles during the 1969–70 season. Part of the problem under study was: How do producers perceive the process of selecting content and the relative importance of their two audiences. Those audiences are the controllers of the occupational and organizational setting and the viewing audience. A producer wishing to make commercial television shows must please both audiences, first the buyer of the films and eventually the viewers.

The little research that is available on those who create television programs points out that several competing factors determine what is seen. These are the occupational group, the medium itself, the organizational setting, reactions from the viewing audience, and professional judgements. For example, Herbert Gans[1] suggests that media considerations, professional judgements, personal and professional values, and audience reactions determine how newsmen identify and broadcast news. Jay Blumler,[2] in a study of television producers in Britain, also found the output to be determined by varying pressures arising from organization rules and policies, perceptions of the audience, and the producer's own attitudes. In an earlier study, I also found

"Producing Television for Children," by Muriel G. Cantor. © 1971 by Muriel G. Cantor. Originally presented at the annual meetings of the American Sociological Association, Denver, September 1, 1971. Reprinted by permission of the author.

An expanded version of this paper may be found in *Television and Social Behavior, Volume I,* ed. by G. Comstock and E. Rubinstein (Washington, D.C.: Government Printing Office, 1971), pp. 259–89. The author extends special thanks to Douglass Fuchs and Susan Lloyd-Jones for their critical reading of earlier drafts of this paper.

1 Herbert J. Gans, "How Well Does TV Present the News?" in *New York Times Magazine,* January 11, 1970, pp. 30–35, 38.

2 Jay G. Blumler, "Producers Attitudes Toward Television Coverage of an Election Campaign: A Case Study," in *The Sociological Review Monograph* 13, 1969, pp. 85–116.

that putting together dramatic television series, producers are influenced by their professional values and their orientations to the viewing
audiences, to the network and to their colleagues.[3]

A few studies on creative persons and technicians employed by commercial enterprises have concerned dance musicians, studio musicians
working Hollywood, commercial artists, Hollywood starlets, Hollywood
television writers and newspapermen and others.[4] These examine how
creators function in organizations which, together with the occupational milieu and audience, limit both creative freedom and autonomy.

A review of the cited literature points out that communicators vary
in their commitment to the value of professional autonomy. (Professional autonomy is the freedom to control decisions concerning the
content and craft-techniques to be used in production.) In my earlier
study, I found that producers vary in their degree of commitment to
the value of creative control. Both the producers of evening dramatic
shows and of the children's shows may choose among several modes of
adaptation in order to operate in the system, as it now exists. At the
extremes, they can conform to network policy by denying a conflict of
values (the networks are primary buyers for films being produced for
television), or if they cannot conform they can quit producing (as several have done). Those who adapt by neither conforming completely
nor quitting, but by trying to deviate from "unacceptable" policy were
seen as most committed to professional values. As this report will show,
few such men are producing shows for children.

The ways in which producers of children's programs perceive their
role in presenting violence demonstrate both how they relate to their
two audiences and the extent to which commitment to professional
autonomy plays a part in the selection process. One reason why the
issue of violent content provides such a good example of the inter-
relationship of the producers to both his audiences and his value of
creative control is that network policy on violence in these shows
changed rather drastically after the deaths of Robert Kennedy and

[3] Muriel G. Cantor, *The Hollywood TV Producer: His Work and His Audience*
(New York: Basic Books, 1971); *Television Producers: A Sociological Analysis*. Unpublished Ph.D. dissertation. University of California, Los Angeles, 1969.

[4] Howard Becker, "Careers in a Deviant Occupational Group," in Howard Becker,
Outsiders: Studies in the Sociology of Deviance (New York: The Free Press, 1963);
Robert Faulkner, *The Hollywood Studio Musician: Their Work and Careers in
the Recording Industry* (Chicago: Illinois Aldine Publishing Co., 1971); Mason
Griff, "The Commercial Artist," in M. R. Stein, A. J. Vidich, and D. M. White,
eds., *Identity and Anxiety* (Glencoe: The Free Press, 1970); Anne Peters, *The Early
Careers of the Hollywood Actress*. Unpublished Ph.D. dissertation. University of
California, Los Angeles, 1971; Joan Moore, *The Hollywood Writer*, unpublished
manuscript; Warren Breed, "Social Control in the Newsroom," *Social Forces* 33
(1955), pp. 226–35.

Martin Luther King. Many of the same people who were making the films before 1968 were making different kinds of films in 1969. In general, network policy and norms about content vary from year to year depending on judgements of what will be popular with the "mass audience" and of the social climate. Writing with particular reference to what is usually defined as violent, Sam Blum[5] noted that the 1966 Saturday-morning television schedule would be viewed as almost "totally a matter of cartoon superheroes beating the brains out of supervillains." Neil Compton,[6] the television critic, considered the Saturday-morning children's cartoon shows an oasis of wit and sophistication in the earlier part of the decade (1960's) but these shows had been replaced by morally repellent pseudo-scientific space fantasies by 1966. According to both a search of the television schedules and the respondents in this study, the nature of programming has since then once more changed radically.

The remainder of this paper is divided into the following sections: Producers and Network, Producers and the Viewing Audience, and Concluding Remarks. The twenty producers and the four writers primarily make films which are either animated or use animals. These are usually shown on Saturday morning (prime-time for the children's shows). A few of those interviewed are making Western adventure series telecast for a family audience during the early evening hours. No producer of a show on the air after 8 o'clock p.m. was included in this series of interviews.

PRODUCERS AND THE NETWORK

PRODUCERS OF SHOWS SPECIFICALLY FOR CHILDREN

The reactions to the networks and to network control of stories, while not the same for all producers, varied little among those making shows specifically for the children's audience. Those making animated films had little trouble conforming to the changing network policy. Because the three large producers of animated films made films for different types of buyers and were engaged in a number of activities each demanding different content, their products were sold on demand. For instance, two of three production houses made animated titles for films

5 Sam Blum, "Who Decides What Gets on TV and Why," in *Social Profiles in U.S.A. Today from the New York Times* (New York: Van Nostrand Reinhold Company, 1970).
6 Neil Compton, "TV Specials," *Commentary* 45 (1968), pp. 69–71.

and live-action television series. One of these titles actually became a main character in a children's animated series with a very successful run. All three make animated commercials and one makes educational films for the classroom. Two smaller companies make the animated segments of *Sesame Street* as well as their commercial offerings. These animation houses had little trouble following network directives. When the network presented them with series ideas they were able and willing to instigate them. In other words, they considered themselves primarily businessmen making films rather than creators of ideas.

The producers who were making shows with live animals also had few problems with the networks because their shows were considered "educational" rather than amusement. There were only a few of these programs in production. One new show using live animals, which could be considered a comedy rather than an educational program, was produced for the first time in 1970. Both the "old" shows and the new one are relatively free of network pressure to change because of the nature of their content. One exception is a program that is a mixture of live-action adventure and has in its cast one live animal. Because its essential ingredient is not necessarily the animal in the cast but rather its stories, it will be discussed later with the Westerns.

Producers for a company involved in the production of animated, live-action and animal and nature shows also had little trouble conforming to network policy. They search for scripts, stories and educational material that lend themselves to visual comedy or visual adventure. To quote one:

> I like to put the accent on the positive and avoid the seamy aspects. I leave that to others. I do fear things so I try for the upbeat.

Because the ratings for their programs has always been high and because their themes were consistently the same, they had no serious doubts about their work. They were not concerned with the network for several reasons. They never had had any trouble except in selling offerings to the network. Here, of course, they along with the others had their share of failure. However, two of the shows they had sold to the networks were record successes both in ratings and length of time on the air. Besides, this production company is one of the few left in Hollywood to be successfully producing both theater films and television series and specials. In all areas they are relatively successful compared to other production companies. Their films, whether for television, for educational purposes (they do some classroom production, as well), or for theater, are similar.

Seven producers are employed by the studio (three of whom were interviewed), and although some are assigned to theatrical projects and others to television production, the philosophy behind their work is essentially the same. The studio is well known for a certain type of product which may or may not get critical acclaim, but the record of success is high and network control minimal. The studio philosophy controls the philosophy of the producers: nothing that would be controversial, either politically or socially, is allowed. Also, while intellectuals believing that certain kinds of adventures can generate fear in children, have discussed the effects of some of their stories, there has been little which violates network policy. This is especially true of their television offerings that have focused on animals in their natural habitat and upon science education. What they have presented to the networks has been approved and accepted with only minor changes.

Another producer is producing a children's series for the first time. His show has an unusual concept; the live animals portray humans. They do "everything people do" to quote their producer, "wash, dress, get into trolley cars, etc." The show is comedy and, according to the respondent, has "absolutely no violence which is *unnecessary* to the plot." Although in real life the animals are dangerous (I had to sign a release to go on the set), in the show they are "like people." The theme is a bumbling detective and his girl friend who have various adventures each week. When the interview took place, none of the episodes had been on the air. The original show was developed from a theatrical film short, made several years before, and has been shown around the country to adult audiences with a feature length film. This short served as a pilot, and the network which bought it decided that the idea would be perfect for a children's Saturday morning series. The producer and the writer-creators had an adult audience in mind when they presented the idea to the networks, but the network purchased seventeen weeks (34 short episodes) to be shown on children's prime time. Because the show was originally planned for adults, there was some concern about its level of sophistication. The writers and producers had in mind several ideas which, though intended to be spoofs, could be considered risque or sexually provocative.

When the interview took place, about one-half of the episodes had been filmed. None had been broadcast. According to the producer, the network had been very cooperative and supportive in its reactions to the scripts. Their only problems came from the Humane Society who by law has someone on the set watching the way the animals are handled. When talking about the networks and script control, the producer said,

> The network has the final say in theory but they have never turned down a script we have submitted. We have had no interference from them for approval; there have been only the most minor changes required. Once in awhile Broadcasting Standards complain about something. We have to be especially kind to the animals. The Animal Rescue League or whatever it

is called is always on the set watching us. But we have one trainer for every animal as you saw.

PRODUCERS OF SHOWS FOR THE FAMILY AUDIENCE*

Those making the Western adventures, which are directed to the family audience and broadcast in the evenings had more problems concerning violence and network interference. Two men in the sample had been previously interviewed in 1967–1968, and their shows had been on the air for a number of seasons. When the network censorship offices informed them at the beginning of the 1969–1970 season that violence would have to be curtailed in their programs, both thought this would be no problem. They considered their shows basically nonviolent. The network thought otherwise, and the two, having had no interference in past seasons, found their shows being scrutinized in what both considered a most arbitrary manner.

The producers protested network interferences. They insisted that their content was not violent just for the sake of violence and that the action sequences in the show were there because the drama demanded it. This was a touchy point because as one put it, "How are you going to have an adventure if nothing is threatening?" Both insisted that formerly the networks had been too lenient with others and that now the censorship offices were going overboard in their search for violence. One told this story about an episode:

> First, I fought with the network over the basic script. The story demanded that several people be killed when a bridge had to be blown up. This was a Revolutionary War story. How can you show war without killings? That would be more dishonest than making war non-violent. Finally they allowed me two killings—new rule two killings in an episode. After that was settled and I thought the script was approved, the second day of shooting, I get a phone call from the network. They were upset because my main character was carrying powder to blow up a bridge. Listen, they said, we are upset about him carrying that powder. Could he (the main character) find it when he arrives at the bridge—have it cached there?
>
> The implication is that the story is violent by nature because he is going to blow up something. I told them I had been shooting for a day and a half—I have already established that they are carrying powder—nothing I can do about it now. You know the networks are moral only up to a point. They are not going to spend money reshooting. OK. That settled it.

In refusing to change the scene, the producer was committed to certain principles of dramatic writing. The mission had to be clearly stated in the first few minutes of the play. The audience had to know what is to be accomplished and how the characters would attempt to accomplish the mission. That, to him, is the essence of the suspense involved in such drama. There can be no suspense if the audience does not know from the beginning what is going on. The producer believed this had nothing to do with violence as such, and he appealed to the network Vice-President. The disagreement was one of seven occurring in the 1969–1970 season, compared to only one request for a minor change in a script due to violence in the 1967–1968 season. In the seven similar situations, the producer reported that several times he was able to convince the networks to do the script according to the original directions and dialogue. The other times he had to yield to the networks to get the show on the air.

During this producer's first few years with the show, his situation had been very much different. The networks always had the right to approve all scripts. However, they usually accepted his material readily, and he was able to operate within a framework he could accept. He said that he gave the networks credit for thinking they hired people to make the show who they believed were artistically and technically able to make decisions about content. According to him, nothing had changed. There had been no adverse response from the viewing audience. (This, of course, could not be confirmed by the method being used.) The letters the program received were for the most part complimentary, and the ratings were high. However, even though all the indicators suggested that the show was being well received, the network's relationship with producers had changed drastically from the 1967–1968 season to the 1969–1970 season. For example, in the 1967 season, this same producer had boasted of his good relations with the networks and of his freedom to produce scripts that were rarely changed. In 1967, he said:

> I haven't found any traditional things that everyone writes about—about sponsor pressure or network pressure. They would like to have the best possible show—and they have never said or done anything with one or two minor exceptions that I felt in any way impeded my creativity. We are doing the best possible show we can do considering the time and money we have to do it with. The network has never turned me down on a script. Sometimes they like some scripts better than others but it is always a matter of conversation. When they don't like something, I say what can I do to make it better. Sometimes I accept what they say, sometimes I don't. I have inherited a successful show. I have become spoiled. Another show on another network may not be as good. I have no problems.

What brought about this drastic change? The network was the same one that the producer had saluted in 1967 for being "secure and supportive." Content that was once acceptable was no longer so because of the change in network policy. Thus, and this point cannot be sufficiently emphasized, *the producers operate in a milieu where the final decisions about stories and content is not theirs.* Network policy on violence had changed in three years. In order to stay with the show, the producer had to redefine his role. Although he fought the networks on specific points, for his purposes he no longer had the autonomy he once had. The authority of the producer is always a delegated authority.

It is impossible for anyone who does not give in to the continuous network pressure to stay on the job. Of course, it is possible for producers to argue and even occasionally win on specific points. But all ideas for series depend first on network approval, and secondly, all stories, characters, music and settings must be submitted for network approval before production can begin on an episode.

PRODUCERS AND THE VIEWING AUDIENCE

Because of its size and distance, the viewing audience cannot feed back direct reactions to the producer. It might be the least important reference group he considers, when he selects content. Since only 17 episodes are made for Saturday-morning viewing, often all are completed before even one can be shown on the air. Therefore, there can be no chance for any audience feedback, and the actual effect of this audience on the producer during production is minimal, if any at all.

Children's shows are often pretested or previewed before purchase. However, this is not really a satisfactory method of discovering audience reactions to content because only still pictures of the characters are shown to the children. Several producers were derogatory about this method; they thought that it gave them no clue as to what children would like to see. The pictures are presented so that children can voice approval or disapproval of material, and according to those interviewed, children are more apt to like characters with whom they are familiar. For example, if Gulliver or Goldilocks were presented among new characters, the more familiar ones would get the approving vote.

If a series becomes a success with the audience (measured by high Nielsen ratings), both the producer and the production company receive many financial benefits. One is using the characters to merchandise clothing and toys. Also, phonograph records of the music can be sold. One producer claimed that a record featuring the musical group in his series had sold over a million copies. Most important, once a producer or a production house has one success, the networks are more likely to contract with them to develop new ideas and to use them to make more series.

Therefore, the ultimate audience the producers hope to please is still the viewing audience. The audience is distant and the feedback is slight. Certain of the producers' conceptions of their audience are more often stereotypical than they are thoughtfully drawn. These stereotypes are derived from several sources, used differently by the different producers. The ratings of the types of shows which had been on the air in former years give the only available "complete" picture of the audience. A second source is direct contact with children and their parents, either from letters received or from the highly particular personal interaction producers maintain with their own children and with those of friends.

Ideas about the audience can be obtained from the ratings and other types of marketing research done by the network and by the advertiser. "Demographics" are most important to the advertiser to make sure that a program is reaching a target audience. Toy and cereal manufacturers are not as interested in such characteristics as income, ethnicity and section of country as the advertisers for the evening shows are. Size of audience, age and sex are more important to them. The advertisers and the producers assume that American parents indulge their children. If children cajole, parents will buy. Accordingly, the major kind of audience the advertiser wishes to capture is the age bracket verbally capable of convincing parents to buy products or having spending-money. Because the ratings suggest that the older children control the sets, advertisers and producers believe the younger children are held captive to the programs their older sisters and brothers wish to watch.

Many times the product to be advertised will determine which sex is the target for the program. If the toy is meant for boys, the show will be an adventure, western or space-fantasy. Girls are reported to prefer comedy and rock and roll groups. However, despite either the theme or the target audience, every show has both masculine and feminine characters, each performing according to the producers' notions of society's notions of proper sex-determined, adult roles. The boys or adult men are always the leaders regardless of the major orientation of the show, and there is always one girl or possibly a woman who acts as his helper. If the show has a villain, this pattern is repeated—although it is not uncommon to find a major villain being portrayed as a woman, especially in the space-fantasies. However, only in alien cultures are women the leaders of society as well as villains, not in middle-class America.

Because the segments for the animated shows are short, just ten minutes in length, each segment is a complete adventure or incident. By necessity the plots must be simple, and the drawings are often crude when compared to the animated theatrical films made in the 1940's and 1950's. One explanation for this is that the fine action necessary for the large screen would be wasted (if not invisible) on the smaller screen of a television set. In any case fine-action drawings are more costly, because they require many more people working on the film. Thus, the main line of action in an animated show is fast and usually noisy. The creators feel the child's attention span is limited, and loud banging noises and quick movements are used to keep the children watching. The animated commercials appearing in the breaks between segments are also made by the same people; therefore, the same techniques are used to keep the children from leaving the set during commercials. Some producers even thought that their commercials were often made with more care and were more interesting than their regular shows.

When in production, the producers rarely consider the effect their shows might have on children. Most (there were exceptions) believed that those considerations were the network's responsibility or maybe the parents'; but not theirs. They often stated that the networks hire psychologists to study whether shows have negative effects (which, if not true, might be a defensive belief). The newer shows are making a special effort to present educational messages to children in the form of entertainment. These messages stress good manners, racial tolerance and, especially, the irrelevance of physical differences. Of course, the "good guys" still always win when there is conflict, and because the characters are rarely presented in shades of gray, there is never any sympathy for "bad guys."

One producer, whose programs were first aired in 1970–1971, stated that he was glad to have the chance to improve television, because the function of television should be to entertain rather than inform. (This is a commonly held belief among those producing for children.) This producer thought his shows would uplift children through entertainment.

Some children's shows have been violent for violence sake, as you probably already know. Here we can be funny, entertain—not hurt anyone. For instance we have one scene where (the main character—an animal) shaves. The kids love that. We try to show everyday occurrences—wives nagging husbands. We discovered people laugh when they see animals do things people do.

We really hope that this program will uplift the kids in certain ways. Certain messages are there. For instance, the main character always brushes his teeth after each meal. And we worry and talk a lot about safety. No one ever goes into a car without fastening his seatbelt. But we don't have any strong messages, nothing controversial. We don't want to antagonize anyone.

Respondents commonly believed that after Robert Kennedy's assassination in June 1968, mothers all over America wrote thousands of letters to the networks to protest the violent programs appearing on television. Producers themselves did not receive these letters, but thought that the networks did. To quote one: "Mothers of America rose in unison to protest." It should be noted that they assume it was the mothers who psychologically opposed the super-hero cartoons, not the fathers.

Also, and in contradiction, producers simultaneously shared a common belief that parents never watch television on Saturday morning. They think the noise level might disturb parents but, according to the producers, most parents have no idea about the actual stories or themes used. Producers see Saturday-morning television in use as a babysitter, especially among the lower and middle class audience. (Parents, as well as the producers and networks, might want their children mesmerized—but for different reasons, the networks to sell products and the parents so that they would not be bothered.) All of this has become part of the folklore that has grown up around and influences the production of morning programming. Of course, there is very little evidence for this folklore. Few producers have personally received unfavorable letters about their programs—at least, they did not admit to receiving such letters in quantity. As far as could be discerned from the interviews, respondents did not know of any specific research concerning parents' uses of and reactions to Saturday-morning programming.

The producers expect a mixed audience, children and adults, for the evening programs (usually Westerns and adventure programs). These are of a higher level of sophistication. The noise level both of the shows themselves and of the commercials is also lower, and because the story can be as long as forty-eight minutes, more attention can be given to content. There is also more possibility of audience feedback, because the series might still be in production while episodes are being broadcast. Even so, producers of these shows are more apt to use personal values about entertainment or the reactions of friends and family as their yardstick to determine whether their programs are being well received than they are to use a more general feedback from the viewing audience. Like the Saturday-morning producers, they often use the Nielsen ratings as their best measure of success. In their case, the ratings determine whether or not the networks will let them stay on the air.

Even when producers of evening programs receive direct critical feedback in letters, they tend to rationalize or ignore the content, considering it idiosyncratic. Moreover, those producing adventure series usually deny they are making shows for children, even though these series are categorized as children's shows by the National Academy of Television Arts, which is responsible for the Emmy awards. One producer in particular (whose audience includes a large number of children under ten, according to ratings and other demographic survey data) stated:

We are not making a children's story. I don't think anyone in the business knows who their audience is. I think it is presumptuous of anyone to claim they know this. Kids don't know anything. They are not discerning. As long as we are on the air I don't care.

This producer received a semi-critical letter shortly before the interview took place. A section of that letter follows:

I am not in the habit of writing to television producers regarding their programs, but in this case I feel I must drop you a line regarding last night. My six year old daughter is a viewer for the past couple of years. Needless to say we have been through many adventures, trials and tribulations, but I have never seen her as shaken as during last night's program. Not only did she cry her eyes out during the show, I had to keep reminding her during the evening it was only a story and (animal character) in several weeks time [will] be fine. She also was worried her own pet would suffer a similar mishap.

His reaction was to disclam responsibility for the emotional health of the children-viewers. Parents should see that their children are not frightened or in any way affected by what is on the air. According to him:

You cannot have it bland—sometimes it has to be upsetting. How can we do it to your kids? What do you mean how can we do it to your kids? We are doing something for entertainment; this is our only purpose. If we are not entertaining the kid, we are failing. The entire thing of throwing the burden on us because the kids cry. This is wrong and unfair. If a parent has the child enjoying our program which they do, then it is the parent's responsibility, when it is brought to a point that the parent is worried, then it is the parent's responsibility to see that in an honest and realistic way this is dealt with.

This producer quoted above is representative of most of those producing all types of children's programming. Concern about the effects of their programming was negligible. However, four producers were exceptions and expressed concern in various ways. One producer thought that the networks should spend more money on psychological research. Another, as mentioned earlier, would no longer produce for commercial television because of the kinds of programs being produced, even though he saw there had been a shift from violence. He thought that the level of the children's shows was still so low that there could be no benefits to the children viewing them. He also protested the lack of freedom to create and was disturbed that he might be forced to work in a medium where the intelligence level required to produce was minimized. Two other producers had publicized their opinions about children's programming. One was an animator who had had limited success in producing. He showed the interviewer several newspaper clippings. They quoted him as essentially saying that the low-level programming, whether or not violent, was an improper use of the medium, and television could be used as a great social force to enhance the intelligence and capabilities of a whole generation of children. Because of the commercial aspects of programs regardless of the content, he was generally anti-network television as well. He believed that when well known personalities sell products to children, the shows themselves lose their credibility.

I think children realize when they are being sold even in a basically good show. This is a universal thing that is wrong with the industry. The networks can't change. The only hope is not to change network television, but we must get more non-commercial TV. *Sesame Street* could not be as successful on commercial TV because of this. The welfare of children must come first. Under present conditions this is impossible.

The other producer, who had made his views public, is extremely successful in both adult and children's programming, working primarily in live-action and using animals in many of his shows. A major concern of his was the effects television programs might have on the minds of children, and he thought that the television industry has definitely not met its responsibilities in several other areas. According to this producer, it is the industry's responsibility to find out what television does to the minds of children and, the industry should use its facilities to make children more loving rather than more violent. He was so concerned about the power of television to mold the minds of the young that he actually suggested that no child under six should be permitted to watch television. Part of his concern was with content, but part was with the hypnotic ability of the medium itself, regardless of the content. He said, although he

considers television an entertainment medium and not a charitable institution, the time had come when all of us, not only the networks, must remember we live in a world dominated by television where a child spends more time in front of his set than in school.

To sum up, producers showed some concern about the effects of television on children, but this was not an overwhelming concern. Producers would rather make nonviolent shows if they had the opportunity. But, producers emphasize that regardless of how they view the home audience, the final decision about content remains with the network. The newer producers in the children's field are the least concerned about both audience effects and network power, because they intend to produce shows for television that meet the networks' demands to fill air time. Their values about programming and their views of the audience are similar to those the networks currently hold.

CONCLUDING REMARKS

Communicators, as John and Matilda Riley point out,[7] must be seen as operating in a social setting, as part of a larger structure, as sending messages in accordance with the expectations and actions of others in the same system. For the television producer, the system is complex. It consists of the organization or studio producing the films, the network and advertisers who buy the films, and the general audience who eventually view the films. Because there is no direct contact with the large viewing audience, the direct feedback comes from the organization buying the films. The network and advertiser seem to be the most important audience to the producer. He sends his messages more directly in accordance with their desires than with the desires of the ultimate viewing audience who is unknown to him. While all the various parts of the system might influence the final product, the most important influence comes from those parts of the system having direct interaction with the communicator.

At this time the reality of the marketplace is: If a producer wishes to make television shows to be shown on commercial television, he must please both of his two audiences first, the buyers of the film, and eventually, the viewers. If a series is to be shown, the buyer is necessarily the most important audience, and he does have the most direct interaction with the producer. No show can ever be judged by the general audience unless it first pleases a buyer. In most cases the buyer is the network.

There are other reasons why pleasing the viewing audience is a secondary consideration. Producers feel that direct expressions of approval or disapproval, such as letter-writing, do not represent the large, heterogeneous audience commanded by television series. Their children and those of their friends are not representative of the audience. Indirect measures, such as market research and rating services are methodologically inadequate, telling nothing about reactions to content. In any case, since television shows appear on the air long after they are made, they could not be changed to reflect audience feedback. The only direct feedback is from the network representatives who watch each step of the production process. Especially with children's programming, the network itself is the primary audience; the content is directed to its desires and its mandates.

[7] John W. Riley, Jr. and Matilda White Riley, "Mass Communication and the Social System," in R. K. Merton, L. Broom, and L. S. Cottrell, Jr., ed. *Sociology Today* (New York: Basic Books, 1959).

Shayon reported elsewhere[8] that producers of children's programs believe they are "the decision-makers, and though they welcome consultation and endorse research, control is properly in their hands." Not one of the producers interviewed for this study believed that he had true creative control. In film television, which may be different from the taped shows made for children, there is an understanding of and, in most cases, a general acceptance of network power and control. As pointed out earlier, the network may not choose to exercise this control, but the network must always be considered whether producers are thinking of story-ideas or series-concepts. The findings from these interviews, at least, indicate that especially producers of animated film-series either actively accept changes in network policy or, more usually, passively accept them. Reporting no trouble from the network is the most usual response to questions concerning freedom and autonomy. But when one examines the content of the responses, one clearly see that producers learn network policy; they give the network what it wants or they produce without specific directives from the network, because they share the network's ideology concerning proper entertainment for children.

The evidence suggests: Those who do not cooperate in the commercial milieu cannot become successful producers and writers for network television. They must leave the medium either voluntarily or involuntarily—when their values are found to be discordant to those of the organization. The content of children's shows has changed several times in the last decade; many of the producers who did sophisticated social criticism in cartoon shows at the beginning of the decade (1960's) later turned to the super-hero shows and space-fantasies and now create the rock and roll and comedy shows. As each new trend sets in, new men whose talents and values tend to fit the programming in demand, are recruited to make shows for children. This might explain why those new to producing children's shows have so few complaints with the networks, their first shows fit the needs of the network at a time when more "educational" and comedy shows are in demand.

Bradley Greenberg[9] has suggested that the men who write, produce and direct television films operate under conditions of high tension and aggression, and that this might account for the intense level of dramatic output. The problem he presents is certainly empirical, but cannot be answered by a case-study method. It should be clarified

8 Robert Lewis Shayon, "Media Mystification," *Saturday Review* 51, October 17, 1970.

9 Bradley Greenberg, "The Content and Context of Violence in the Mass Media" in Robert K. Baker and Sandra I. Ball, eds., *Violence and the Media: A Report to the National Commission on Cause and Prevention of Violence* (Washington, D.C.: Government Printing Office, 1969), pp. 425–52.

whether the working conditions for television's creative people are more highly charged than for other creative people, whose products are not as violent in nature, for example, musicians and artists. Some of the evidence in this study is not in agreement with Greenberg's speculation. As pointed out, the men are not restricted just to violent content, and they can and do make both educational and often highly artistic shows for commercial television, film and public television when required. *Sesame Street* is the best example. The production companies discussed here have a variety of films in production, ranging from polar coordinates on a graph to a new non-violent detective story about a boy detective and his girl Friday. The evidence also indicates that the men who make violent films, not only are able to make films which are non-violent, but they prefer to. Ultimately, though, they make what they can sell.

The highest priority in future studies should be given to the decision-making processes of the networks themselves. Only when this process has been examined can the important questions about who determines content be answered. The present study must conclude that the networks determine the content of children's programs. How they make their decisions, what publics they try to satisfy, and which publics are thereby denied access to the kinds of programs they want are still open questions, which could be subjected to research.

chapter seven

Assembling a network talk-show

GAYE TUCHMAN

"How do innovations arise?" is an old question, as familiar to the student of organizations as it is to the student of culture. Recently, Hirsch[1] suggested a fusion of these two fields to explain the introduction of innovations into popular culture. Noting that the manufacturing and dissemination of "cultural products" is beset by economic uncertainty, he suggests that the "culture industry" be analyzed as a system. (Cultural products are " 'non-material' goods directed at a public of consumers for whom they generally serve an esthetic or expressive, rather than a clearly utilitarian function . . . each [product] is non-material in the sense that it embodies a live, one-of-a-kind performance and/or contains a unique set of ideas.")[2] Using systems theory, he suggests that media "decision makers" decrease uncertainty by promoting their products.

This paper addresses itself to Hirsch's identification of the television talk-show as a system's gatekeeper whose cooptation facilitates the economic success of a cultural product, such as a new movie. It argues that television talk-shows are beset by the same problems Hirsch ascribes to the book-publishing, record, and motion-picture industries. After examining the ways in which economic uncertainty influences the assembly of a talk-show, this paper suggests that the problem of introducing innovations has yet to be solved.

SPECIFICATION OF THE PROBLEM

The basic rule governing the creation of television programming is well-known. Briefly put, it states: Plan programs that will attract a

"Assembling a Network Talk-Show," by Gaye Tuchman. © 1974 by Gaye Tuchman. Used by permission of the author.

An earlier version of this essay, "Consuming Roles at a Network Talk-Show," was presented at the meetings of the American Sociological Association, New Orleans, 1972.

1 Paul Hirsch, "Processing Fads and Fashions: An Organization Set Analysis of Cultural Industry Systems." *American Journal of Sociology 77,* Number 4, 1972, pp. 639–59.
2 *Ibid.,* p. 647.

large audience (as indexed by rating services) so that the audience may be sold profitably to commercial advertisers. Expressed even more succinctly, the same rule governs show business that governs all large business: Make money.

However, unlike many other large businesses, the "culture industry" in general and television programming in particular are high risk affairs. Although media personnel may imitate past success[3] or adopt any one of the several organizational strategies delineated by Hirsch,[4] they cannot, with any degree of certainty, locate formulas for success. As Hirsch notes in his discussion, there is "wide-spread uncertainty over the precise ingredients of a best-seller formula" and an "ignorance of relations between cause and effect." [5] Put more simply, media personnel cannot predict what characteristics a cultural product may have or even should have to become "popular."

Television programming provides a clear example of this problem in prediction. At best, television programmers and producers are beset by correlations. These indicate that certain kinds of persons sorted by specified demographic characteristics, such as age, sex, and area of residence, tend to watch certain types of television programs. However precise these correlations may be,[6] they do not enable personnel to predict *which* program will be economically successful, nor to state precise rules for creating a successful program.

According to Hirsch,[7] one of the methods used by decision-makers to cope with this uncertainty is coopting mass media gatekeepers—programs and newspapers (among others) who control access to a wide audience. "Cultural products provide 'copy' and 'programming' for newspapers, magazines, radio stations, and television programs; in exchange, they receive 'free' publicity. . . . Public awareness of the existence and availability of a new cultural product often is contingent on feature stories in newspapers and national magazines, review columns, and broadcast talk shows. . . ." [8]

---

[3] Hortense Powdermaker, Hollywood: *The Dream Factory.* (New York: Grosset and Dunlap); Denis McQuail, "Uncertainty about the Audience and the Organization of Mass Communications," *The Sociological Review: Monograph No. 13,* January, 1969, pp. 75–84.

[4] Hirsch, *op. cit.*

[5] *Ibid.,* p. 644.

[6] The *Evaluation of Statistical Methods Used in Obtaining Broadcast Ratings,* prepared for the Committee on Interstate and Foreign Commerce (U.S. Government Printing Office, 1961), suggests "When there are important disagreements among the rating services, when program or station ratings do not differ by large amounts but the differences are treated as significant, when decisions are made on the basis of cost per thousand [audience members reached] and the ratings are fairly low and the sample fairly small, it is questionable whether the ratings provide an adequate basis for important decisions," p. 17.

[7] *Op. cit.*

[8] *Ibid.,* p. 647.

Peculiarly, Hirsch does not point out that these gatekeepers, are themselves cultural products. If newspapers, national magazines, and national television talk-shows as cultural products are themselves beset by the same problems of prediction, how open are they to promoting cultural innovations? The answer indicated here is, they are not very open at all.

To reach this answer, this paper examines the assembly of a television talk-show. Based upon backstage observations of one of three network talk-shows televised weeknights in the summer of 1970, it emphasizes the extent to which media personnel plan programs to deliver what they think the audience will buy. Inasmuch as the members of the talk-show staff do not know what the audience will tune in to see, staff members must proceed to plan *as if* they knew what they were doing and *as if* their preferences were those of the audience. This paper describes some of the typifications or characterizations staff members believe to be associated with conditions of economic success.

Typifications are examined for several reasons. For one, typifications are first-order or existential constructs.[9] As Schutz puts it, ". . . as I confront my fellowman, I bring into each concrete situation a stock of preconstituted knowledge which includes a network of typifications of human individuals in general, of typical human motivations, goals, and action patterns." [10] Theoretically, the examination of the typifications used to assemble a television talk-show should provide a picture of the way that members of the talk-show staff perceive their activities.

Second, recent research on typifications suggests the centrality of typifying to the construction of rules for social action under conditions of uncertainty. By "conditions of uncertainty" is meant conditions not governed by known rules of a binding or coercive nature. Thus Sudnow[11] demonstrates the utility of typifications in plea-bargaining, a process not governed by legal rules and even dissociated from them. Elsewhere,[12] I suggest that typifications enable news organizations to

[9] See John C. McKinney, "Sociological Theory and the Process of Typification." Pp. 235–69 in J. C. McKinney and E. Tiryakin (ed.), *Theoretical Sociology*. (New York: Appleton Century Croft, 1970); cf. Aaron V. Cicourel, *The Social Organization of Juvenile Justice* (New York: John Wiley, 1968); David Sudnow, "Normal Crimes: Sociological Features of the Penal Code in a Public Defenders Office." *Social Problem 12* 1965, pp. 255–72; John C. McKinney and Linda Brookover Bourque, "Further Comments on 'The Changing South': A Response to Sly and Weller." *American Sociological Review 37* 1972, pp. 230–36; Gaye Tuchman, "Making News by Doing Work: Routinizing the Unexpected." *American Journal of Sociology 79* (July, 1973), pp. 110–31; Alfred Schutz, *Collected Papers I* The Hague: Martinus Nijhoff, 1962, pp. 37–56; Roger Jehenson, "A Phenomenological Approach to the Study of the Formal Organization," pp. 219–47 in George Psathas (ed.), *Phenomenological Sociology*. (New York: John Wiley, 1973).

[10] Schutz, *op. cit.*, p. 29.

[11] Sudnow, *op. cit.*

[12] Tuchman, *op. cit.*

cope with the problem of planning for and processing information about unexpected events. Inasmuch as talk-show staffers operate under conditions of uncertainty, the use of typifications should facilitate planning.

Third, talk-show staffers themselves emphasize the use of typifications in planning programs, although they do not employ that term. Rather, talk-show personnel take for granted the need to achieve decent ratings and view the rating system as providing boundaries for their programming activities. They assume, for instance, that "celebrities" attract large audiences and that "unknowns" do not. They feel that their programming activities are particularly difficult to carry out, because the format of the talk-show stresses lively and "revealing" interaction between the program's host and his guests. To achieve this interaction (and attract viewers) staffers feel that they must recruit guests in terms of "interactionally-usable" attributes, judging which guest might "go well" with another. This is problematic for two reasons. First, staffers estimate that only 200 celebrities are capable of providing lively and revealing interaction on a talk-show, so that there is a limited pool from which to draw. Second, staffers recognize that try as one might, *one cannot accomplish an interaction for someone else.* To introduce an analogy, one might dress one's child in his best clothes, caution him to be on his best behavior, and leave him at the door of a birthday party, but be totally incapable of governing his behavior at that party. Indeed, although present at the party, one might still be totally incapable of knowing what one's child is going to do.

After reviewing my collection of observational data, I will describe the "natural history" of preparing a guest for a television talk-show. Then, I will discuss staff typifications of celebrities as a group, emphasizing typifications that are relevant to the interaction of celebrities and staff. Next, I will turn to typified attributes of individuals usable for interaction on the air. Finally, I will examine the relevance of staff practices to the original problem: How open are talk-shows, themselves cultural products, to presenting innovations?

THE RESEARCH METHOD

This research was carried out backstage at a talk-show televised weekday evenings. It was one of three programs of this type that originated in New York City in the summer of 1970.

Observations on the talk-show were gathered in the holding room (green room) in which guests, their managers, agents, and friends sit with talk-show staffers as the guests wait to appear on the program. The green room was not the research site by choice. Rather, it was the only site to which I could gain more or less continual access. On several occasions, I watched the taping from the host's dressing room, viewing with the executive producer, some writers, and secretarial assistants. Once I sat in the clients' room, the most elegant of the backstage areas (it had been designed to accommodate advertisers and their representatives).

After two months, I was asked to stop observing, since the green room was extremely crowded and occasional whispers backstage were interfering with the taping. The producer presented this request as part of a larger effort to decrease backstage visitors. (Irregularly shaped, the green room was approximately 175 square feet and usually held between 15 and 25 seated and standing persons.) Although given the option of resuming in several months (after the contractural renewal of the program), I chose not to do so.

Though I observed backstage over a comparatively brief period, I believe the information presented here to be accurate; it is substantiated by reports on the talk-shows published in such popular magazines as *TV Guide, Life, McCalls, Esquire, Saturday Review* and the *New Yorker*. Like this report, the popular articles emphasize the importance of celebrities and of staff attempts to create "lively interaction." Accordingly, by "accurate" I mean that a variety of observers identify similar if not identical processes and practices as central to assembling a talk-show.

PREPARING A GUEST

As might be expected, talk-show staffers try to predict, as much as possible, whether an individual will be a good guest. And, they try to plan the interaction that will occur on the televised program. These attempts are implicit in the natural history of preparing a guest.

If an individual has not previously been viewed on a talk-show by a sufficiently powerful staff member, he or she will be given a pre-interview to determine whether he or she is "good TV." [13] If the person qualifies as a good guest, a researcher (one of two women) seeks additional information about his/her life and background and passes it on either to talent interviewers (female) or to writers (male).[14] The interviewer or writer then speaks extensively and privately with the "potential guest" to discover what aspects of his/her past, present, or projected future will be entertaining to the viewing audience. In gen-

---

[13] Unfortunately, the staff could not explicate their method of determining that someone would be "good TV." I did not have access to those interviews. Like all interviews used to prepare the program, they were only attended by the interviewer and the celebrity. Many show business personalities are exempted from the first pre-interview.

[14] Some of the writers also wrote the host's monologue. The writers (male) held higher status than the interviewers (female). As best as could be estimated from patterns of consumption, the writers also earned more money.

eral, the staff member draws upon his own notion of entertainment, since he knows relatively little about the notions of the audience.[15]

Next, the interviewer or writer composes an introduction for the guest, which will be read by the host, and prepares a series of questions to be asked of the guest. The expected answers are also indicated to the host. Both questions and answers are structured before the program goes on the air; that is, the questions and expected answers are arranged not only in some type of sequence, but also around "segments" of airtime delineated between scheduled commercials. Before taping, in either the make-up room or the backstage green room, the guest will be told some, if not all, of the questions to be asked. While the program is being video-taped, the guest waiting to appear watches it on closed-circuit television, both to see how it is progressing and to see how his interests tie in to comments made by the guests who precede him. This supposedly increases program continuity. After the program has been taped, the interviewer congratulates the guest, providing comfort and reassurance that the performance was adequate, scintillating, splendid, or whatever. Such reassurance, like the long-stemmed roses presented to all female guests with the compliments of the host, supposedly disposes the guest to appear on future programs and so to reenter the "guesting process."

Although indicative of the staff's attempt to orchestrate interaction for others, this natural history of the process glosses over the staff's actual practices and strategies.[16] For those practices sort persons-as-guests in terms of their typified interactionally-usable-attributes-to-glean-ratings. This may be simply demonstrated by considering the staff's emphasis upon those celebrities who attract a large audience. For instance, in planning programs, staff members try to schedule a big celebrity two weeks in advance to meet the deadline of *TV Guide* and the Sunday newspaper's television section. Staff members hope that viewers, deciding which program to watch, will read the big celebrity's name and be attracted to their program. In their discussions, staff mem-

---

15 Although the staff members viewed the studio audience as a "prop" to recording the program, some would make guesses about the home-viewing audience by commenting upon the age-range of those whom they saw waiting to sit in the studio audience.

16 Harold Garfinkel and Harvey Sacks explain "glossing practices" by stating, "The interests of ethnomethodological research are directed to provide through detailed analyses, that accountable phenomena are through and through practical accomplishments. We shall speak of 'the work' of that accomplishment in order to gain emphasis for it as an ongoing course of action. The work is done as assemblages of practices whereby speakers in the situated particulars of speech mean something different from what they can say in just so many words, that is, as 'glossing practices.'" p. 342 in Garfinkel and Sacks, "On Formal Structures of Practical Actions," pp. 337–63 in McKinney and Tiryakin (ed.), *op. cit.*

bers view the celebrity as a well-known person whom viewers will want to hear talk about his life and work and of whom viewers wonder, "What is this person really like?" [17] By implication, staff members view celebrities as "persons who might make partial on-the-air revelations that are interesting to viewers."

TYPIFIED ATTRIBUTES
OF CELEBRITIES RELEVANT
TO INTERACTION
WITH THE STAFF

As planners of programs, staff members have *expectations* of how celebrities will interact as they pass through the recruitment and pre-interviewing processes. Highly interdependent with the staff's notions of how celebrities in general and how a celebrity in particular should interact on the air, these expectations are based upon the staff's participation in show business and their on-the-job experience of dealing with celebrities.[18] Although the staff recognizes an exception, here are some of their expectations:

A. Celebrities want to appear on talk-shows to promote their most recent show-business activity and view appearances as a form of advertising. No matter how dull the movie, how uneventful the making of the movie, how bad the critical reviews (or how good), the movie actor as celebrity wants to discuss that movie. (The staff's expectations of guests resemble the "aims" of "cultural executives" as discussed by Hirsch.)[19]

B. But staff members do not expect that "established celebrities" voluntarily expose themselves to the talk-show host and his audience. Instead, they assume that celebrities—actors and actresses in particular —are uncomfortable with *unscripted self-exposure*, the apparent for-

[17] In part, the staff bases this assumption upon the questions asked of them by lay acquaintances. Academics are not exempt from this seemingly peculiar interest. While I was doing the field work, supposedly intellectual friends frequently asked me what specific celebrities "were really like."

[18] Sudnow, *op. cit.*, emphasizes expectations based upon experience in his discussion of "normal forms." Normal forms differ from typifications in that they are more specific constructions of typicality, such as the typical features of crime and criminals attended to by public defenders. The expectations listed here are not normal forms. Cf. Jehenson, *op. cit.*

[19] As Hirsch put it, selective coverage by the mass media, including talk-shows, is the functional equivalent of advertising. "Cultural products provide 'copy' and 'programming' for newspapers, magazines, radio stations, and television programs; in exchange [those products] receive free publicity. The presence of absence of coverage, rather than its favorable or unfavorable interpretation, is the most important variable." *Op. cit.*, p. 647.

mat of the talk-show. Seemingly, the staff subscribes to the old Hollywood view, detailed by Powdermaker,[20] that actresses and actors are either children or maladjusted individuals more comfortable with delineated prewritten roles than with the "odious" task of "being oneself." That is, the staff accepts at face value celebrities' statements that they dislike performances in which their lines are not prewritten, and staffers ignore in assessing celebrities the implications of their own activities as staff members. Among these implications are that being oneself is itself a constructed activity (as discussed by Goffman in regard to spies and double-agents[21]) and that a child's version of being himself (e.g., a temper tantrum or the statement of his parents' activities to a stranger) is too spontaneous or unprogrammed. Indeed, a child's version of being oneself is so unprogrammed that it is not suited to a talk-show.

Identifying the "self" as a private attribute, staff members fear that celebrities may want to take refuge in discussions of work, the activity that makes them self-less public figures. So too, they suppose—citing booking problems to bear them out—"real celebrities, big celebrities" are not particularly willing to engage in the self-promotion deemed necessary to the establishment of a hit, and they have sufficient power vis-à-vis producers to refuse to appear on talk-shows. For instance, learning that a big star appears in a soon-to-be-released movie, a staff member may say, "We should try to get him for the show." One common response is, "We should try, but he'll never do it."

C. Accordingly, the staff expects real stars to be a scarce commodity, for they are, by this logic, the celebrities most unwilling to appear on the television talk-show. And because the audience is assumed to be interested in the revelations of all celebrities, they are expected to be most interested in the revelations of real stars. In sum, those stars who are most difficult to recruit for an appearance are assumed to have a special ability to raise the program's ratings. (The extent to which such expectations involve the tautological manufacturing of stars, real stars, and high ratings as scarce commodities will be discussed later.)

D. The staff expects celebrities to act differently from the proverbial man on the street, for as celebrities they are, by definition, different. Yet, there are many roles that might be called different or deviant. To be sure, although many celebrities seem to inspire the awe and personal services befitting royalty (such as people earning over $20,000 a year fetching their drinks and checking their underarms for undue perspiration stains), the staff follows the traditional notion of stars as

20 Powdermaker, op. cit.
21 Erving Goffman, Strategic Interaction. (Philadelphia: University of Pennsylvania Press, 1969).

children and expects both spurts of temperament and a dearth of politeness. However, since these people are stars, they may not be reprimanded.

Consider these examples, all taken from the taping of one program. Two stars, prominent years ago, one male and the other female, were booked, along with a rock group. The male actor arrived in Bermuda shorts, sandals, a sports shirt, and a safari hat. When asked, he explained that is how he feels one should dress for a New York summer day. The interviewer responsible for his performance said nothing then, but made an ascerbic comment later. She might have located more "suitable" clothing, but did not even suggest it. Later, when the male star made a denigrating comment about his ex-wife on the air, she commented to another staff member that this was an awful program. Now, she suggested (attributing motives to the ex-wife), they would never be able to talk her into appearing on the show, as they had been trying to do for months. Similarly, the female star and her friends chatted throughout the time the rock-singers were being interviewed. The male star was included in their conversation. As this was the first time I had observed people chatting through the interview portions of the program, I asked an interviewer about it. She expected such "bad manners" and explained, "They don't care about [the singers], but they'll be quiet when one or another of them is on." [22]

Staff discussions prompted by celebrities who are exceptions to the rule reveal the strength of this expectation. For in these discussions, the voices of staff members seem pleased and even surprised. Yet, even when engaging in "exceptionally" nice behavior, celebrities are expected to fit into the all-encompassing role of "being a celebrity." For instance, the evening one actress was to appear on the program, a member of the staff walked into a boom microphone. The actress sent for and then applied an ice-pack to his head. She also sent for a doctor before the producer had even been informed of the accident. The staff widely praised the actress as a warm and lovely woman, but they dealt with her as a warm and lovely woman who was a celebrity. For while she was ministering to the young man, the staff photographer took her picture for their "celebrity collection."

E. Yet, although celebrities as celebrities are always on stage,[23] the staff recognizes that they do have human attributes like other people. And, inasmuch as celebrities are like other people and appear on talk-shows for promotional purposes, staff members fear that celebrities will

[22] The norms for television-watching differ in the clients' room. There, people may speak during the interview segments, providing they do not disturb the censor who also uses this room, but they are silent during commercials.

[23] Sammy Davis, Jr. and Jane and Burt Boyar. *Yes I Can!* (New York: Pocket Cardinal Books, 1966).

be boring. Accordingly, they expect to have to take more than the "usual everyday precautions" to ensure that celebrities will not, for example, engage in "meaningless" chatter. To combat this possibility, celebrities must be pre-interviewed, much as the nervous cook hosting a French dinner might practice a recipe before serving a known gourmet.

Pre-interviewing also decreases the probability that a celebrity will introduce a political topic on the air. For staff members also fear that celebrities will want to discuss political issues, since the staff's experiences suggested that celebrities were becoming politicized. The staff particularly expects the introduction of politics by celebrities who do not have a cultural product to promote. In this case, the staff may either refuse the celebrity access to the audience by not booking him or her or may caution the celebrity to avoid politics while on the air. For whatever reasons the staff wishes to de-politicize the discussions of celebrities on the air,[24] the expectation the staff shares sets up an adversary relationship between them and some of their guests and implies that the celebrity is subject to social control like anyone else. That is, the staff will not pander to the willful guest's desire to set the topic of the interview beyond permitting him to plug his latest cultural product. During the video-taping of the one exception to this rule that I witnessed, a writer chided the interviewer who was responsible for the exception by asking, "Why did you let him talk about that?"[25]

F. Finally, inasmuch as celebrities are like everyone else, the staff expects them to conform to social roles. For example, the staff differentiates between "girls" (attractive young starlets supposedly incapable of intelligent conversation) and "women" (mature authors who are accomplished conversationalists). Role-typing of this sort, including sex-role typing, follows conventional stereotypes. It permits more specific role-typing than merely classifying celebrities as author, cook, star,

24 Bella Abzug, Abbie Hoffman, and Gore Vidal reported examples of both types in response to a question asked from the audience after a panel discussion of newsmakers talking about newsmen, held as part of the [MORE] counter-convention, New York City, April, 1972. Staff members argue that (1) celebrities may have strong political opinions, but be poorly informed, (2) celebrities talking about politics may be boring, (3) celebrities may embroil the program in a problem with the F.C.C. Fairness Doctrine and necessitate the appearance of an "opposing spokesman" in a future program, and (4) celebrities making controversial statements may anger viewers and the executive officers of local stations that carry the program. Staff members feel that they are the appropriate persons to plan political discussions on-the-air.

25 The actor was discussing the characterization of youngsters as revolutionaries by the mass media. Using masking tape, he had layed out a diagram on the stage floor. A shaded portion was to represent radical young people. The interviewer had "permitted" this line of questioning, because she felt that use of another area of the studio-set would help to enliven the program.

director, or producer, and this role-typing influences staff expectations of how guests will interact on the air.

TYPIFIED CHARACTERISTICS OF INDIVIDUALS USABLE FOR INTERACTION ON THE AIR

Let me introduce another analogy involving an attempt to plan interaction for others, the dinner party. As staff members themselves put it, a "good program" is more than a composite of individual guests, just as a successful dinner party is more than a collection of individual diners and good food. Both involve an undefinable spirit, a process of "hitting it off" that makes "guesting" enjoyable.[26] In the case of the television program, the "spirit" should somehow appeal to viewers. The staff assumes that this spirit is a function of a lively interaction that makes viewers unwilling to turn off their television and go to sleep. Three staff practices, of the many available, reveal how staff members go about designing a lively interaction. All three of these practices typify attributes of celebrities that are "interactionally-usable-to-glean-ratings."

A. GOING THE "ED SULLIVAN ROUTE"

One method of maximizing the interaction is to book a big star and to plan the program around him or her. Planning may involve booking people who will both highlight the star through their dissimilar characteristics and set off one another. Such a plan is like using rich velvet to call attention to a gem and *vice versa*. This practice is also believed to attract a large audience, because dissimilar audience members may watch the program to view the celebrity who best matches their interests.

For example, one program was "balanced" around a Hollywood sex symbol whose latest movie, a film with intellectual pretensions, was generating some controversy within show business. At the opening night party for her film, the sex symbol revealed to a staff member that the two women whom she most admired were Jackie Kennedy and a young female singer, a sex symbol for the acid-rock set. The singer was invited to appear on the program with the film star. The appearance of the women was then "balanced" by booking a national newscaster and an old Hollywood star, the son of a famous actor-father.

The staff expected the male star to be somewhat dull, a "poor talker,"

---

26 One talk-show host commented on the air that three factors led him to believe his program was becoming more popular: the studio audience was more diverse, their applause at his entrance was lasting longer, and guests told him after the taping that they had enjoyed being on the show.

but hoped that he might interest some of the audience by talking about the "old days in Hollywood." Besides, he could be (and was) put on the air first, so that the audience might wait through his segments of the program to see eventually one of the other guests. In using the newscaster, the staff hoped he would be "cute" and display his wry humor. They felt the Hollywood sex symbol was dumb, but would attract an audience, and they were confident that young people would tune in to see the acid-rock singer.

B. FOSTERING FOIBLES

The staff choreographed another "lively" program by locating the interactionally-usable-attributes of one star and then planning to accentuate them. As one staff member explained of this popular nightclub singer and ladies' man, "He doesn't have too much information at his finger tips so we ask him about other things." The man's manager bluntly characterized him backstage by saying, "He'll screw anything and just put a bag over her head." A song writer-actor-singer was booked to appear with this man. He had achieved a reputation as a more discriminating, yet active man-about-town. As the staff anticipated, the men used one another as foils to joke about women and sex.

The other guests that night were a Hollywood plastic surgeon and a New York actor known for his delivery of jokes about his personal appearance. Although the staff hoped the plastic surgeon could be induced to discuss his treatment of celebrities by name, the doctor was paired as a foil for the actor-comic and *vice versa*.

C. CREATING AND CONTROLLING CONTROVERSY

Just as staff members may try to accentuate typified interactionally-usable-attributes, so too they may try to locate attributes amenable to interactional conflict, a sub-type of lively interaction. For instance, the staff planned a controversy between a representative of the Daughters of the American Revolution and a soft-spoken black singer who had been involved with civil-rights activities for some years. The staff scurried about researching the D.A.R., paying particular attention to its charter and its notoriety for refusing to let black opera singer Marian Anderson perform in its Washington hall. They expected the black singer booked for the program to interject quiet arguments to keep the program lively and to discredit tactfully the racism and elitism credited to the D.A.R.

On another occasion, the staff booked a radical actress to attract an audience, so that they might invite less-famous politically oriented persons to debate the Vietnam war. Each participant had been carefully coached. The actress complained volubly backstage about the "male chauvinist" advice she had been given by a female staff member—to keep quiet and let the men carry the political conversation. While the actress and her colleague, a radical lawyer, were onstage, their opponent, a conservative psychiatrist, was encouraged to take notes on any inaccuracies in their statements. (Generally, guests are encouraged to pay attention, but not to take notes on previous segments of the program.) As the psychiatrist left to go on stage, the writer who had pre-interviewed him reminded him to follow the staff advice—stay calm and "let them destroy themselves."

But, both these attempts to generate liveliness through conflict failed and ultimately revealed again that one cannot plan an interaction for anyone else, a hazard of staff work. In the first case, rather than interject soft critical comments, the singer made faces off camera as the D.A.R. spokeswoman held forth. He prompted the studio audience to peals of laughter. Because his expressions were rapid and could be neither anticipated nor telecast, the viewing audience would be left with the impression that the studio audience was laughing at the woman from the D.A.R. Indeed, at the end of the program, the host offered an on-the-air apology to the woman. In the second case, the controversy got out of hand, because the female radical was not content to sit on the sidelines and let the men argue. In both cases, the staff was distressed. Why had the singer not offered verbal objections as they had expected? What had happened recently to the actress? Previously, she had been so much calmer and so pleasant to interact with. Though resembling idle gossip (albeit professional gossip), staffers' comments about the actress, her husband, and her complexion were much more. Having used a previous typification, the staffers had been confronted by unexpected behavior. They needed to develop some *ad hoc* and potentially reliable explanation, to construct some revised notion of the actress's character, before she could reappear on the program.

CONCLUSION

This description of the process of assembling a talk-show has several implications concerning typifications, attacks on the mass media by social movements, and the question of innovation.

A. ON TYPIFICATIONS

The last examples—programs constructed to control conflict and controversy—stress both the difficulties of, and the extent to which, staff members depend upon locating celebrities with the proper typified interactionally-usable-attributes-to-glean-ratings. One might even suggest that the natural history of the talk-show process is the natural history of locating, preparing, and choreographing the typified personal characteristics of celebrities for public consumption.[27] That this process

27 This characteristic of the talk-show appears to be a continuation of the trend toward consumption delineated by Leo Lowenthal ("Biographies in Popular Maga-

depends so heavily upon typifications confirms the concentrality of typification to the control of work scenes and work processes, as variously discussed by Sudnow, Cicourel, Jehenson, and myself.[28] The talk-show presents a particularly clear example of the importance of typifications, for without them, staff members would be working in a void. They cannot, to any *significant* extent explain the relationship between their program's ratings and with their own activities. Nor can they control most of the factors that supposedly influence their ratings, such as the size of the audience that they inherit from preceding programs. And so they fall back upon typifying as a central process through which they may impose order upon an otherwise unstable work situation.

**B. ON ATTACKS ON THE MEDIA MADE
BY SOCIAL MOVEMENTS**

A second point needs to be made. Many of the examples used here involved some aspect of sex roles, in particular the expectation that men and women who are celebrities should conform to stereotypic age-sex roles and interests. But staff members will use any typified attribute of celebrities, including eccentricities born of personal unhappiness, to glean ratings and sell an audience to sponsors. A final and somewhat extended example speaks to this point.

A young actress was invited to be on the show after she had accepted a professional award with a peculiar and incoherent speech. Show business circles buzzed with gossip about what might have prompted her curious speech. The staff, curious about her, invited the star to appear. Also, the staff reasoned, since the speech had been delivered on national television, members of that viewing audience "should" also be curious about her behavior.

The actress arrived at the program's offices in the mid-afternoon. Following her pre-interview, she asked to stay in the offices, explaining plaintively that she had no place to go. When the staff moved from the offices to the studio, she came too. She sat quietly as people began to filter into the green room, and then under the guise of speaking with the woman who had pre-interviewed her, she began a loud monologue occasionally interspersed with cackles. When people in the room looked

---

zines" in Paul Lazarsfeld and Frank Stanton (ed.), *Radio Research 1942–43* (New York: Duell, Sloan, and Pearce, 1944). Using biographies to index the transformation from an economy of production to an economy of consumption, Lowenthal implies—but does not explicitedly state—a concern with the packaging of celebrities. He suggests the biographies reveal a concern with the celebrities' habits of consumption that captures Veblen's notion of vicarious consumption. Lowenthal implies that the biographies of celebrities are themselves vicariously consumed. Many of Lowenthal's findings are reinterpreted by Daniel Boorstin (*The Image: A Guide to Pseudo-Events in America* (New York: Harper-Colophon, 1964) in a somewhat over-simplified manner.

28 Sudnow, *op. cit.,* Cicourel, *op. cit.,* Jehenson, *op. cit.,* Tuchman, *op. cit.*

her way, she countered, "Why are they staring at me?" Until the actress went on stage, the stage manager had to enter the room repeatedly to ask for silence. On the air, she gave a modified (i.e., more restrained) version of her backstage behavior.

After the program, as the staff left for the day, there was only one topic of conversation—the behavior of this young woman. The next day, when the staff arrived at the studio, the actress was mentioned in another context: the overnight ratings taken in Los Angeles and New York placed the program significantly ahead of its nearest competitor. As revealed by this retrospective reasoning, what ultimately counted was the influence of the woman's appearance upon the ratings. Her personal problems were the stuff that programs and ratings are made of.[29]

This example forces a reconsideration of popular attacks upon the mass media. In the past decade, it has become increasingly popular to indict the mass media as perpetrators of racism, sexism, militarism, and the other assorted "isms" that afflict American society. But these separate attacks upon the media by social movements must, within the context presented here, appear naive. To single out the "harm" done to any one group or to any one individual is to ignore processes central to American television programming. When hundreds of thousands of dollars ride on a rating point, people take as few chances as possible. They use typifications that will help them deliver what they guess the audience might like, using their own reactions as a barometer of public taste. Show business is big business, and so long as entertainment is business, the assorted "isms" will be perpetuated by people who have a show to do.

C. ON THE TALK-SHOW AND CULTURAL INNOVATIONS

The typifications discussed are grounded in the staff members' experiences with celebrities, their participation in show business networks, and their agreement with values in the larger American culture. They are not grounded in knowledge of the viewer's preferences, but rather in fears of offending too many potential viewers. The relevance of the mass audience is simple, straight-forward, and economic: how many people can be exposed to a product, whether it be a magazine, a record, or a dog food? How many people can be induced to keep their television tuned to a program?

Hirsch suggests that some of the cultural industries use the talk-show as a systems gate-keeper which may be coopted to introduce product

---

[29] That this actress may have identified her "personal problems" as her "selling point" for the purpose of appearing on talk-shows does not mitigate my argument. As implicit in the notion of an adversary relationship between star and staff, the talk-show interview is the product of negotiation between the star and a staff member.

innovations.[30] Yet I have argued that television talk-shows are beset by the same economic uncertainty characteristic of other segments of show business. How open, then, are the talk-shows to innovations?

I have already suggested that the talk-shows perpetuate the assorted "isms" of American society. In addition, typifications used by staff members suggest that they try to maintain audience ratings by the artificial maintenance of stars as a scarce commodity. They suppose that there are only 200 or so persons in the country who are capable of being good guests; that the less often a celebrity appears on the talk-shows, the more audience members would like to view an appearance. They suspect celebrities who want to appear, but who do not have a cultural product to promote, of having "ulterior political motives." Besieged by the recording, book-publishing and motion-picture industries (among others) to introduce their new products, the staff members want to present the singer who has already sold a million records, the author who has already been on the best-seller list, the movie star with whom the audience is already familiar. The talk-show staff wants to present the cultural product that "everyone" is *already* talking about. Glutted with available products, the staff members prefer relatively inaccessible products. Although the talk-show may be identified as institutional gate-keeper and surrogate consumer,[31] it acts to perpetuate the fame of those who are already famous and to mitigate the introduction of cultural innovations.

How, then, are cultural innovations introduced? Schutz suggests that the social meaning of the term "everyone" is "everyone who belongs to us." [32] An identification of how institutional gate-keepers and surrogate consumers come to agree that "everyone is talking about" a cultural product probably rests upon a closer examination of communication channels and networks within show business. After all, the analysis reported here emphasizes the extent to which talk-show staffers base their decisions upon their participation in show business networks, not upon their familiarity with the mass audience.

Since Hirsch's key point is correct—show business is an organized business, the invention of innovations within show business is probably similar to that found in other businesses and professions. But, if this is so, one should not discuss the ways in which "cultural organizations deploy contact men . . . at their output boundaries, linking the organizations to . . . retail outlets and . . . surrogate consumers [such as talk-shows]." [33] Rather, it might be profitable to focus upon those who are *marginal* participants at *every* step of the production process.

30 Hirsch, *op. cit.*
31 Hirsch, *op. cit.*
32 Schutz, *op. cit.*, p. 75.
33 Hirsch, *op. cit.*, p. 651.

Marginal members of a network are more likely to adopt innovations.[34] It is possible that by concentrating upon national industries, including people occupying key positions within national networks, both Hirsch's analysis and this one have ignored processes that are vital to the development of cultural innovations.

[34] For a partial review, see Mark S. Granovetter, "The Strength of Weak Ties," *American Journal of Sociology* 78, May, 1973, pp. 1360–80.

III

Hegemony: the long-range effect

Tackling slightly different aspects of the same problem, all three chapters in this section are concerned with the domination of both institutions and intellectual and moral thought by ideas that legitimate the existing social order. Wilensky's article considers the impact of television upon "high culture." Sallach concentrates upon the educational system and the mass media as ideological institutions within American society. Schiller maintains that the American media-conglomerates are extending the American cultural hegemony throughout the world, endangering the cultures of other lands. Ultimately, all three articles ask, What is the relationship of mass culture to social structure?

Wilensky notes that the relationship of mass culture to social structure has long been a problematic issue for sociologists. Reviewing the various theoretical and empirical stances taken to examine this issue, Wilensky affirms that the key problem has been whether the mass media are not only encouraging the homogenization of culture, but also the waning of voluntary associations. In the terms of the sociological debate, is a supposed once-dominant pluralism disappearing? Is mass culture leading to a basic sameness among religious groups? among workers? Are the standard sources of social differentiation and stratification being rendered obsolete with the increasing importance of mass culture?

Wilensky suggests that the terms in which this debate have been waged are incorrect. Rather than identifying either the older structural roots (such as the division of labor) or the new sources of differentiation (such as the mass media) as the more crucial to contemporary social structure, Wilensky argues that both the newer and the older structural roots of social organization may gain strength simultaneously. Indeed, Wilensky concludes, while the social structure is becoming more differentiated, the culture is becoming more homogeneous.

According to Wilensky, the dominance of the mass media poses a very serious threat to high culture. Educated persons, who would have been opera buffs and serious readers in former times, instead use the mass media, including television. And the mass media pose an even more serious threat to political democracy. Mass media and mass culture lead to the development of coherent life styles, the style of the "Happy Good Citizen-Consumer" being a major one. Reviewing this life style, Wilensky suggests, "To be socially integrated in America is to accept propaganda, advertising, and speedy obsolescence in consumption."

Sallach's article examines two of the mass institutions discussed as new sources of social differentiation by Wilensky: the mass media and the educational system. Sallach's particular interest is the extent to which these institutions are open to a diversity of ideas and viewpoints; for rather than viewing them as sources of social differentiation, he analyzes them as ideological institutions, central to the diffusion and propagation of ideas. Sallach argues that these institutions in general and television in particular both limit the kinds of ideas that can be presented and create confusion, fragmentation, and inconsistency in belief systems. By accomplishing these tasks, Sallach maintains, the mass media operate as a system of social control, upholding the existing class structure and preventing the development of support for dissident views, not to speak of revolutionary movements. In essence, Sallach argues, this hegemony truncates the range of notions that may be admitted to the "free market place" of ideas.

Schiller's selection also concerns the "free market place of ideas." After demonstrating that the American corporate media are invading both the developing and the industrialized nations, Schiller asks what the consequences of this invasion are. Insisting that the sale of American programs to developing nations is not a manifestation of free speech, Schiller argues that these sales pervert the aims of developing countries. While destroying indigenous cultures, they propagandize for American consumerism as a way of life. In so doing, they divert funds and energies from the development of capital goods and hamper processes of industrialization. Less equipped to develop their own capabilities, these nations remain dependent upon the industrialized powers. The sale of these programs to developing nations is not a matter of free speech, but rather is the sale of harmful ideologies that both limit economic development and level folk cultures throughout the world. Ultimately, Schiller suggests, the United States is imperialistically extending its hegemony over other lands.

Taken together, these three articles suggest that the long-range effect of television is (1) to level high culture, (2) to increase propaganda, (3) to limit the range of ideas accessible to citizens, (4) to introduce ideas as transient phenomena, (5) to fragment belief systems, (6) to support the established class system, and (7) to export American consumerism and mass culture to whomever will mistakenly identify it as "neutral entertainment" and the expression of free speech. In short, the long-range effect of this all-pervasive medium is to transform cultures throughout the world, to create a common mediocrity.

chapter eight

Mass society and mass culture: interdependence or independence?

HAROLD L. WILENSKY

Several major questions about the social impact of affluence have come to dominate intellectual discussion concerning the shape of modern society. Some of them involve the nature, extent, and impact of mass culture and mass leisure. Everyone agrees that abundance everywhere brings a rise in mass communications, through radio, tele-

Excerpted from "Mass Society and Mass Culture: Interdependence or Independence?," by Harold L. Wilensky. From *American Sociological Review* 29 (April 1964), pp. 173–96. Excerpted and reprinted by permission of the author and publisher.

vision, and press; the development of mass education and the concomitant spread of literacy; and, finally, mass entertainment on a grand scale. I propose to deal with these trends in the context of ideas about the "mass society." I will (1) analyze the interplay of high culture and mass culture, with special attention to the structural roots of cultural standardization and heterogeneity in rich countries; (2) present data on the quality of media exposure in a variety of occupational groups and strata in the Detroit metropolitan area—so that we may both gauge the extent of cultural uniformity and locate the sources of resistance to mass culture. My general aim is to fill in gaps in theories of the mass society and to arrive at a more valid vision of modern society.

THEORIES OF MASS SOCIETY
AND THE FUNCTIONS OF THE
MASS MEDIA

Traditional theorists of "urbanism" or of the "mass society" tend to be pessimistic in ideology and macroscopic in sociology; their empirical critics tend to be optimistic—some would say fatuous—in ideology and microscopic in sociology. Both seek to interpret the impact of industrialism and urbanism on social structure and culture. Together they have given us most of the imagery with which we construct our picture of the affluent society . . .

The main theme of the theorists is this: the *mass society* develops a *mass culture*, in which cultural and political values and beliefs tend to be *homogeneous* and *fluid*. In the middle and at the bottom—in the atomized mass—people think and feel alike; but thoughts and feelings, not being firmly anchored anywhere, are susceptible to fads and fashions. At the top, poorly-organized elites, themselves mass-oriented, become political and managerial manipulators, responding to short-run pressures; they fail to maintain standards and thereby encourage the spread of populism in politics, mass tastes in culture—in short, a "sovereignty of the unqualified." [1]

The empirically-minded critics of such theories are impressed by the diversity of modern life. Concerning the leveling and fluidity of culture, they point to an extraordinary variety of cultural products, assert that it is easier to prove that mass tastes have been upgraded than that such tastes have been vulgarized, and protest that high culture has not declined but merely become more widely available. Concerning the role of the mass media in politics and culture, the

[1] Cf. Philip Selznick, "Institutional Vulnerability in Mass Society," *American Journal of Sociology,* 56 (January, 1951), pp. 320–331; Bernard Rosenberg and David Manning White (eds.), *Mass Culture,* Glencoe, Ill.: The Free Press, 1957; and William Kornhauser, *The Politics of Mass Society* (Glencoe, Ill.: The Free Press, 1959).

critics cite considerable diversity of media content as well as persistence in habits of exposure. And where diversity of *content* falls short, they argue, there is everywhere enormous diversity in *response*. While the optimists are well aware of the limits of their studies, they seem always to come to the same punch line: the burden of evidence indicates that the media are not omnipotent; they are absorbed into local cultures via the two-step flow from media to local group to person; and this absorption involves a self-selection of exposure corresponding to previous attitude.[2]

It is a pity that these students of the media who know mass communications best are not more ideologically sensitive and not more concerned with general characterizations of society; equally unfortunate is it that the theorists, at home in the world of ideologies and utopias, are not more sophisticated in the handling of data. For systematic observation and theoretical problems must be brought together if we are to understand the interplay of social structure, high culture, and mass culture.

MASS CULTURE AND HIGH CULTURE

For my purposes here the most useful definition that distinguishes high culture from mass culture is one that emphasizes the social context of production. "High culture" will refer to two characteristics of the product: (1) it is created by or under the supervision of a cultural elite operating within some aesthetic, literary, or scientific tradition (these elite are the top men in the sphere of education, aesthetics, and entertainment who carry the core values and standards of that sphere and serve as models for those working in it); (2) critical standards independent of the consumer of the product are systematically applied to it. The quality of thought or expression of the cultural object and the social milieu in which it is produced define high culture. This definition has the advantage of leaving open questions about the organization and recruitment of cultural elites, the social controls to which they are subject (e.g., pressures from patron, market, or mass), the conditions under which a high-quality product—a Shakespearian play, a Mozart symphony—can become popular, the ways in which the product is or is not absorbed into the culture of the consumer.

"Mass culture" will refer to cultural *products manufactured solely for a mass market*. Associated characteristics, not intrinsic to the definition, are *standardization* of product and *mass behavior* in its use. Mass culture tends to be standardized because it aims to please the average taste of an undifferentiated audience. Common tastes shape mass culture; critical standards sustained by autonomous producing groups shape high culture. . . . The definition leaves open

2 See e.g., Joseph Klapper, *The Effects of Mass Communication*, Glencoe, Ill.: The Free Press, 1960, and Raymond A. and Alice H. Bauer, "America, 'Mass Society' and Mass Media," *Journal of Social Issues*, 16 (1960), pp. 3–56.

questions about the relation of mass culture to high culture; the conditions under which a product of mass culture can meet the standards of high culture; the degree to which mass culture is fluid or, like folk culture, stable (characterized by little original creation in each generation); whether traditions of expression and performance develop in it; the extent to which the impact of the mass media is mediated by audience standards and the extent to which those very standards are themselves anchored in the media.

In short, these concepts permit sociological analysis of cultural products in the social contexts in which they are created and used. They have the disadvantage of being difficult (but not impossible) to apply in empirical research.

THEORETICAL PROBLEM AND ASSUMPTIONS

Our problem is the relation of the main structural trends associated with abundance to the form and content of high culture and mass culture. The main research question is, "which groupings of modern populations acquire a 'mass' character and which do not—with what net effect on culture, high and low?" More precisely, will the heterogeneity of culture rooted mainly in the division of labor give way to the homogeneity of culture rooted mainly in the centralized state, mass education, the mass media, and mass entertainment?

Five assumptions about modern society have guided my approach to this question: (1) Social differentiation persists, even increases; (2) cultural uniformity also grows; (3) in rich countries there is more independent variation of social structure and culture than in poor ones, although some of this incongruity is due to imprecise measures of structure; (4) developments in the aesthetic-recreational sphere as well as the political sphere may remain isolated from those in the economy and locality for some time, so that in the short run mass behavior in one sphere may not become mass behavior in another; but (5) over several generations, and as rich countries grow richer, there is a strain toward consistency between structure and culture and between behavior in one institutional sphere and that in a second. . . .*

SOCIAL STRUCTURE,
HIGH CULTURE, AND MASS CULTURE:
AN EMPIRICAL APPROACH

. . . Let us apply the larger debate about modern society to the mass media and mass entertainment in America. We must first grasp

---

* At this point in the original essay, a four-page theoretical discussion spells out these assumptions about the disjunction of social structure and culture in contemporary society.

the fact that the mass media are the core of American leisure and that television has become the core of media exposure. The sheer arithmetic is striking. Nine in ten American homes average five to six hours daily with the TV set on. And it is not just turned on; it is generally being watched. Eight in ten Americans spend at least four hours a day viewing television, listening to the radio, or both.[3] Additional time goes to reading newspapers and magazines.

The trend is up. An increasing fraction of the daily routine is devoted to the products of the mass media. Mainly due to the rise of television, the media together and on the average now take up almost as much time as work; substantial minorities log more hours a year in TV viewing alone than in working.

Both cause and consequence of this trend is the development of an enormous machinery of promotion. Today, our outlays for advertising are almost equal to our current expenditures on public schools (elementary and secondary)—about $11 billion annually.[4] Additional billions go to PR and the like. The more abundance, the more activity to increase the desire for it.

So far we are on safe ground. The size of this frenzied promotion effort and the astonishing amount of exposure are well known. The *impact* on the quality of American culture, however, is difficult to judge.

In tackling the problem I have tried to be specific: in approaching the *standardization* of culture I have looked for media exposure and response cross-cutting social classes, educational levels, age grades, and religious and nativity categories. In handling the *heterogeneity* of culture I have searched for variations in media exposure and response with special attention to structural facts obscured by these traditional categories of sociological analysis—e.g., the quality variations within broad levels of education; the variations in tasks, work schedules, occupational groups, workplaces, and job patterns within broad occupational strata. The picture that emerges is more complicated than the assertions and counter-assertions of theorists and critics, but it is also a more realistic reflection of modern life.

I will first present findings bearing on the structural roots of cultural heterogeneity, and then findings that suggest the perhaps more powerful roots of cultural uniformity. I will draw from data on the quality of media exposure among 1,354 men ranging from highly-educated professors, lawyers, and engineers and executives matched for age and income, through a cross-section of the lower middle and upper working classes (the "middle mass") of the Detroit area, and

---

[3] G. A. Steiner, *The People Look at Television,* New York: Alfred A. Knopf, 1963, pp. 4, 112; and citations in footnote 9 below.

[4] Fritz Machlup, *The Production and Distribution of Knowledge in the United States,* Princeton, N.J.: Princeton University Press, 1962, p. 104.

down through 186 men unemployed and on relief[5] We listed all their favorite TV shows, periodicals and newspapers read regularly, and all books they could name which they had read in the last two months. We then classified each program, each magazine, and each book in three "brow" levels—high quality, trash, or neither.

In coding for quality we were tolerant. The aim was to classify according to some fixed aesthetic standard, applicable to the medium, the more-or-less best performances and the clearly worst. Thus, the bias was that of Gilbert Seldes' *Seven Lively Arts*—sympathetic to the media. The product does not have to be aggressively educative to get by as highbrow, but if it is drama, the contrast is "Playhouse 90" vs. the most stereotypical detective, western, and adventure shows; if it is a paperback mystery, the contrast is Agatha Christie or Chandler vs. Spillane.

On *television programs* our staff made an effort to keep in touch with criitcal opinion and pooled judgments.

On *books, periodicals,* and *newspapers,* we compiled an initial classification and checked with experts. For the book code, for instance, two English professors reputed to have opposing views about the modern novel independently agreed on 97 per cent of the 200-odd high-quality titles. (That this code, like the others, is tolerant is suggested by the reaction of a literary critic who judged that perhaps half of the highbrow books would better be labeled "middling" or "upper middle;" clearly the list would not withstand the scrutiny of a Dwight MacDonald. But by that token it has the advantage of

[5] The analysis is based on detailed interviews with probability samples or universes of six professional groups (100 solo lawyers; 107 firm lawyers in the 19 Detroit firms with ten or more partners and associates; 31 professors at "Church University"; 68 professors at "Urban University"; 91 engineers at "Unico" and 93 at "Diversico"—generally research and development specialists, supervisors, or executives); a probability sample of the middle mass ($N = 678$); and as a sharp contrast, two samples of underdogs, 81 Negro and 105 white, who were severely deprived. The interviews took place in the first half of 1960. Only males who were in the labor force, 55 years old or younger, and currently or previously married were interviewed. All the professionals had college degrees. The special selection criteria are described in Harold L. Wilensky, "The Uneven Distribution of Leisure: The Impact of Economic Growth on 'Free Time,' " *Social Problems,* 11 (Summer, 1961), p. 38; "Orderly Careers and Social Participation," American Sociological Review 26 (August 1961), pp. 529–530, and "The Moonlighter: A Product of Relative Deprivation," *Industrial Relations,* 3 (October, 1963), pp. 106–108. It is important to note that the leading colleges and universities are well represented in the backgrounds of men in the professional samples. Three-quarters of the firm lawyers, for instance, are graduates of one of five elite "national" law schools—Chicago, Columbia, Harvard, Michigan, and Yale. Like the professors—full-time faculty in the humanities and physical sciences (including mathematics) in two arts and sciences colleges—these lawyers may be assumed to have had as much opportunity to acquire discriminating tastes as their counterparts in other cities.

not understanding the fallout from the "cultural explosion" as it appears in these samples—which, as it turned out, was scanty.)

In general these codes do *not* reflect a snobbish understatement of quality exposure, and there is less disagreement at the extremes than one would expect.[6]

To establish the coherence, independence, and economy of my measures, I combined all samples and carried out two factor analysis —one of the content, social context, and psychological functions of exposure; the other, of media uses as part of leisure style. A resulting factor from each analysis will be used as a dependent variable below.

1. *"Much exposure to poor TV"* is a strong factor (12 per cent of the variance) in the media analysis. It is defined by: (1) high number of hours per week of television viewing; (2) many westerns as "favorite TV programs—the ones you almost always watch;" and (3) many detective and adventure programs as favorites. These defining items not only go together in the media experience of our 1,354 men but they are independent of such other factors as "privatized TV-viewing," "vicarious participation via television," and a variety of uses of print. The men who score high here are neither ardent sports fans nor devotees of panel, quiz, giveaway, audience participation, and general entertainment shows. But so far as one can become involved with the western-detective-adventure triumvirate, these men are: when they watch, they watch with others; when they are away from home they are likely to discuss television often with friends or relatives.

2. *"Low leisure competence"* (or *"compulsive absorption of much poor TV as a time filler"*) is a strong factor (22 per cent of the variance) in the analysis of leisure style, which included data from all areas—social participation, consumption, politics, as well as media exposure and response. It is defined by (1) much exposure to poor TV (above); (2) absorption of media, especially television, into groups beyond the nuclear family; (3) compulsive TV-viewing (when watching he often feels he'd rather do something else, but he just can't tear himself away); and (4) much restless, aimless, aggressive leisure (he "blows his top" often, does a great deal of aimless Sunday driving, says he would not watch TV more if the day were 26 hours long, but meanwhile names the late show or the late-late show as TV favorites.

Other correlates of this factor are: *deviance* (the man who is low

---

[6] Two independent studies, using impressionistic judgments to rank magazines, arrived at results so similar to one another (a rank order correlation coefficient of .93 for 49 magazines) that one is tempted to defend a ranking of the entire range, not merely the validity of three categories. Babette Kass, "Overlapping Magazine Reading: A New Method of Determining the Cultural Level of Magazines," in Paul F. Lazarsfeld and Frank N. Stanton (eds.), *Communications Research: 1948–1949*, New York: Harper, 1949, p. 133, Table 1.

in leisure competence is likely to be a McCarthyite, a cross class iden-
tifier, have a deviant perception of his standard of living—i.e., he is a
blue-collar worker who thinks he is better off than office workers or a
white-collar worker who thinks he is worse off than blue-collar workers
—and he hangs on to his cars longer than most people); *leisure malaise*
(often feels he has time on his hands, doesn't know what to do with
himself); subjectively *weak attachments to secondary associations* and
fluid friendships; and, as I shall show below, a *short work week.*[7]

The most precise summary phrase I can think of to describe the
psychology of this leisure style is, "coping with restless malaise by an
unsatisfying retreat to violent, escapist television." . . . Other, sim-
pler measures of media behavior will be self-evident as I use them. I
now turn to the sources of variation in the quality of exposure.

STRUCTURAL ROOTS OF CULTURAL HETEROGENEITY

The paradox of structural differentiation and cultural homogeneity is
in part a spurious product of our weak concepts and measures of the
attributes of social organization. If we pinpoint the groups and events
that grip men in the daily round, some of the cultural phenomena
which at first blush appear standardized turn out to be somewhat differentiated.

This can be seen in an analysis of the sources and correlates of (1)
the number of media areas (television, newspapers, magazines, books)
in which our respondents were exposed to any high-brow material and
(2) their score on "much exposure to poor TV." In each case, 17
variables were related to these two media exposure variables. (See
Table 1.) To determine the relative effect of each variable and to
locate the incidence of high- and low-brow exposure within each class
of each variable, I used a regression technique called "multiple classification analysis" which permits the use of non-continuous variables
like religion and does not assume linearity in their effect. . . .

. . . Only 85 of these men were exposed to any high-brow material
in three or four areas; 157 score in two areas, 305 in one; 807 men reported no quality exposure in any area. At the other extreme 138 men
reported very high exposure to poor TV—25 and 30, even 35 hours of
westerns, detectives, and adventure programs a week; 524 have medium scores; 692 avoid large doses of this type of program.

7 These are items whose loadings on the Low Leisure Competence factor rank
high, but which are either too weak or appear on two or more factors; they are
sufficiently associated with the defining items to be taken as subsidiary meanings
of the factor, but they may measure other phenomena as well. The results of this
leisure style analysis are reported more fully in Harold L. Wilensky, *Work, Leisure,
and Freedom,* New York: The Free Press of Glencoe, forthcoming. Correlation
matrices were factor analyzed by the method of principal axes. Factors were rotated
according to Kaiser's varimax criterion. In interpretation, loadings below 25 per
cent of the average commonality of the factors were ignored.

Although the main story is the general scarcity of quality exposure, which I will explore in detail later, Table 1 tells us something important: with sensitive measures of social position we can go far in explaining what cultural variation we do uncover. *The 17 variables explain over 46 per cent of the total variance in the number of areas in which quality exposure is reported and 25 per cent of the variance in exposure to poor TV.*

Both the measures and samples of the larger study were designed to permit projections of social and cultural trends in the affluent society based on comparisons of vanguard and rearguard groups at the same stage of the life cycle and the same social level. Does modernization increase the level of education? Then compare college graduates of growing mass institutions with those of elite colleges, which produce a declining percentage of the educated. Does economic development bring rising levels of mass aspiration? Then compare the aspiring with the less aspiring. Does it bring the dominance of large, complex organizations? Then compare the self employed with men in workplaces of various sizes and structures. Does it make for an uneven distribution of leisure? Then compare the long hours men with the short. Does modernization change the social composition of elites? Then compare established Protestant elites with rising Catholic populations.

My findngs underscore the importance of education and the persistence of older bases of differentiation—descent (religion and nativity), age, and work situation. When we really peg the meaning of these as indicators of social position and discover their variable effects, however, we cannot help but be struck with the difficulty of predicting their future functions for the maintenance or decline of cultural diversity.

The three top predictors of quality of exposure in both "number of areas of highbrow exposure" and in amount of poor TV are: (1) an index of level and quality of formal education which I interpret as degree of exposure to the liberal arts—by far the single most important variable in both cases; (2) an index of "generation American, religion, and status of religious preference;" (3) work context (size of workplace and self-employment status). The more education, and within educational levels, the higher the quality, the higher the level of taste. Among religious-nativity categories Jews, those with no preference, and established Catholics (four grandparents born in the U.S.) stand out in taste while the most ardent consumers of low-brow TV are Catholics of more recent American vintage (three or fewer grandparents born in the U.S.); however, two of those same high-brow categories—established Catholics and men with no preference—also produce more than their share of enthusiasts for the Western-detective-adventure shows. Jews and established high-status Protestants tend to avoid big doses of poor TV. As for work context, the good-taste cate-

TABLE 1: RANK ORDER OF 17 SOURCES AND CORRELATES OF QUALITY OF MEDIA EXPOSURE AND ADJUSTED MEANS FOR SUB-CLASSES IN A MULTIPLE CLASSIFICATION ANALYSIS*

		Quality of Media Exposure			
		No. Areas High-Brow		Much Exposure to Poor TV	
	N	Adjust. Mean	Rank as Predictor	Adjust. Mean	Rank as Predictor
I. Pre-Adult Socialization					
A. Generation American, Religion, and Status of Religious Preference					
Protestant					
Above average status of religious preference and four grandparents born in U.S.	98	.752		49.046	
Above average status of religious preference and three or fewer grandparents born in U.S.	133	.807		49.454	
Average or below average status of religious preference and four grandparents born in U.S.	144	.719		48.779	
Average or below average status of religious preference and three or fewer grandparents born in U.S.	217	.702		49.239	
Catholic					
Average or below average status of religious preference and four grandparents born in U.S.	70	.895		49.608	
Average or below average status of religious preference and three or fewer grandparents born in U.S.	351	.700		49.990	3
Jewish	77	.922		48.337	
No Preference	66	.943	2	49.774	
B. Early Farm Isolation (number of years lived on farm, nature and number of activities while in school, and teen-age club memberships)†					
Non-farm activist (40–49)	693	.772	17	49.752	4
Mixed farm-non-farm, isolation-non-isolation (50–59)	373	.751		49.093	
Much farm isolation (60–79)	90	.710		48.105	
C. Level and Quality of Formal Education (degree of exposure to liberal arts)					
Less than high school graduate	235	.278		53.004	1
High school graduate	255	.303		52.391	
Some college (1–3 years)	124	.409		50.745	
Baccalaureate degree, low quality	173	.722		48.344	

TABLE 1—(Continued)

		Quality of Media Exposure			
		No. Areas High-Brow		Much Exposure to Poor TV	
	N	Adjust. Mean	Rank as Predictor	Adjust. Mean	Rank as Predictor
Baccalaureate degree, high quality	63	1.040		46.865	
Graduate or professional degree, low quality	152	1.502		44.805	
Graduate or professional degree, high quality	154	1.729	1	44.707	
II. Work Context, Schedule, and Attachment					
A. Size of Workplace					
Less than 49 employed	249	.655		48.475	
50–499 employed	194	.748		49.558	
500 or more employed	543	.940	3	49.306	
Self-employed	170	.337		50.950	2
B. Work Schedule					
Has orthodox work schedule	1039	.767	15	49.547	7
Has deviant work schedule	117	.696		48.206	
C. Long Hours: Chooses Work Over Leisure (many hours per week and weekends, and has control over work schedule)†					
Short work week (30–49)	575	.660		49.626	8
Medium work week (50–59)	446	.812		49.464	
Long work week (60–69)	135	1.013	4	48.320	
D. Work Alienation					
None	979	.755		49.362	
Some	126	.728		49.401	
Much	51	.928	10	50.377	13
III. Age, Aspirations, Mobility, and Career					
A. Age of Respondent					
21–29	121	.609		50.196	6
30–39	478	.818	6	49.710	
40–55	557	.744		48.981	
B. Worklife Mobility Pattern					
Up	385	.726		48.967	10
Stable	420	.776		49.672	
Fluctuating	335	.780	14	49.650	
Down	16	.727		48.238	
C. Intergenerational Climbing of Couple (Respondent's father's occupational stratum → respondent's; respondent's father-in-law's occupation → respondent's; and educational level of respondent compared with father's)†					
Much status loss of couple (20–39)	99	.695		50.131	12

TABLE 1—(Continued)

	N	No. Areas High-Brow Adjust. Mean	Rank as Predictor	Much Exposure to Poor TV Adjust. Mean	Rank as Predictor
Little or no status loss of couple (40–49)	407	.753		49.327	
Some status gain of couple (50–59)	484	.800	9	49.347	
Much status gain of couple (60–69)	166	.700		49.375	
D. Occupational Aspirations (past, present, and for the next generation)†					
Low Aspirations (30–39)	52	.670		48.659	
Medium-low aspirations (40–49)	398	.737		49.450	
Medium-high aspirations (50–59)	505	.778		49.466	16
High aspirations (60–69)	201	.784	13	49.390	
IV. Participation, Community Attachment, and Miscellaneous Leisure Correlates					
A. Primary Range (index of range of values, interests, and status levels represented by relatives, neighbors, friends from workplace or in same line of work, and other friends)†					
Low primary range (00–04)	158	.706		49.006	
Medium primary range (05–12)	764	.738		49.500	15
High primary range (13–19)	234	.867	8	49.395	
B. Effective Mediating Attachments (much time and wide range of contacts in formal assns.; numerous assns. clearly attached to; and high political affect and strong mediation of campaigns)*					
Weak mediating attachments (30–39)	183	.766		49.391	
Medium-weak mediating attachments (40–49)	251	.778	12	48.966	
Medium-strong mediating attachments (50–59)	492	.775		49.443	
Strong mediating attachments (60–79)	230	.702		49.844	11
C. Community Attachment, Good Citizen Style (voted in recent elections; voted for school taxes; gives high percentage of family income to churches and charity; feels neighborhood is "real home" and reasons show local attachment)†					
Weak local citizen (30–39)	61	.820	7	49.310	
Somewhat weak citizen (40–49)	354	.792		49.370	

TABLE 1—(Continued)

		Quality of Media Exposure			
		No. Areas High-Brow		Much Exposure to Poor TV	
	N	Adjust. Mean	Rank as Predictor	Adjust. Mean	Rank as Predictor
Somewhat strong citizen (50–59)	676	.760		49.478	17
Strong local citizen (60–69)	65	.531		49.030	
D. Leisure Malaise: Time on Hands					
Never have time on hands	610	.793	11	49.009	
Not very often	461	.720		49.743	
Fairly or very often	85	.741		50.500	5
E. Leisure Style as a Status Criterion: Taste (mentions manners and speech, books, music and art, and refinement of taste in defining class differences)†					
Few references to taste (40–49)	376	.692		49.411	
Some references to taste (50–59)	649	.754		49.520	14
Many references to taste (60–69)	131	.985	5	48.871	
F. Leisure Style as a Status Criterion: External Symbols (mentions houses, amount of money, clubs and organizations, and clothing in defining class differences)†					
Few references to external symbols (40–49)	637	.748		49.080	
Some references to external symbols (50–59)	425	.765		49.848	9
Many references to external symbols (60–69)	94	.817	16	49.678	
Total N	1156				

*For explanation see "Appendix on Method." [not reprinted here]: For details on measures which are not self-explanatory, see text. For participation measures (e.g. of the range of values, interests, and status levels represented by the respondent's social relations) see "Orderly Careers . . . ," *op. cit.*

† Items are combined in a factor score; the cutting points for scores are in parentheses.

gories are salaried men employed in big organizations; the poor-taste categories are self-employed or are employed in medium-sized work-places. Long hours, a factor measuring choice of work over leisure, ranks fourth as a predictor of high-brow media exposure; short hours ranks eighth as a predictor of low-brow television exposure. Men 21–29 years old (all in the middle mass) stand out in low-brow exposure; men 30–39 stand out in high-brow exposure.

What can we make of such findings? We began with the macro-scopic assumption that the division of labor, religious institutions, and age-grading systems persist as powerful sources of cultural differentiation and that mass education is a source of standardization. Now that we have pin-pointed the effect of these variables, slicing things a bit finer, the picture is not so simple. Take one of our favorite sociological clues to social structure: education. Will rising education levels bring an upgrading of taste, or will mass education mean an efflorescence of *kitsch?*

. . . The main findings are these:

1. For the number of media areas in which high-brow exposure is reported, *amount* of education makes little difference from grade zero through "some college"; thereafter, both quality of education and sheer level count heavily. The biggest jump in mean scores is between baccalaureate level and graduate level (.462), but the difference between men with high- and men with low-quality undergraduate education (.318) is greater than the differences between less than high school vs. high school (an infinitesimal .025), high school vs. some college (.106) or even some college and low-quality baccalaureate degree (.313).

Ultimately the mere rise in the average education level will do little for the cultivation of taste in reading and in the broadcast media; what counts is the number who complete college, and especially the number fortunate enough to go through a few favored colleges.

2. For the avoidance of big slugs of poor TV, sheer level of education counts slightly more than quality, although the differences are tiny until we come to college populations. Here the three largest differences are between "some college" and the low-quality baccalaureate (2.401), high-quality baccalaureate and low-quality graduate school (2.060), and low-quality and high-quality baccalaureate (1.479).

In sum: when we conceptualize "education" even at this crude level of "exposure to the liberal arts" and devise measures to match, we can gauge the cultural impact of abundance with more precision. These data suggest that the rising average level of education will protect against enervating amounts of the very shoddiest media content but it will not cause large populations to break the mediocrity barrier. As for the graduates of quality institutions, they will decline as a percentage of the educated and, as I shall show below, their exposure to quality print has declined and perhaps will continue to decline as a fraction of their leisure routine.

A final demonstration of the ambiguous effects of education and of the structural roots of cultural heterogeneity [involves] the impact of the organization of work and the level and quality of education on "leisure competence." In modern economies, group propensity and opportunity to work vary greatly even among occupational groups at the same social level. . . .

[The data] show first that a simple structural fact—group schedules of work—is a powerful source of diversity in leisure style. "Low" leisure competence ranges from 17 per cent in long hours groups to 65 per cent in short hours groups. The underdogs are similar to short-hours engineers and blue-collar workers; 61 per cent score low competence. Within various work contexts, how does the education of the individual affect his leisure competence? Exposure to the liberal arts has a heavy effect, which increases with shorter hours. For instance, among the short hours groups, a high-quality bachelor's degree brings the low competence rate down to 25 per cent; a low-quality bachelor's degree yields 45 per cent incompetence; some college or less yields a whopping 73 per cent. The 343 men comprising that 73 per cent are the largest group and have the lowest rate of competence in the table. Among men not accustomed to the wider universe made available by demanding work, it takes a long, expensive education to avoid an impoverished life. For students of American culture who look forward to the leisure-oriented society, in which we retreat from work to the more diversified joys of ever-shorter hours, the moral is that those who have most leisure have least resources for its creative use.

STRUCTURAL ROOTS OF CULTURAL HOMOGENEITY

So far I have asked, "who in all these samples is exposed to high culture and who avoids the very worst of mass culture?" I have not dealt with the *extent* of high-brow exposure, the effects of diverse *types of media*, and above all, the *interaction between high culture and mass culture*. How much do men who could be expected to have cultivated tastes expose themselves to high culture? To what extent are intellectuals insulated from mass culture? Which media of communication have most and least impact on the standards of cultural elites and educated laymen?

Not everything that is wrong with our intellectuals, as Shils reminds us, can be attributed to the media or to mass culture; high culture has always been precarious.[8] But what *is* new, unique to our time, is a thorough interpenetration of cultural levels; the good, the mediocre, and the trashy are becoming fused in one massive middle mush.

Structural trends in the organization of intellectual life are at the root of the problem; among *intellectuals* and their educated publics we see: large numbers, spatial scattering, intense professional specialization, and a loss of a sense of autonomy and intellectual community. . . . For both *intellectuals and the general population*, as I have suggested earlier, the cultural atmosphere is permeated by the mass media.

8 Edward A. Shils, "Mass Society and Its Culture," *Daedalus*, 89 (Spring, 1960), pp. 288–314.

These are all in some measure requisites ui consoquency of abundance. Hundreds of thousands, eventually millions, of specialized experts and intellectuals are indispensable in a complex society. And the spread of higher education to the average man is both a manpower requirement of modern economies and a great achievement in equality.

The problem is not that the taste of the masses has been debased, but rather that the creators and maintainers of high culture in the humanities, the arts, the sciences, have an increasingly difficult time doing their proper work. Intellectuals are increasingly tempted to play to mass audiences and expose themselves to mass culture, and this has the effect of reducing their versatility of taste and opinion, their subtlety of expression and feeling.

There is little doubt from my data as well as others' that educated strata—even products of graduate and professional schools—are becoming full participants in mass culture; they spend a reduced fraction of time in exposure to quality print and film. This trend extends to the professors, writers, artists, scientists—the keepers of high culture themselves—and the chief culprit, again, is TV.[9]

[9] Any assertion about long-term trends is inferential; we lack good base-line data. My position rests on three considerations. First, there is scattered evidence that the broadcast media in competition with print generally win out—in attraction, number of hours, perhaps persuasiveness, too. Reading, especially of books and magazines, declines. T. E. Coffin, "Television's Impact on Society," *The American Psychologist,* 10 (October, 1955), p. 633; L. Bogart, *The Age of Television* (2nd ed.), New York: Frederick Ungar, 1958, pp. 133 ff.; James N. Mosel, "Communications Patterns and Political Socialization in Transitional Thailand," in Lucien W. Pye (ed.), *Communications and Political Development,* Princeton, N.J.: Princeton University Press, 1963, pp. 184–228; and Klapper, *op. cit.,* pp. 107 ff. Second, among the educated, total exposure to broadcast media has recently increased. Before television, radio listening among set owners averaged 4.9 hours daily; evening listening averaged 2.6 hours for all, 2.4 hours for college graduates. Program preferences did not vary much by education. P. F. Lazarsfeld, *The People Look at Radio,* Chapel Hill, N.C.: The University of North Carolina Press, 1946, pp. 97–98, 136. Today, even excluding highbrow FM, radio listening has not declined to zero. (The typical radio family that acquired a television set cut radio listening from four or five hours to about two hours a day. Bogart, *op. cit.,* p. 114.) Meanwhile, television viewing for the average product of a graduate or professional school rose from zero to three hours daily. Steiner, *op. cit.,* p. 75. If we assume no major increase in the work week of the educated, and no change in life style that can remotely touch television in sheer hours, their exposure to undifferentiated broadcast media has risen as a portion of the daily round while their exposure to serious print has declined. And the small differences in amount and quality of television exposure reported in the text indicate that the educated are not especially discriminating. Finally, the argument about the effect of intellectuals' participation in mass culture on their standards of performance and appreciation proceeds through example and counter example without the benefit of much systematic evidence. "Raymond Aron's thought," says Edward Shils, "does not deteriorate be-

You will remember that media researchers emphasize the limited power of mass communications by invoking the idea that the audience sorts itself out according to predisposition. By that formula, we should find the highly-educated listening to Gerry Mulligan, watching [public television], and reading the *Partisan Review* (or at least *Harper's*); and the less educated should be listening to Elvis Presley, watching "Gunsmoke," and reading *True Detective*. The evidence is that the educated display, on balance, a mild tendency toward more discriminating tastes.

Studies consistently demonstrate that college graduates compared to the less educated have somewhat less exposure to the broadcast media, which are more uniform in their content, and somewhat more to print, which is more diversified. They are a bit more choosey in the regular programs they watch on television; they definitely read more quality magazines and newspapers; and they listen to more serious music.[10] [My data] emphasize the efforts of educational and occupational groups to be selective in their use of newspapers, periodicals, and television. . . . For instance, over two-fifths of the professors, a third of the lawyers, and a tenth of the engineers compared to one in a hundred of the middle mass and none of the underdogs read a quality newspaper. And in reading the newspaper, the professional groups are somewhat more cosmopolitan and serious; they include world and national news as sections important to them more often than do the middle mass or underdogs. Similar differences appear for quality magazines read regularly. But the differences in exposure to print among my samples, as well as those in other studies based on broader samples, are not great. . . . [If] we pin-point the groups and take interest in political news as a clue to wider perspectives, the most privileged, well-educated firm lawyers have only a 10 per cent edge over the middle mass; and engineers are about the same as lower white-collar workers. In his interest in world news, the solo lawyer has only a 7 per cent edge over the younger blue-collar worker. The

---

cause he occasionally writes in the *New York Times Magazine.*" *Op. cit.,* p. 306. Unfortunately, we cannot know what the quality of Aron's thought would have been if as a young man he had been watching "situation comedies" instead of reading books. As a master of ambiguous polemic, Shils presents the best defense of the view that mass culture has little effect on high culture; but in listing the structural forces that threaten high culture, he gives inadequate weight to them and no weight at all to the major problem we confront here—central tendencies in the life styles of educated strata. Shils, *op. cit.*

10 Cf. Paul F. Lazarsfeld, *Radio and the Printed Page,* New York: Duell, Sloan, and Pearce, 1949; B. Berelson and M. Janowitz, *Reader in Public Opinion and Communication,* Glencoe, Ill.: The Free Press, 1953, Part 7; L. Bogart, "Newspapers in the Age of Television," *Daedalus* (Winter, 1963), pp. 116–127, and other essays in that issue; and the citations in footnote 9 above.

differences in the proportion of diverse groups who rank local news as important to them in their daily reading are similarly small.[11]

Even more uniform from group to group are media habits tapped by more subtle measures of involvement with mass culture . . . being a loyal rooter for sports teams, rating comics as an important daily experience, becoming deeply involved with media heroes. And when we come to television, at least in America, the constraint of structural differentiation seems doomed; uniformity of behavior and taste is the main story. Nowhere else has a "class" audience been so swiftly transformed into a "mass" audience.

A recent nationwide survey of TV-viewers, sponsored by CBS, reports that those with more than four years of college average about 3 hours a day of viewing compared to the 4.3 hours of those with only grammar school education.[12] Admitted prime-time viewing is unrelated to education. When the CBS survey asked them to name their favorite programs (those watched regularly), over half of those at the top of the educational range named light entertainment shows, the overwhelming preference of everyone else. Comedy, variety, and action (i.e., western, adventure, crime, police, private eye)—there were only slightly less common favorites among the college educated than among the less privileged.

Unfortunately, the actual record of viewing—in diaries, for instance —reveals even fewer differences.[13] Education has a lot more to do with how people *feel* about TV than what they *do* with it. College graduates criticize TV programming, but they choose to watch extensively, and in doing so, find themselves in [Newton] Minow's wasteland, unable, because of the limited high-brow fare available, to exert much more selectivity than the general population. They clearly display more signs of guilt and uneasiness at this state of affairs, but apparently it's not so punishing that it makes them flick the dial to "off."

Perhaps the most telling data demonstrating the interpenetration of brow levels, not merely in television viewing but also in reading, come from my samples in the Detroit area. Most of those who read at least one high-brow magazine, also read middle- or low-brow magazines. Only 3 per cent of all these men read only high-brow magazines. How about books? *Among college-educated professionals, only one in four claimed to have read a high-brow book in two months.* Only

---

[11] If you are inclined to use the British as a case on the other side, you will receive little support from Mark Abrams' careful study of the media habits of the socio-cultural elite of Great Britain. "The Mass Media and Social Class in Great Britain," paper presented at the Fourth World Congress of Sociology, Stresa, Italy, September, 1958.

[12] Steiner, *op. cit.*, p. 75.

[13] *Ibid.*, p. 161.

about three in five of the professors and lawyers, the most highly educated, entirely avoid low-brow TV favorites. The typical professor crosses one or two levels of TV exposure. The engineers and executives, middle mass, and the underdogs on relief are quite similar in their TV-viewing habits. Television, again, appears to be a powerful force for cultural standardization, since these groups include men making more than $100,000 and others who have been unemployed for years. The department chief at GM, his foremen, and the unemployed autoworker on relief are bound together in the common culture of Huntley-Brinkley, "Restless Gun," and Mr. Clean.

If we consider magazines, books, newspapers, and TV together, what portion of these groups are exposed to any quality product in more than two areas? The answer: a minority of each group. Forty-three per cent of the professors score high on at least one item in each of three or four areas, 13 per cent of the lawyers, 5 per cent of the engineers and executives, 1 per cent of the middle mass, none of the underdogs.

The fact that the professors did so well in this generally dismal picture encouraged me to carry out a special analysis of deviant cases —those who use print and television for enlightenment and stimulation, and seek the quality product for entertainment.

PORTRAIT OF THE MEDIA PURIST

Who are the media purists—men who insulate themselves fully from mass culture? We could not find one case in 1,354 who was not in some area exposed to middle- or low-brow material. By relaxing the definition, however, we located 19 men who make rather heroic efforts to cultivate the best in the media. They either (1) report some highbrow exposure in all four media areas (magazines, books, newspapers, TV) *and* are exclusively highbrow in one or more reading areas; or (2) have no TV set or never watch TV, have some high-brow exposure in the three reading areas, and are exclusively high-brow in one reading area.

The characteristics of the 19 men suggest that one must be a very odd fellow in America to avoid mass culture. All but two were educated in high-quality liberal arts colleges and graduate schools or were educated abroad—a very rare pattern. In occupation, 16 were professors (13 of high rank, especially in the humanities, mathematics, and physics); three were prosperous corporation lawyers. As a group, the media purists have inherited higher occupational status than their colleagues (their parents tend to be established professionals and executives)—which suggests that it may take rather close family supervision over more than a generation to inculcate a taste for high culture. In religion they are more often Jewish or have no preference or are inactive Protestants. Several are intermarried or in other ways have experienced cultural discontinuity. In origin, training, and position, then, this group is at once high status and marginal.

What constitutes the style of life of media purists? In consumption, they are almost ascetic; among the professors, the relatively high incomes are spent only minimally for luxury possessions, homes, cars, vacations, or charity. They are apartment-dwellers more often than home owners. They tend to be ambitious, independent-minded, like to "go-it-alone." Their media exposure is not only more high-brow; it is more extensive.

Although these media purists stand outside American society ideologically, they are well-integrated socially and politically. As one would expect, they are to a man highly critical of the media. They are also generally estranged from the major power centers in the United States —except for the federal courts, which they feel are doing an excellent job. In participation patterns, however, they belong to more organizations and are attached to more than their colleagues. The professors among them are almost all active, liberal Democrats; the lawyers are conventional, moderate Republicans.

In short, it takes such an unusual set of experiences in family, school, and career to produce a media purist that they are practically nonexistent.

IMPLICATIONS FOR
SOCIOLOGICAL THEORY

In applying the larger debate about the shape of modern society to the mass media and mass entertainment in America, I have brought systematic survey data to bear on the problem of the interplay of social structure, mass culture, and high culture. I have tried to resolve the paradox of a simultaneous growth of structural differentiation and cultural uniformity by re-examining the structural roots of media exposure and response. These data point up the need for a merger of the main characterizations of modern society—"mass," "industrial," and "urban." Specifically, these lessons can be learned.

1. The sketchy treatment of mass culture in theories of the mass society and the very limited idea of the two-step flow of mass communications, which accents the healthy absorption of the media into local cultures, demand more sophisticated treatment of the social structures in which the media are received. My data suggest that we need to slice up social structure in ways that capture both the persistence of older divisions (age, religion, occupation) and the emergence of newer ones (the quality and content of education) and to do it more precisely than usual. To say "white collar" or "working class" is to obscure most of what is central to the experience of the person and the structure of society. To say "professional, tech-

nical, and kindred" captures more of social life but not much more. "Lawyer" and "engineer" move us closer to social reality, for these men develop quite different styles of life, rooted in diverse professional schools, tasks, work schedules, and organizational contexts. To say "independent practitioner" is to say even more, and finally, to particularize the matter with "solo lawyer" vs. "firm lawyer" is to take account of the sharp contrasts in recruitment base (social origins, religion, quality of professional training), career pattern and rewards which divide the two.

In general, data both here and in other studies suggest that as predictors of life style variables—especially cultural tastes and ideology —sex, age, and social-economic stratum are far weaker than religion, type of education, work and career—variables that represent positions in established groups. The implication is clear: return to the study of group life.

2. Television, the most "massified" of the mass media, the one with the largest and most heterogeneous audience, has become central to the leisure routine of majorities at every level. The usual differences in media exposure and response among age, sex, and class categories— easy to exaggerate in any case—have virtually disappeared in the case of television. Even here, however, where we pinpoint social groups—an occupation supported by an occupational community, a religion buttressed by a religious community—some differences do remain. And among the printed media, where most competition prevails, the chance of such groups to stylize their uses of mass communications remains strong.

3. The paradox of the simultaneous growth of structural differentiation and cultural uniformity is thus partly a matter of our weak concepts and measures of social structure and our consequent failure to spot group-linked variations in life style. But it may also reflect the state of an affluent society in transition. In order to pin down the cultural impact of continued economic growth, we require data not now in hand. For countries at similar levels of economic development, having diverse cultural traditions and systems of education and communications, we need data on levels of mass taste, organization and self-conceptions of cultural elites, distance between educated and less educated in exposure to mass culture and high culture. Until we have such systematic comparisons, I will assume that structure and culture are congruent and massified in rapidly developing new nations and that they become increasingly *in*congruent at levels of development thus far achieved. Finally, as rich countries grow richer, homogenizing structures in politics, education, and mass communications combine with an already high level of cultural uniformity to reduce the hold of differentiating structures of age, religion, work, and locality, and bring about greater consistency of structure and culture—a new combina-

tion of "mass" society and "industrial" society, mass culture and high culture.

4. Many leads in my data point to the need for synthesis not only of ideas about industrial society and mass society but also of ideas about pluralism and totalitarianism. I can here merely indicate the direction of these findings. Briefly, what takes place in the economy and the locality—work, consumption, and participation in formal associations—forms coherent styles of life, one of which I have come to label "Happy Good Citizen-Consumer." The style includes these pluralist-industrial traits: strong attachment to the community (supporting increased school taxes, contributing generously to churches and charity, thinking of the neighborhood as one's "real home," voting in elections); consumer enthusiasm (planning to buy or to replace many luxury possessions); optimism about national crises; a strong belief that distributive justice prevails (feeling that jobs are distributed fairly). It also involves long hours at gratifying work, little or no leisure malaise; wide-ranging, stable secondary ties and, to some extent, wide-ranging, stable primary ties—the very model of a modern pluralist citizen. But this benign pattern of work, consumption, and participation is independent of participation in and feelings about mass culture. And both happy good citizenry and the uses of the mass media are more or less independent of approaches to national politics—or at least go together in ways not anticipated in received theory. Thus, the good citizen-consumers tend to be unusually prone to personality voting (party-switching, ticket-splitting), dependent on the media for opinions on issues, susceptible to advertising and to mass behavior generally (e.g., they score high on a measure of susceptibility to manipulation by the media in politics and consumption). Men who have confidence in the major institutions of American society distrust "TV and radio networks"; men who trust the media distrust other institutions. Finally, men whose social relations are stable tend to have fluid party loyalties. *To be socially integrated in America is to accept propaganda, advertising, and speedy obsolescence in consumption.* The fact is that those who fit the image of pluralist man in the pluralist society also fit the image of mass man in the mass society. Any accurate picture of the shape of modern society must accommodate these ambiguities.

chapter nine

Class domination and ideological hegemony

DAVID L. SALLACH

CLASS DOMINATION AND IDEOLOGICAL HEGEMONY

The problem of social order has been of persistent interest to social and political theorists. The most fundamental issue in the theoretical debates has been whether coercive or ideational forces provide the more central basis for social order. Two well-defined positions have emerged: 1) Following Durkheim, Parsons and his followers have asserted that ideational factors (e.g., cultural values) provide the bedrock of social order; 2) The Marxist position has held that the ideological superstructure emerges in response to the existing social structure defined in terms of coercive economic and political social relations. In the latter view, the dominant class in the society is able to reinforce its material control through the successful extension of that control to the ideational arena, specifically within the institutions of civil society.[1]

Both views rest upon assumptions which if undermined raise doubts about the viability of the perspective in general. Specifically, the view that social order is based upon a consensus of cultural values requires that a consensus of values exist in the empirical world. On the other hand, the Marxist view of social order assumes 1) the existence of a ruling class which 2) permeates the cultural and ideational institutions

"Class Domination and Ideological Hegemony," by David L. Sallach. Reprinted from *The Sociological Quarterly* 15 (Winter 1974), pp. 38–50, with the permission of the author and publisher, footnotes renumbered.

This article is a revision of a previous paper presented at the 1971 meeting of the American Sociological Association in Denver. I have profited greatly from the critical commentary provided by a number of people, including: John R. Ainlay, Nicholas Babchuk, Larry Hazelrigg, Peter K. Manning, Hugh Mehan, Clyde Z. Nunn, Whitney Pope and Austin T. Turk.

[1] Cf. Marx and Engels, *The German Ideology*. New York: International Publishers, 1947, p. 39.

of the society. It is not the purpose of the present paper to exhaustively examine these assumptions; however, a brief exploration of the empirical literature is in order.

PRELIMINARY QUESTION: IS THERE A VALUE CONSENSUS?

Does the concept of value consensus describe existing patterns on an empirical level? Previous studies indicate clearly that the conception of consensus simply does not describe social reality within the U.S. Protho and Grigg[2] find that general consensus on the idea of democracy disappeared when specific issues were considered. McClosky[3] asserts that while the political views of influentials are relatively ordered and coherent, "millions of people continue to possess only the most rudimentary understanding of democratic ideology." Mann[4] reviews a range of studies and draws a similar conclusion: "Value consensus does not exist to any significant extent."

Rather, the available evidence suggests that the value and belief systems of the majority of the U.S. population are underdeveloped, fragmented, and inconsistent. As we have seen, McClosky's data is generally supportive of such an interpretation. Further support is provided in an insightful article by Converse.[5] In his analysis of belief systems in mass publics, Converse finds that an abstract and contextual grasp of belief systems characterizes only 10% of the adult population of the U.S. Even within that tenth, the majority either do not rely heavily upon conceptual dimensions or else appear limited in the breadth of their understanding of such dimensions.

In addition to the differential distribution of conceptualization ability, Converse finds the level of analysis changes as one moves down the ideological spectrum: "Moving from top to bottom of this information dimension the character of the objects that are central in a belief system undergoes systematic change. These objects shift from the remote, generic, and abstract to the increasingly simple, concrete, or 'close to home'." [6]

The different "levels of conceptualization" are related to education and political participation.[7] As these relationships suggest, the variance

2 James Protho and Charles Grigg, "Fundamental Principles of Democracy: Bases of Agreement and Disagreement." *Journal of Politics* 22 (May 1960), 276–294.

3 Herbert McClosky, "Consensus and Ideology in American Politics," *American Political Science Review*, 58 (June 1964), 361–82, p. 289.

4 Michael Mann, "The Social Cohesion of Liberal Democracy," *American Sociological Review*, 35 (June 1970), 423–39.

5 Philip E. Converse, "The Nature of Belief Systems in Mass Publics," in D. Apter, ed., *Ideology and Discontent*. New York: Free Press, 1964, pp. 206–61.

6 *Ibid.*, p. 213.

7 *Ibid.*

in belief systems is patterned, also, along class lines. Mann's[8] survey of research notes two trends which document this point: 1) there is a greater degree of consensus among the middle class than among the working class, and 2) working class individuals exhibit less internal consistency in their values than middle class people. Mann feels that the evidence suggests that "only those actually sharing in societal power need develop consistent values"[9] and further, that working-class compliance with the political order is based upon a *lack* of consensus and a *lack* of internal consistency that prevents that class from translating its experiences into a political framework.[10] All of the above evidence appears to be more compatible with a perspective that emphasizes the relationship between ideational institutions and the structure of control than a perspective which asserts that cultural values are consensually held and emergent.

PRELIMINARY QUESTION: IS THERE A RULING CLASS?

The sociological literature concerned with demonstrating or refuting the existence of a ruling class is almost infinite, certainly it is beyond the scope of this paper to fully explore it. Among the many conceptual problems which arise is the issue of whether domination is a class phenomenon as opposed to other formulations: a power elite,[11] strategic elites,[12] the rise of the managers[13] or in the vague terms of Rose,[14] different elites dominating different areas. Further, if a dominant class is seen to exist does it rule (Marx), govern (Domhoff), or exert superordinant influence? Such questions, however important, cannot be resolved here.

We can note, however, several well-documented empirical trends. In the first place, all available data on the distribution of income and wealth reveal the continued existence of sharp income differentials.[15] Most important in terms of control of production, one per cent of the U.S. population (or less) owns between 58 and 61 per cent of the

---

8 Mann, *op. cit.*, p. 432.
9 *Ibid.*, p. 435.
10 This is a fundamental aspect of the concept of hegemony, which will be discussed below.
11 C. Wright Mills, *The Power Elite*. New York: Oxford University Press, 1956.
12 Susan Keller, *Beyond the Ruling Class*. New York: Random House, 1963.
13 See A. A. Berle and G. C. Means, *The Modern Corporation and Private Property*. New York: Macmillan, 1932; James Burnham, *The Managerial Revolution*. New York: G. P. Putnam's Sons, 1941; and many others.
14 Arnold Rose, *The Power Structure*. New York: Oxford University Press, 1967.
15 See, for example, S. M. Miller and Pamela Roby, *The Future of Inequality*. New York: Basic Books, 1970; and Herman P. Miller, *Rich Man, Poor Man*. New York: Crowell, 1971.

corporate stock[16] (most experts feel that corporate control is established by ten per cent of the voting stock, or less). Moving from distribution of wealth to actual corporate control, Kolko found that the
board of directors of the 100 largest industrial corporations owned or
represented an average of 9.9 per cent of that company's shares. Further, Kolko feels that such an index greatly understates the concentration of corporate control. In Kolko's words:[17]

The splitting of blocks of stocks among family members for tax purposes,
or the placing of the stocks in professionally managed trusts and investment
companies, where identities can be obscured, may have practical value for the
corporate elite. But these moves can hardly be regarded as significant changes
in stock ownership.[18]

Further, corporate interests are significantly represented in a number of vital political and ideological areas. Kolko[19] finds that between
the years of 1944 and 1960, 59.6 per cent of all high level governmental
policy positions in the departments of State, Defense, Treasury and
Commerce were held by men from big business, investment and (corporate) law. In the area of higher education, Foster[20] finds that nearly
40 per cent of all college trustees are executives or administrators of

[16] Gabriel Kolko, *Wealth and Power in America*. New York: Praeger, 1962.

[17] Given the numerous studies of the distribution of wealth, the discrepancy in
conclusions is surprisingly small. Thus, a 1951 study by the Brookings Institution
concludes that only 2.1 per cent of the common-stock shareholding owned 58% of
the common stock (Lewis H. Kimmel, *Share Ownership in the United States*.
Washington, D.C.: Brookings Institution, 1952). If one takes into consideration
the fact that a relatively small proportion of the population owns stock—Kolko
indicates that the stock-owning sector has ranged from 5.1 to 7.9 per cent of the
population (Gabriel Kolko, *Wealth and Power in America*. New York: Praeger,
1962)—then clearly less than 1 per cent own the majority of common stock.
Similarly, a government-sponsored study published in 1966 found that 1 per cent
of the sampled households owned 61 per cent of corporate stock (Dorothy S.
Projector and Gertrude Weiss, *Survey of Financial Characteristics of Consumers*.
Washington, D.C.: Federal Reserve System, 1966). For a more general discussion
of the significance of such figures see Kolko, *op. cit.*; G. Williams Domhoff, *Who
Rules America?* Englewood Cliffs, N.J.: Prentice-Hall, Inc.; and Frank Ackerman,
Howard Birnbaum, James Wetzler, and Andrew Zimbalist, "Income Distribution in
the United States," *The Review of Radical Political Economics*, 3 (Summer 1971)
20–43.

[18] To the extent that "management-controlled" corporations exist, a study by
Robert Larner ("The Effects of Management Control on the Profits of Large
Corporations" in M. Zeitlan (ed.), *American Society, Inc.* Chicago: Markham; 1970,
pp. 251–62) indicates that such firms differ little from owner-controlled firms on
the crucial question of profit-orientation.

[19] Gabriel Kolko, *The Roots of American Foreign Policy*. Boston: Beacon, 1969.

[20] Julian Foster, "The Trustees and Protest," in J. Foster and D. Long, eds.
Protest! Student Activism in America. New York: William Morrow and Company,
Inc., 1970, pp. 383–93.

various types of businesses. In contrast, only 3.6 per cent were faculty members and only 0.1 per cent were labor union officials. When Foster examined the trustees of 30 prestigious private universities, only 4.9 per cent reported incomes under $20,000. The broadcasting industry, of course, constitutes a significant part of the corporate structure and, further, is tied to other corporate interests by advertising revenues.[21]

The above evidence is not conclusive or exhaustive; however, it does provide tentative support for the Marxist view that extant culture and ideology is an outgrowth of class domination rather than an emergent and consensually shared product of social interaction. Despite such easily available evidence, the Marxist concept of ideological hegemony is foreign to sociological analyses of social order.[22] The following discussion, therefore, undertakes to develop the concept of hegemony and relate its dynamic to two specific institutional areas: education and the mass media.

THE CONCEPT OF HEGEMONY

In *The German Ideology,* Marx states the basic idea contained in the concept of hegemony:

> The ideas of the ruling class are in every epoch the ruling ideas: i.e., the class which is the ruling material force of society is at the same time its ruling intellectual force.[23]

Marx's analysis is further elaborated by the brilliant Italian theoretician, Antonio Gramsci.[24] Gramsci used the concept of hegemony to refer to the way in which "a certain way of life and thought is dominant, in which one concept of reality is diffused throughout society in all its institutional and private manifestations." [25] The process that Gramsci describes is one in which a dominant class, which controls the economic and political institutions of a society, also possesses privileged access to the primary ideological institutions of that society (religion, culture, education, communications media). The dominant class uses its privileged access to ideological institutions to propagate values which reinforce its structural position. Such propagation involves not

[21] G. Williams Domhoff, *Who Rules America.* Englewood Cliffs, N.J.: Prentice-Hall, Inc., 1967.

[22] Actually, this fact constitutes evidence of the hegemonic process within sociology itself. For a related discussion, see Sallach "What Is Sociological Theory?" *The American Sociologist* 8 (August 1973), 134–39.

[23] Marx and Engels, *op. cit.,* p. 39.

[24] Antonio Gramsci, *Prison Notebooks.* New York: International Publishers, 1971.

[25] G. A. Williams, "Gramsci's Concept of Egemonia," Journal of the History of Ideas 21 (1960), p. 587 cited in John Cammett, *Antonio Gramsci and the Origins of Italian Communism.* Stanford: Stanford University Press, 1967, p. 204.

only the inculcation of its values and the censorship of heterodox views, but also and especially the ability to *define* the parameters of legitimate discussion and debate over alternative beliefs, values and world views. Actually, censorship and direct inculcation are extreme instances in the hegemonic process (and frequently may be counter-productive). The most effective aspect of hegemony is found in the suppression of alternative views through the establishment of parameters which define what is legitimate, reasonable, sane, practical, good, true, and beautiful.

The consequence of the hegemonic process is that the majority of the population is largely unaware of alternative values and alternative readings of history. The hegemonic process does not create a value consensus but confusion, fragmentation and inconsistency in belief systems. Garson[26] in a study of beliefs and attitudes among auto workers, comes to precisely this conclusion: "Rather than possessing a coherent ideology, whether reactionary, liberal or radical, one finds them to be full of ambiguity and overlays of consciousness. Different and seemingly contradictory orientations will be evoked depending upon the context." The fragmentation of consciousness among the larger population and existence of ideological parameters on public discussion and debate are but two sides of the same hegemonic process, the former being a consequence of the latter.

For Gramsci (and for most Marxists[27]), a major source of social control rests in this process of ideological hegemony. Garson[28] describes the result. "Satisfaction is perpetuated on a superficial but en-during basis by the absence of attractive models capable of raising expectations beyond the level presently satisfied by the firm." In this view, the suppression of ideological alternatives is an integral exten-sion of the legal apparatus which systematically expelled revolution-aries from the trade unions in the late forties and early fifties; the two processes seek the same result at different levels. In the absence of visible alternatives, no mass-based opposition emerges and the struc-ture of control is able to continue unchallenged.

---

26 David G. Garson, "Automobile Workers and the Radical Dream," *Politics and Society,* 3 (Winter 1973), p. 164.

27 There is another strain of Marxism which appears to treat the hegemonic process as one of inculcation. This view tends to rest on assumptions similar to those of the "value consensus" perspective, i.e., that subordinate classes accept and internalize the values of the dominant class. An excellent example of this per-spective may be found in Marcuse's *One-Dimensional Man* (Boston: Beacon Press, 1964) in which Marcuse speaks of a "happy consciousness" coming to prevail. He writes (p. 32), "The novel feature is . . . the depth of the preconditioning which shapes the instinctual drives and obscures the difference between false and true consciousness." In my view, such a position is not appreciably superior to the "value consensus" position and is equally subverted by the evidence presented above.

28 *Ibid.,* p. 174.

Previously we have examined evidence that bears upon two aspects of the hegemonic process: 1) the influence of the wealthy and the corporate elite within the ideological sectors of society; and 2) the tendency for belief systems to be increasingly fragmented and inconsistent as one descends the class structure. The evidence in both cases provides tentative support for Gramsci's view of social order. It is now necessary to determine the viability of the third aspect of the hegemonic process: the tendency for debate and discussion to be circumscribed within parameters which preclude the development and propagation of alternative values and world views. A complete exploration of this issue would necessarily focus upon a large number of relevant arenas: art and culture, science and technology, social science, religion, labor unions, education and mass media. The present effort will focus upon the latter two. To the extent that hegemonic parameters are found to exist within these two ideological institutions, there is some reason to hypothesize similar findings in the other institutional areas. Ultimately, of course, it will be necessary for ideological hegemony to be treated in its entirety.

POLITICAL SOCIALIZATION

Recent political socialization studies indicate that the elementary school experience is central to the formation of political orientations.[29] Further, the same research consistently indicates that controversial or deviant perspectives are omitted from consideration by teachers and texts. Greenstein[30] suggests that children's perspectives are "sugarcoated" through the books to which they are exposed. Key notes a similar trait in history texts: "Those episodes that redound most to our national glory receive emphasis; and the picture of the past is deficient in cracks and crevices." [31]

A similar tendency is found in the treatment of minorities and minority struggles. Kane, after a study of forty-five junior and senior high school social studies textbooks, concludes, "a significant number of texts published today continue to present a principally white, Protestant, Anglo-Saxon view of America's past and present, while the nature and problems of minority groups are largely neglected." [32] Dual patterns of racism and sexism are reported in a study of children's readers conducted by Women on Words and Images:

29 See Fred I. Greenstein, *Children and Politics*. New Haven: Yale University Press, 1965; Robert Hess and Judith Torney, *The Development of Political Attitudes in Children*. Garden City, N.J.: Anchor, 1968; and Kenneth P. Langton, *Political Socialization*. New York: Oxford University Press, 1969.

30 *Ibid.*

31 V. O. Key, *Public Opinion and American Democracy*. New York: Alfred A. Knopf, 1961, p. 317.

32 Michael B. Kane, *Minorities in Textbooks*. Chicago: Quadrangle, 1970, p. 138.

Indians are the race we meet most often in these stories and the readers are very ambivalent about them. Now they are courageous, marvelously skilled at meeting the challenges of the wild, and the friend of the white man. The terms "good Indian" and "bad Indian" are used here exclusively in the sense of what's good or bad for the white settlers . . . But there is not ambiguity about who is the bravest sex of all. Indian males are as achievement-oriented as any palefaced male. The Indian girl, no matter how resourceful or courageous, is no better off than the rest of her sex. . . .[33]

In general, the 88 readers which the study examined continued the pattern of omission: "ignored are one-parent families, adopted children, divorced and/or fighting parents." [34]

Teachers, as well as texts, insulate children from political conflict and deviant values or traditions.[35] As Dawson and Prewitt [36] summarized:

The evidence about the public school teacher in United States forms a consistent picture. Teachers are expected to, and do, propagate political views and beliefs appropriately labeled 'consensus values.' Teachers should not use the classroom as a forum for discussion of 'partisan values' and controversial positions.[37]

Conflict populism, and alternative traditions are thus extracted from consideration within the educational process. The consequence, as Mann observes, is that in later years the child has difficulty expressing his increasing cynicism in abstract concepts.[38]

MASS MEDIA

That the mass media possess potential for the manipulation of public thought is not exactly an original insight. As early as 1942, Schumpeter stated, "The ways in which issues and the popular will on any issue are being manufactured is exactly analogous to the ways of

[33] Women on Words and Images, *Dick and Jane as Victims: Sex Stereotyping in Children's Readers*. Princeton, N.J.: Women on Words and Images, 1972, p. 31.

[34] *Ibid.*, p. 30.

[35] Cf. Edgar Litt, "Civic Education, Community Norms and Political Indoctrination," *American Sociological Review*, 28 (1963), 69–75; and Richard M. Merelman, *Political Socialization and Educational Climates*. New York: Holt Rinehart and Winston, 1971.

[36] Richard E. Dawson and Kenneth Prewitt, *Political Socialization*. Boston: Little, Brown and Company, 1969.

[37] It is *not* being suggested that public school teachers are conscious "agents" of the hegemonic process. Rather, they are, like the vast majority, subject to hegemonic parameters, and thus contribute to the overall process.

[38] Mann, *op. cit.*, cf. Greenstein, *op. cit.*

commercial advertising." [39] However, an emphasis upon the techniques of direct manipulation obscures the more pervasive aspect of the relationship between the media and the "mass". Janowitz captures this significant aspect well when he says, "The influence of mass media, supported by networks of interpersonal contacts among opinion leaders, is not in dramatic conversion of public opinion, but rather *in setting the limits within* which public debate on controversial issues takes place" (emphasis mine).[40]

Evidence supporting this conclusion is not scarce. Analysis of media content indicate that, in biography and fiction, positively portrayed figures approximate cultural ideals.[41] Further, some writers see the most general impact of media content to be support for "accepted" social goals.[42] The converse is also true. Partisans of controversial political positions have recently attempted to document bias in the news. Efron[43] attempts to document bias against conservative positions; Cirino attempts to document a "shackling of antiestablishment ideas." [44] Both present figures which illustrate the way in which controversial positions are ignored or distorted by the mass media.

As important as the content *per se* is the process by which content is tailored. In this area, Cantor discusses the way in which television producers internalize network controls and exercise self-censorship. The vast majority of respondents commented about how racial and political themes can result in network interference. Further,

According to several producers, the networks are essentially apolitical and *within certain limits* seem little concerned with the ideology or philosophy of a show *if* the ratings are high *and* the advertisers are satisfied (emphasis mine).[45]

Another example of the process of control is provided by Breed,[46] who examined social control in the newsroom and concluded that the

[39] Joseph Schumpeter, *Capitalism, Socialism and Democracy*. New York: Harper & Row, Publishers, 1962, p. 263.

[40] Morris Janowitz, *The Professional Soldier*. New York: Free Press, 1960, p. 402.

[41] See L. Lowenthal, "Biographies in Popular Magazines, in P. Lazarsfeld and F. Stanton, eds., *Radio Research 1942–43*. New York: Duell, Sloan and Pearce, 1943, pp. 507–43; and Charles R. Wright, *Mass Communication*. New York: Random House, 1957, pp. 78–84.

[42] Cf. Theodore Peterson, Jay Jensen and William Rivers, *The Mass Media and Modern Society*. New York: Holt, Rinehart and Winston, 1966.

[43] Edith Efron, *The News Twisters*. Los Angeles: Nash, 1971.

[44] Robert Cirino, *Don't Blame The People*. Los Angeles: Diversity, 1971.

[45] Muriel G. Cantor, *The Hollywood TV Producer*. New York: Basic Books, 1971, p. 127.

[46] Warren Breed, "Social Control in the Newsroom," *Social Forces*, 33 (May 1955), 323–35.

results of the process were inadequate for wider democratic needs. However, Breed's discussion needs further elaboration. As Brown points out, "The internal dynamics of this particular milieu are also part of a larger system that both rationalizes and defines itself in terms of ideological positions." [47]

In both print and electronic media economic influence and control constitute a central aspect of that larger system. Domhoff [48] suggests that the upper class exerts a predominant influence on the mass media, indirectly through corporate advertising and directly through ownership. Skornia takes a similar position when he says:

> The repressive influences, taboos, and other blockages which *economic* pressures bring result in unfreedoms which may not be *called* censorship but which, no less effectively than government censorship, determine what can be said and learned through the broadcast media. [49]

Skornia's statement is similar to the conclusion of Klapper. [50] In a comprehensive study of the effects of mass communication, Klapper indicates that mass communication is a contributory agent to a process of reinforcing socially prevalent attitudes. One of the factors which he identifies as responsible for this effect is the nature of commercial mass media in a free enterprise society, which leads media *to expose only such attitudes as are already virtually universal.*

Mass media content, economics and criteria of selection all seem to indicate that this ideological institution is subject to parameters that are quite clearly defined. A further question might concern the way in which regulatory agencies circumscribe media functioning. Do such agencies serve as insurance of a broad and unrestricted ideological arena? A clear and revealing example is provided by the Federal Communications Commission's illustration of how the "fairness doctrine" is to be applied. The FCC cites an example in which a station broadcasted a program entitled "Communist Encirclement" in which it was asserted (*inter alia*) that U.S. foreign policy, "the alleged infiltration of our government by commmunists and the alleged moral weakening in our homes, schools and churches have all contributed to the advance of international communism." The station maintained that since it did not know of any communist in its community it was unable to afford air time to those who might want to present opposing views.

The FCC's ruling is instructive and worth quoting at length:

[47] Roger L. Brown, "Some Aspects of Mass Media Ideologies," *The Sociological Review*, 13 (January 1969), 166.

[48] Domhoff, *op. cit.*, pp. 79–83.

[49] Harry J. Skornia, *Television and the News.* Palo Alto: Pacific Books, 1968, p. 70.

[50] Joseph Klapper, *The Effects of Mass Communication.* Glencoe, Ill.: Free Press, 1960.

In situations of this kind, it was not and is not the Commission's intention to require licensees to make time available to communists or the communist viewpoint. But the matters listed above raise controversial issues of public importance on which persons other than communists hold contrasting views. There are responsible contrasting viewpoints on the most effective methods of combating communism and communist infiltration.[51]

The above interpretation of the "fairness doctrine" in no way challenges the assumption that communism (however defined) must be fought or that communist infiltration is a realistic threat to national security. Consequently, the interpretation not only prevents the airing of communist perspectives but also the presentation of the perspective of a pacifist perspective, not to mention any revolutionary opposition. In sum, the evidence presented here clearly suggests that Janowitz[52] correctly describes the role of the mass media: to set the limits within which public debate on controversial issues takes place.[53] Since the establishment and maintenance of the parameters of debate and discussion is a central tenet of the Marxist theory of hegemony, that theory would appear to be reinforced accordingly.

LIMITATIONS OF HEGEMONY

It is common for theories concerned with social control and social order to become so infatuated with the processes under study that they

---

[51] Federal Communications Commission, "Applicability of the Fairness Doctrine in the Handling of Controversial Issues of Public Importance," *Federal Register,* 29 (July 25, 1964), 10415–27.

[52] Janowitz, *op. cit.*, p. 402.

[53] Because the focus is upon the way in which the media *sets the limits* of public debate, the present discussion is forced to ignore very real and stormy issues which arise within those limits. The history of relations between the Nixon administration and the electronic news media certainly illustrate the volatility of such issues. Yet, they continue to take place within the context of well-defined ideological parameters. A newscaster may imply that Nixon has overstepped the bounds of the office; however, he does not imply that the office of President never actually answers to the American people. He may suggest that specific contributions may have influenced specific policy decisions but not that the government continually functions to protect U.S. corporate interests and that those interests are not those of the majority of the American people. Nixon may accuse the media of slanting the news and being "out to get him," but he does not object to the power which the corporate dollar has over programming, nor does he call upon the media to provide a forum for community and labor groups and movements to express their views. The issues concerning the power of the executive branch of government relative to the power of the media and the other branches of government are important and controversial to the concerned parties. They do not, however, raise fundamental issues of class interests and the structure of U.S. society, and they do not escape or expand the normal limits of public debate which the corporate media help to maintain.

become incapable of anticipating or explaining fundamental social change.[54] It is important for sociologists to realize that however strong ideational control might be, it yet retains the potential to generate opposition.

Gitlin[55] makes just that point regarding the effects of television when he suggests that, once simplified and stereotyped presentations are seen to be just that, the effect backfires—the more so when the coverage distorts an event one has experienced. A similar point could be made concerning the effects of political socialization: when a sugar-coated world-view conflicts with subsequent experience and insight, the power of that original world-view may be reduced accordingly.[56] Habermas has said, "Perhaps the process of petrification of our ad-ministered consciousness has progressed so far that (it) can only be broken through today under the socio-psychologically exceptional conditions of university study." [57] More likely, and the point is under-scored by the rise of militant minorities and the reemergence of the rank-and-file caucus movement, the university is a special case of a more general phenomena: the demystification of a regulated and frag-mented world-view imposed in the interest of social control.

Vital to an understanding of the limitations of hegemonic control is the ethnomethodological point that "the meanings of situations and actions are interpretations formulated on particular occasions by the participants in the interaction and are subject to reformulation on subsequent occasions.[58] To the extent that social structure is thus continually emergent, a perspective which reifies normative or control structures is incapable of explaining the breakdown of those struc-tures.[59]

The point is not that ideational control is omnipotent or without limitations, but rather that the mechanisms which reinforce an ideo-logical hegemony become themselves a focal point of struggle. This explains the (recent) renewed interest in Gramsci and Lukacs as well

54 Cf. Herbert Marcuse, *One-Dimensional Man*. Boston: Beacon, 1964.

55 Todd Gitlin, "Fourteen Notes on Television and the Movement," *Leviathan*, 1 (July/August, 1969), 3–9.

56 The limited effects of media and political socialization could be described as process of selective perception and retention. Such a formulation leaves unan-swered the crucial question: What, in concrete day to day experience, shapes the selection process itself. This issue is explored in greater depth in Sallach, "Critical Theory and Critical Sociology," *Sociological Inquiry*, 43 (2, 1973), 131–40; and "Class Consciousness and the Everyday World in the Work of Marx and Schutz," *Insurgent Sociologist*, 8 (August 1973), 134–39.

57 Jurgen Habermas, *Toward a Rational Society*. Boston: Beacon, 1970, p. 30.

58 Thomas P. Wilson, "Conceptions of Interaction and Forms of Sociological Ex-planation." *American Sociological Review* 35 (4, 1970); 697–710.

59 Cf. Sallach, "Critical Theory and Critical Sociology." *Sociological Inquiry*, 43 (2, 1973), 131–40.

as the popularity of Dutschke's[60] call for a "long march through the institutions." [61] In theory and in practice a major thrust of the New Left opposition has been the mechanisms of the ideological hegemony.

CONCLUSION

The purpose of this analysis has been to examine the viability of two alternative views of social order: the normative and the Marxist. The former was found to be seriously compromised by failure of empirical studies to reveal an underlying value consensus which might serve as a basis for social order. The Marxist view of social order, as developed by Gramsci in his concept of hegemony, hypothesizes three fundamental aspects of the relationship between class structure and ideological institutions: 1) that a dominant class exists and has privileged access to cultural and ideological institutions; 2) that discussion and debate within these institutions is circumscribed within limited parameters; and 3) that public belief systems reflect such ideological constraints in the form of fragmentation, inconsistency, and disinterest. The first and last of the three aspects were given support by the preliminary evidence reviewed. The second aspect of ideological hegemony was explored within the areas of education and mass media. In each instance, the available literature consistently indicated that the range of positions and perspectives tolerated within those institutions was truncated severely. A fuller analysis is required to trace the dimensions of ideological hegemony in the U.S. Such an analysis must include the entire gamut of ideological institutions. In the meantime, the thesis that ideological hegemony is an integral component of a larger system of social control is not only tenable, but consistent with the available empirical evidence.

[60] Rudi Dutschke, "On Anti-Authoritarianism," in C. Oglesby, ed., *The New Left Reader*. New York: Grove Press, pp. 243–53.

[61] Cf. Carlo Donolo, "Politics Redefined," *Leviathan* 1 (June 1969), 35–40; and Richard Flacks, "Strategies for Radical Social Change," *Social Policy* 1 (March/April 1971), 7–14.

c h a p t e r   t e n

Mass communications and american empire

HERBERT I. SCHILLER

THE GLOBAL AMERICAN
ELECTRONIC INVASION

Canada's radio and television air waves are dominated by American programs. Many Canadians feel, consequently, that much of the broadcasting they see and hear is not serving Canadian needs. Such is the finding of a government-appointed Committee on Broadcasting[1] . . .

. . . The heavy exposure of Canadian audiences to American radio-TV culture is to some extent a matter of geography. After all it is estimated that almost three-fifths of the Dominion's households are within range of American stations. Certainly the three thousand mile common boundary offers no barrier to electromagnetic impulses originating in U.S. broadcasting studios. But the American mass media's penetration (perhaps saturation is more accurate) of the Canadian scene cannot be explained fully as merely a matter of adjoining real estate. The Canadian experience only represents a sector, and a small one at that, of a staggering global invasion by American electronic communications.

How completely the international community is being blanketed by radio-television programming produced in the United States or in U.S.-financed facilities overseas, has never been fully documented. An inventory would soon become obsolete because the use of American materials and American foreign broadcast holdings are expanding rapidly and continuously. Each new electronic development widens the perimeter of American influence, and the indivisibility of military and commercial activity operates to promote even greater expansion.

The Department of Defense, for instance, possesses a broadcasting

"Mass Communications and American Empire." From *Mass Communications and American Empire*, by Herbert I. Schiller (New York: Augustus M. Kelley, Publishers, 1969), pp. 79–122. Reprinted by permission of the publisher.

[1] *Report of the Committee on Broadcasting,* Ottawa, Canada, 1965.

network across the world with 38 television and more than 200 radio transmitters. Philip Coombs, former Assistant Secretary of State for educational and cultural affairs, reported that "the foreign audience is believed to outnumber overseas American listeners by about twenty to one." [2] There is, in addition, a huge civilian governmental broadcasting establishment, the United States Information Agency (U.S.I.A.), which concerns itself, among other things, with transmissions to foreign audiences. The Voice of America, the radio arm of the U.S.I.A., transmits some 845 hours in 38 languages weekly to an overseas audience of unknown size. The Agency also distributes taped programs and scripts to local stations throughout the world and estimates that its materials are broadcast by more than 5,000 stations for some 15,000 hours a week.

Besides forty-three powerful domestically-based transmitters, the Agency operates 59 transmitters overseas, including broadcasting installations in Liberia, on the Isle of Rhodes and in England. The Agency's Berlin radio, RIAS, located in the middle of the German Democratic Republic (unrecognized by the West), operates around the clock with an annual budget exceeding $3,000,000. More than half its broadcast time is occupied with political commentary, news, and cultural programs that are transmitted to and heard by an East German audience 24 hours a day. [3] Additional facilities are being constructed in Greece, Thailand and the Philippines. [4]

Regular TV series programs are prepared for Japan, Nigeria, Thailand and all of Latin America, though "most of the U.S.I.A. programs . . . are not identified as such in the 97 countries in which they are shown." [5] Some of the shows are commercially sponsored by American or local companies and enjoy prime evening television time. Latin Americans, for example, receive *Panorama Panamerico,* a weekly fifteen minute news review presented over 114 stations in the hemisphere. Japan used 8,000 U.S.I.A. programs and news clips in 1966.

But official broadcasting efforts, military and civilian, are only a limited side of America's international communications activities. The private sector has come along rapidly in recent years. Former National Association of Educational Broadcasters' president, Harry J. Skornia, not too long ago wrote: "Probably few Americans are aware of the extent to which American television programs, films, advertising agen-

2 P. H. Coombs, *The Fourth Dimension of Foreign Policy,* Harper & Row, New York, 1964, p. 63.

3 Hearings Before a Subcommittee of the Committee on Appropriations, House of Representatives, 89th Congress, First Session, Washington, 1964, *U.S. Information Agency,* Appropriations for 1966, p. 146.

4 Hearings Before a Subcommittee of the Committee on Appropriations, House of Representatives, 89th Congress, Second Session, *U.S. Information Agency,* September 13, 1966, Washington, pp. 345, 368, 625.

5 *The New York Times,* March 24, 1967.

cies, and other communications and entertainment efforts and activities now encompass most of the globe." [6]

The American interest in overseas communications extends from direct ownership of broadcast facilities (still limited but expanding), to equipment sales, management service contracts, and program exports. The magnitude of the involvement is illustrated best perhaps, but by no means exhausted, in the foreign activities of the major United States broadcast corporations.

No one needs to be persuaded of the domestic communications importance of the Columbia Broadcasting System (CBS). Its international efforts may be less familiar. According to its 1966 Annual Report, "CBS has become a worldwide communications enterprise whose services and products are distributed in 100 countries. . . . Its products are distributed through 72 overseas subsidiaries . . . 10 per cent [of its employees] are foreign nationals . . . distribution of [its] programs expanded to 94 countries, including for the first time India, Greece, Ghana, Liberia, Aden, Gabon, the Ivory Coast and the Congo." [7] CBS also is providing consultation and advisory services for the creation of a government-operated television network in Israel. It owns investments in three Latin American production companies; *Proartel* in Argentina, *Proventel* in Venezuela and *Pantel* in Peru.[8] Additionally, CBS owns television stations in Trinidad and Antigua and CATV systems in several Canadian communities.

RCA is a two billion dollar giant electronics conglomerate, which serves as the corporate supershelter for NBC, another major domestic radio-television communications system. The global communications interests of RCA and its subsidiary NBC, already considerable, are enlarging annually. In 1965, NBC reported that its international activities included "syndication of 125 film series and services in 83 countries for more than 300 television stations. . . . The leading export was "Bonanza," distributed to 60 countries for viewing by approximately 350 million people every week . . . NBC International dubbed programs in Spanish, Japanese, Portuguese, German, Italian, French and Arabic.[9]

In 1966, NBC Enterprises, the internationally-oriented affiliate, was active in 93 foreign countries. Other involvements included investment in a new television station in Hong Kong and a contract for RCA Communications to install, operate and maintain the first communications satellite earth station in Thailand. Also, "in anticipation of regular color broadcasting in Europe, a new company, RCA Colour

[6] H. J. Skornia, "American Broadcasters Abroad," *Quarterly Review of Economics and Business*, Vol. 4, No. 3, Autumn, 1964, pp. 13–20.

[7] Columbia Broadcasting Company, *Annual Report*, 1966, p. 2 and p. 19.

[8] Columbia Broadcasting Company, *Annual Report*, 1965, p. 22.

[9] *NBC Year-End Report*, 1965, p. 28.

Tubes Ltd., was formed in England in association with the British firm of Radio Rentals, Ltd., to produce RCA color picture tubes for the British and European markets." [10]

NBC also has partial interests (over 10 per cent but less than controlling) in two Australian TV stations in Brisbane and Sydney, a radio and television station in Caracas, Venezuela, a TV station in Monterrey, Mexico, and memberships in consortia that operate a TV station in Jamaica, a radio station in Barbados and Hong Kong's UHF station.

More important to date than its overseas broadcast holdings, has been NBC's provision of technical and administrative expertise to developing (and some developed) countries in the last ten years. "It is in the management-services area, where strictures against government-owned operations do not hold," writes one reporter, "that NBC has had the greatest influence on television abroad." Countries in which NBC has been active in this respect since 1957 included Saudi Arabia, "the largest single TV project undertaken by an American firm," South Vietnam, West Germany, Wales, Mexico, Lebanon, Sweden, Peru, the Philippines, Argentina, Yugoslavia, Barbados, Jamaica, Kenya, Nigeria ("the largest project except for Saudi Arabia") and Sierra Leone.[11]

RCA, the parent company, is also one of the major shareholders, along with AT&T, and IT&T, of Comsat, the Communications Satellite Corporation, and plays therefore a considerable role in the international space communications consortium, *Intelsat*.

The American Broadcasting Company, the third major network company in the United States, has been the most active in the international field, perhaps compensating for its somewhat less influential position in the domestic market, where it ranks behind CBS and NBC. ABC has organized an international TV network, *Worldvision*, which, at latest estimate, "can reach 60% of all world TV homes [outside the United States] where sponsorship is permitted (a total of 23 million TV homes)." [12] In the 26 nations where *Worldvision* operates, ABC has some financial involvement in telecasting in the following countries: Canada, Guatemala, El Salvador, Honduras, Costa Rica, Panama, Colombia, Venezuela, Ecuador, Argentina, Lebanon, Japan, Ryukyus, Philippines, Australia, Chile and Bermuda.

Direct financial interest, however, as one writer sees it, is not "the cement that holds *Worldvision*'s 56 TV stations [now 64] and 30 radio stations together. The essence of the relationship is a worldwide contract that provides the stations with three major services: pro-

10 Radio Corporation of America (RCA), *Annual Report*, 1966, p. 24.
11 R. Tyler, "Television Around the World," *Television Magazine*, October, 1966, pp. 32 and 59.
12 *Ibid*.

gram buying, sales representation and networking." [13] ABC itself reports that in 1966 "its programs were sold in over eighty foreign markets." [14] ABC also has interests in production companies in Germany and Mexico and Britain.

Other American broadcasting groups besides the "big three" have moved into the international field. Most important to date is *Time-Life Broadcast Stations*, which is involved in two situations with CBS and former Cuban broadcaster Goar Mestre. These are

the *Proventel* production company, which provides programs for Channel Eight network in Venezuela, with headquarters and a station in Caracas, plus additional stations in Valencia, Barquisimeto and Maracaibo, and the *Proartel* production company in Buenos Aires, which produces programs for the city's channel 13. In both cases *Time-Life* and CBS own 20% each, with the rest split between Mestre and local interests. . . . Elsewhere in South America, *Time-Life* is furnishing technical and financial assistance to two Brazilian stations, TV Globo in Rio de Janeiro and TV Paulista in Sao Paulo.[15]

Time-Life's Brazilian tie-in has created concern in that country because the Brazilian constitution prohibits foreign ownership of the nation's communications media, and the link that has been established seems clearly to violate this provision. Moreover, the dollar infusion has encouraged TV Globo to attempt the acquisition of a nationwide chain of radio and TV stations in all the nation's major cities.[16]

Whatever the outcome in this case, the communications penetration is familiar and insistent. National laws are being changed to accommodate expanding American investments in international broadcast communications. New Zealand, for example, which has had only state-controlled radio-tv broadcasting, is preparing to revise its statutes to sanction a private commercial television system. A new group, New Zealand Television Corporation Ltd. of Auckland, which intends to establish private TV stations throughout the country, is expecting to have $3.8 million of its initial $7 million capital subscribed by NBC International and Time-Life Broadcast Stations.[17]

A special case of American influence exists in Saudi Arabia where there are two TV services, one of which is government controlled

13 *Ibid.*, p. 33.

14 American Broadcasting Companies, Inc., *Annual Report*, 1966, p. 11.

15 Tyler, *op. cit.*, p. 33.

16 E. Blum, "Brazil's Yankee Network," *The Nation*, May 29, 1967, pp. 678–681. See also, *Variety*, June 14, 1967, p. 45.

17 Tyler, *op. cit.*, p. 58.

and financed (constructed with the assistance of NBC). The other, ARAMCO TV, is financed and run by the Arabian American Oil Company, the overseas holding company of an American oil consortium comprising the Standard Oil companies of New York, California, and New Jersey and the Texas Oil Company. ARAMCO TV is operated largely for American oil personnel in the area but its signals are picked up by local set-owners.

PROGRAM EXPORTS

Though equity investment in facilities offer American broadcast companies direct outlets, the bread and butter revenues, as well as the significant political-cultural impact of the American overseas involvement, still comes from the export of U.S. programming. Commercial television has become an important and flourishing national export. A former United States Information Agency (U.S.I.A.) official, Wilson P. Dizard, made this appraisal of such transactions:

> American TV products, for better and for worse, are setting the tone for television programming throughout the world in much the same way Hollywood did for motion pictures 40 years ago. The United States now leads all other countries combined twice over as a program exporter. . . . Foreign sales were, until a few years ago, a source of random profits peripheral to revenues from syndication at home. . . . Today, overseas sales account for 60 per cent of all U.S. telefilm syndication activities and represent the difference between profit and loss for the entire industry.[18]

American broadcasters are beginning to complain that obstacles are being placed in the way of U.S. commercial television exports. Examples cited are the United Kingdom's stipulation that a minimum of 86 per cent of air time must be of Commonwealth origin, Canadian air time must be 55% locally produced and Australia 50%. Broadcasters have noted similar trends in Japan, Argentina, Italy, Mexico, Brazil and many other countries.[19] But the limitations on American programming frequently appear more severe than they actually are. Generous interpretations of permissible import categories and local production that is financed by American companies are two loopholes that have been used successfully in motion picture production to circumvent superficially tough national quotas. Similar arrangements may be anticipated in telefilms.

18 W. P. Dizard, "American Television's Foreign Markets," *Television Quarterly*, Vol. III, No. 3, Summer 1964, p. 58.
19 "The Global Market: Tough Nut," *Television Magazine*, August, 1966, pp. 90–92.

In any event, U.S. television activity abroad intensifies. U.S.I.A. official Dizard told a congressional committee in 1967 that

"The amount of [TV commercial] exports, now approaching $100 million a year, is such that the television screen is becoming the main source of the 'American image' for increasing millions of people abroad." He noted also that "It has been said that TV will replace Hollywood films in this respect. However, television, unlike Hollywood, deals not only in fictional entertainment but also in reporting current developments. This adds a dimension to television that Hollywood has never taken on in its products, and it is one that gives television special meaning in the patterns of our communications with other countries. Because our domestic television system is largely commercial, the quantity and quality of American television exports rests primarily in the hands of private broadcasters.[20]

In 1964, Dizard found that "the daily schedule of a typical Australian television station is, particularly in prime listening hours, virtually indistinguishable from that of a station in Iowa or New Jersey." [21] In 1967, *Television Age* reported that "the majority of the shows still on (the Australian) air are still U.S. imports." [22]

The situation, with local variations, is much the same all around the non-Sino-Soviet world. Even the communist area is not entirely immune to American imagery. Consider the weekly television fare in these widely separated countries. In Argentina, "U.S. imports continue to maintain high popularity. Among the favorites and number one in the top income audience group, is *Man From U.N.C.L.E.* followed by *The F.B.I., Batman,* and *Peyton Place. Beverly Hillbillies* continue to get high scores. . . ." In Belgium, "current and recent U.S. network film fare dominates Belgium's Top Ten, with *The Jetsons, The Fugitive, Dr. Kildare, Love On a Rooftop,* and *Voyage To The Bottom of the Sea* all up there." In Canada, "it's news when a Canadian program gets in Nielsen's top 10." In Finland, on the commercial channel, 45 per cent of the shows are live and 55 per cent are filmed. "Imported U.S. half-hour series account for 85 per cent of the filmed variety." In Hong Kong, the new Time-Life and NBC International TV station will use U.S. shows exclusively. In Mexico, "programming, according to an American syndicator, is a 'carbon copy' of the United States network fare . . . U.S. shows dominate Mexican prime time, right through the evening." [23]

[20] W. P. Dizard, Office of Policy and Research, U.S.I.A., Before the Subcommittee on International Organizations and Movements, "Modern Communications and Foreign Policy," 90th Congress, 1st Session, Washington, May 4, 1967, p. 59.

[21] Dizard, *Television Quarterly, op. cit.,* p. 63.

[22] *Television Age,* global report, July 3, 1967, p. 34.

[23] *Ibid.,* pp. 34–69.

Though American telefilms currently are obtaining their largest revenues from the high-income countries whose audiences are pro-spective customers for the advertising messages that accompany and finance the film showings, the developing world receives some atten-tion too. Dizard points out that "Almost every U.S. distributor is sell-ing films at cut-rate prices (in Latin America, Africa, and Asia) against the day when these markets will become stronger" [24] . . .

. . . THE MECHANICS OF CULTURAL LEVELLING

Gunboat diplomacy is now an item in the antiquities showcase but communications diplomacy is a very thriving business of the moment. Consider the rich possibilities for maneuver that accompany the estab-lishment of radio-television broadcast facilities in a society lacking an industrial base.

The actual physical equipment must be secured from abroad. Cap-ital to pay for it usually must be coaxed from reluctant treasuries with tempting promises and enticing conditions. No less a problem to the impoverished state is the matter of trained technicians and personnel to run the broadcast structures once they are in place. Labor that is skilled in these techniques must initially come from or be trained abroad, and the training is usually, as one would expect, in how to run French, English, or American style broadcast enterprises.

But the elemental, and barely acknowledged, issue in contemporary communications appears only *after* broadcasting, however it is organ-ized, begins. What messages will the new instrumentation transmit? The content of the programming is all that really matters, for what is broadcast may determine, in large measure, the cultural outlook and the social direction of the new nations for generations.

Mistakes and failures in agriculture and industry, if momentarily disastrous, are still remediable. Cultural patterns, once established, are endlessly persistent. The opportunity to freshly mould a new nation's outlook and social behavior is historically unique and merits the most careful deliberation. Yet in modern mass communications hard and inflexible laws, economic and technological, operate. If these are not taken into account *in the beginning,* and at least partially overcome, courses of development automatically unfold that soon become un-questioned "natural" patterns.

A few examples indicate the character of the forces at work. For instance, the ability to produce local broadcast programming is an extremely demanding business, one which requires skill and experi-

[24] Dizard, *Television Quarterly, op. cit.,* p. 63.

ence, not easy to come by. Furthermore, live programming is expensive and the question of how it will be financed becomes critical, not only for the considerable costs involved but for the direction of the medium the character of the financing imposes. Shall broadcast budgets be met by state subsidy with the implicit accompaniment of crippling state control? Can license fees cover the costs, as they hardly do in already-developed Britain and France? Or should commercial sponsorship be permitted? The last is always tempting in countries with empty treasuries, especially since decision makers often seem unaware of the long run *quid pro quo* that private sponsorship exacts.

Though financing is the overriding issue to be settled, another, more mundane, factor cannot be overlooked. Once individuals have made their investments for receivers they will press for longer viewing (and listening) intervals. The pressure to keep the sets playing seems to be irresistible. This demand, if even partly met, creates programming needs far exceeding most local production. This is true even in the most technically advanced societies.

As a result of the limitations to easily expanding the domestic production of programming and TV's enormous appetite for material, the door is opened to foreign program suppliers. The United States is by far the most important of the few states capable of exporting television material. What is more, the program suppliers are willing to distribute their wares at lower than production costs (sometimes at only a tiny fraction of cost) because the foreign sales are bonus revenues, profits made from programs which have already more than covered their production costs. Dumping further discourages domestic program production in all but the richest countries.

Once a developing society gets caught up in the impersonal imperatives of television operations, its broadcast structure rapidly becomes a vehicle for material produced outside its territory with an outlook and a character generally irrelevant, if not injurious, to its development orientation. Already the inroads are vast. For example, Dr. Lloyd A. Free, Director of the Institute for International Social Research, describes this situation in the most heavily populated country in Africa:

I did a study in Nigeria a couple of years ago. During that time I watched Nigerian television. Do you know that most of the prime hours of programming time on Nigerian television was made up of filmed television shows from the United States, many of them of a soap opera variety? . . . The Nigerians apparently watched because there was nothing else to watch. But of all the sheer waste of program time in a country faced with very grave problems as we see today, it just seems atrocious that this medium with the potential of television was utilized in that way. The reason that it is utilized that way is that it is cheaper for the Nigerian television networks to buy American films than produce their own or get other types of material.[25]

. . . The cultural homogenization that has been underway for years in the United States now threatens to overtake the globe. Mordecai Gorelik, long-time student of the theatre, asserted in 1965 that "The era of mechanized and centralized communication via the syndicated press, radio, movies and TV, has created a *gleichschaltung* unprecedented in history."[26] Everywhere local culture is facing submersion from the mass-produced outpourings of commercial broadcasting. Television in the United States is tailored almost exclusively to fit the market needs of the consumer goods producers who sponsor and finance the programming. The program material is designed especially to secure and hold mass audiences in thrall to the delights of consumerdom. . . .

Resources directed into consumer goods in the poorer countries represent materials channelled away from education and capital expansion. The stimulation of personal consumption wants diverts painfully scarce materials from group projects and long range improvement possibilities. Also, it creates or at least intensifies attitudes of individual acquisitiveness that go poorly with the community's desperate need of far-reaching social co-operation . . .

The view that complete free trade in goods and services between states unequal in economic strength may be detrimental to the health of the weaker society is now only at the point of partial recognition, certainly not total acceptance, in the powerful industrial nations. Those who are willing to grant *this* possibility have by no means conceded that the proposition can be broadened considerably.

Just as the folklore of commerce supposes that diverse trading groups will be drawn together amicably and beneficially in the exchange of goods, a stronger mythology insists that interpersonal and intergroup communications, whatever their nature, must have a positive and benevolent impact on world-wide human affairs. Open up communications between peoples, the belief goes, and humankind must prosper. The most extravagant claims are made in that connection. Margaret Mead, discussing the survival of man, is optimistic because, among other things, ". . . of the huge recent advances in communications and the possibilities for sharing knowledge."[27] Jerome Frank, simi-

[25] "Modern Communications and Foreign Policy," Subcommittee on International Organization and Movements of the Committee on Foreign Affairs, House of Representatives, 90th Congress, 1st Session, May 4, 1967, p. 42.

[26] *The New York Times*, April 11, 1965.

[27] *The New York Times*, April 20, 1965.

larly, in a different context but also considering the question of human solidarity, writes: "The reason there has not been a feeling for mankind is because we have not been able to communicate fully and intimately with mankind. One of the great new hopes of the world is that the media of mass communications, and the shrinkage of the world in terms of transportation and so on, are going to lead to a rapid buildup of a worldwide network of communications and of mutual rewards, out of which, I think, can grow a feeling for all mankind." [28]

These are sentiments with which everyone would like to agree, and their commonsense character seems solid enough to be acceptable. But as with conventional trade theory, they set aside the structural and social divisions that now characterize the global community. They assume that everything the well-to-do states have to say is useful and of concern to the destitute nations—an assumption that must be very carefully scrutinized.

The fact and paradox of this age is that technical advances have made electronic communications capable of massive global penetration by the advanced countries, while the socio-economic differentials that still separate nations require, at this stage of world development at least, the maintenance of distance between states and systems. In the poor world, leaderships work frantically to secure domestic integration, to recreate cultural identities, and to maintain national individuality in the face of domestic and internationally-generated resistance.

Communications media could be of great assistance in the realization of these aims, if they functioned in a public educational role. If programming objectives coincided with the nation's developmental goals, massive campaigns of literacy, manpower training programs and honest forums for popular discussion would receive the highest priorities. Broadcasting's responsibility in the emergent states, if identified and accepted, would require a complete reversal of radio-TV's function as it is now performed in America. No such reversal is in sight. . . .

. . . Sometimes the issue of freedom is invoked to defend the flow of cultural materials within and across national borders. Tariffs on shoes or woolens or whiskey may be acceptable at times, but, so the argument runs, how can anyone advocate measures which strike at the creations of the human mind? Does not all mankind suffer thereby? If human creativity literally were involved, there could be no other conclusion. But a confusion of individual effort with corporate activity obscures the actualities. It is assumed that films and television and radio programming are the inspired efforts of talented individuals. Yet only in the exceptional case is this so. Most often, the television pro-

---

28 "On the Developed and the Developing," an Occasional Paper, published by the *Center for the Study of Democratic Institutions,* 1965, pp. 18–19.

gram or the typical American movie is merely another commodity, designed carefully, in the same sense that soap and cars and cosmetics are prepared, to satisfy artificially stimulated wants.

Identifying the products of the United States film and broadcasting industries with human freedom can be misleading. Individual expression and talent are difficult to discover in most of the offerings of the information and entertainment industries in the West. What comes out of these faceless complexes today generally are neat packages of stereotyped dramatic ingredients, formalistically arranged. Fortunately, it is not often the artist who is injured if the mass media's artifacts are rejected.

Two decades ago the Commission on Freedom of the Press rejected the easy assumption that the espousal of free speech in the American Constitution was the basis for insisting on an unrestricted international free flow of communication. "The surest antidote for ignorance and deceit," it noted, "is the widest possible exchange of objectively realistic information—*true* information, not merely *more* information; *true* information, not merely, as those who would have us simply write the First Amendment into international law seem to suggest, the *unhindered flow* of information! There is evidence that a mere quantitative increase in the flow of words and images across national borders may replace ignorance with prejudice and distortion rather than with understanding." [29]

Some African leaders are aware of the issues at stake. The Senegalese Ambassador to the United Nations recently suggested:

> We should, without delay, proceed to take an exhaustive inventory of the artistic and cultural stock of all peoples in order to conserve it so that it may become a part of the universal civilization. . . .
> We must become acquainted with all civilizations and all original cultures of all the races before they perish under the increasingly overwhelming pressure toward the international standardization of man. [30]

If there is a prospect that cultural diversity will survive anywhere on this planet, it depends largely on the willingness and ability of scores of weak countries to forego the cellophane-wrapped articles of the West's entertainment industries and persistently to develop, however much time it takes, their own broadcast material.

It is already uncertain whether this remains a serious possibility for the world's "have not" states. Roger Revelle, discussing the bio-

29 Llewellyn White and Robert D. Leigh, *Peoples Speaking to Peoples,* A Report on International Mass Communications from the Commission on Freedom of the Press, University of Chicago Press, Chicago, 1946, p. 2.

30 Ousmane Soce Diop, "Communications in Senegal," *The American Scholar,* Spring, 1966, p. 221.

logical imperatives of a broadly-based and international scientific ecology, writes that "Especially we need to learn how to avoid irreversible change if we are going to be able to assure future generations the opportunity to choose the kind of world in which they want to live." [31] No less important, in this respect, is the preservation of cultural options to peoples and nations only now becoming aware of their potential . . .

[31] Roger Revelle, "International Biological Program," *Science*, 24 February 1967, Volume 1955, Number 3765, p. 957.